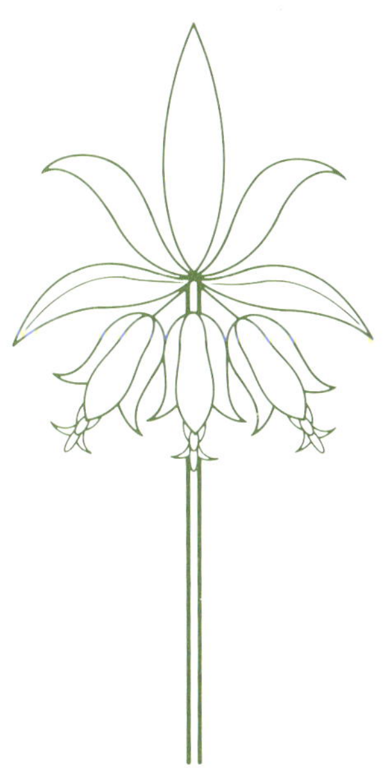

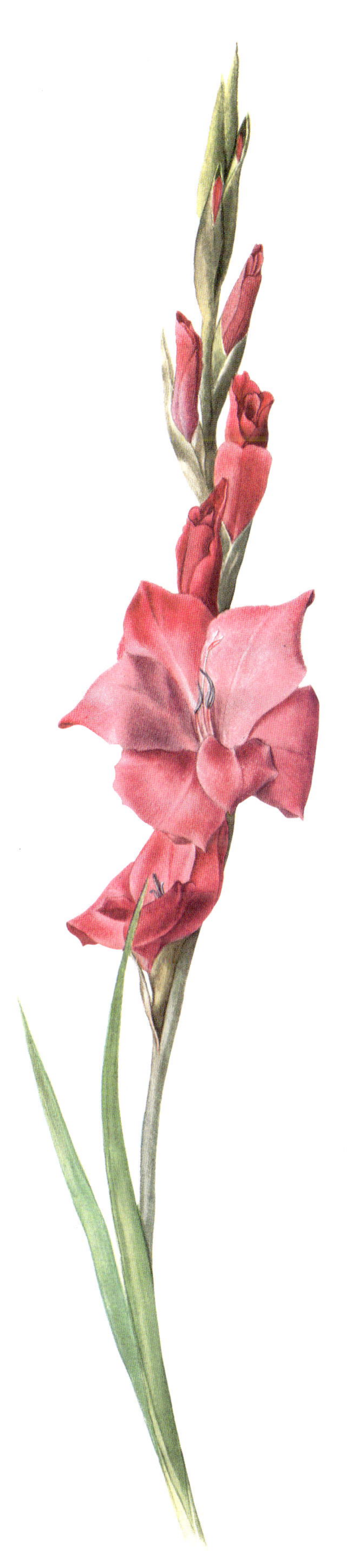

Carnegie-Mellon University

The Hunt Institute

for Botanical Documentation

Pittsburgh, Pennsylvania

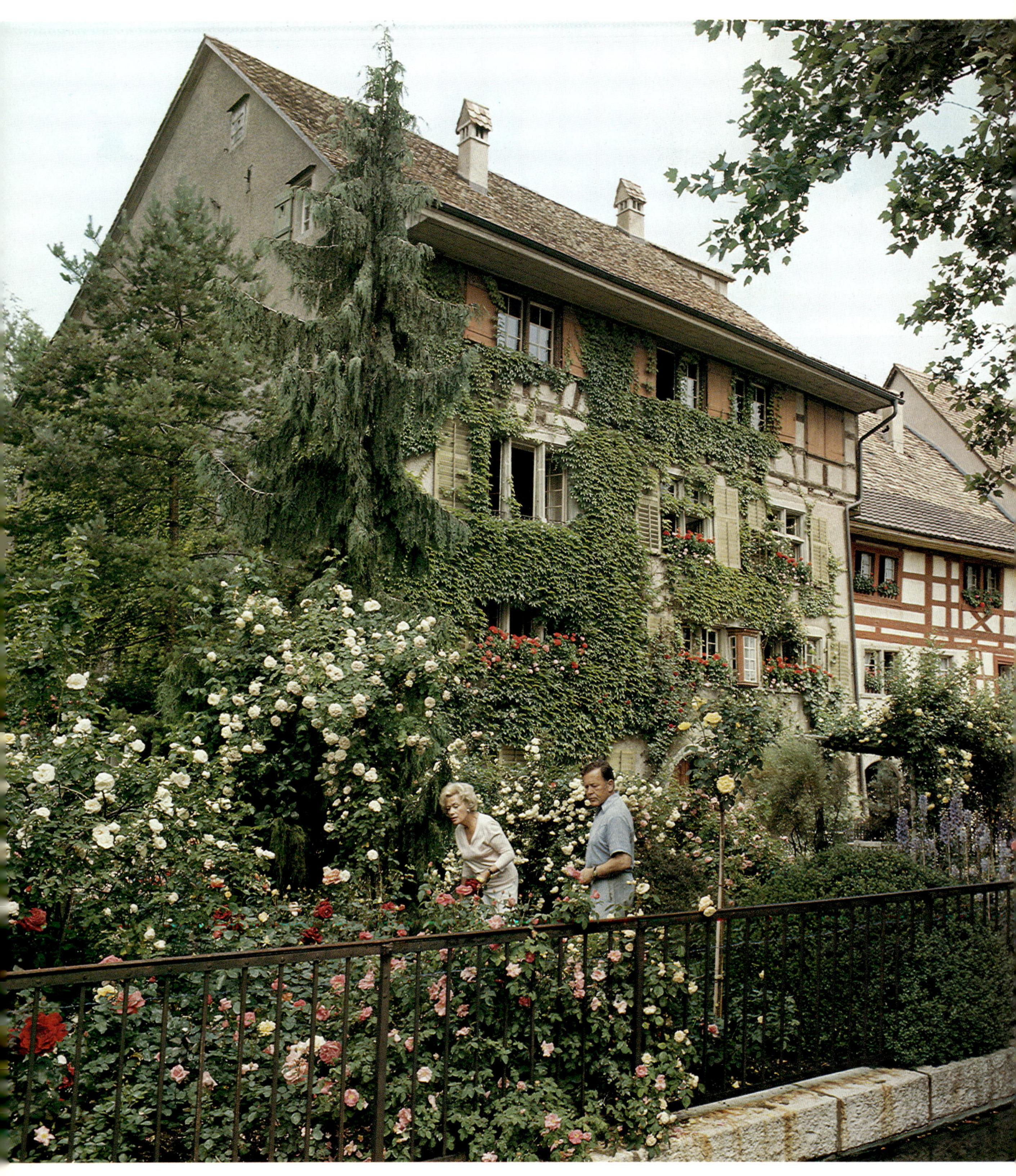

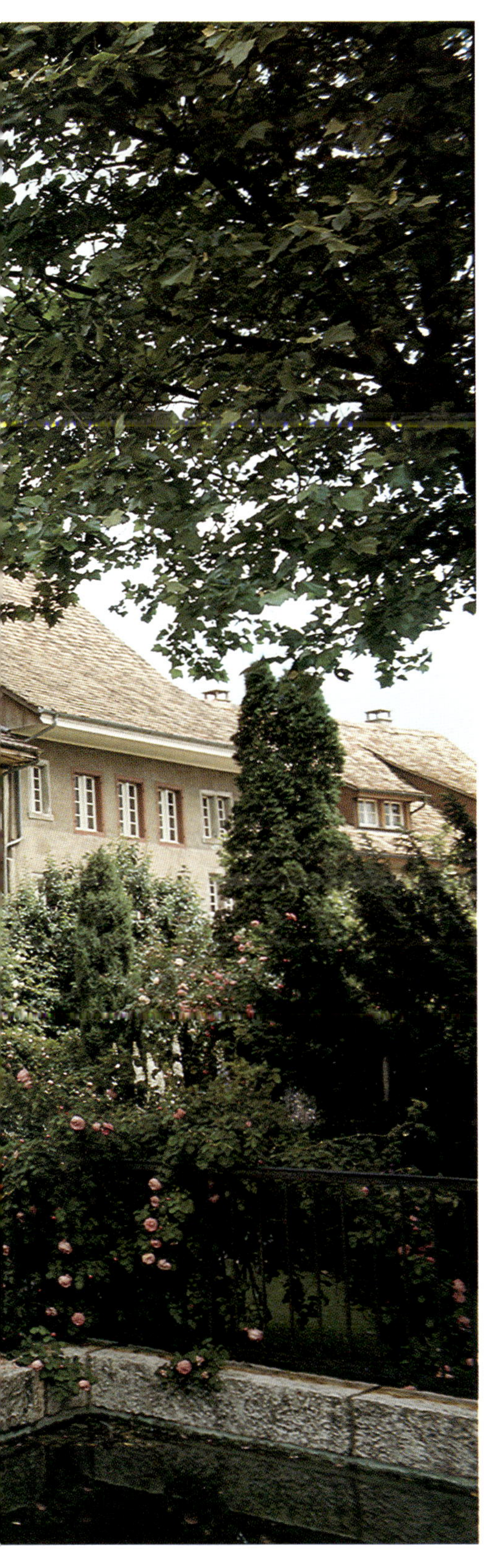

Lotte Günthart

Linger golden Light

Engelfried House.
The 700 year old house where Lotte and Willi Günthart
live in Regensberg, and the seat of the
Foundation Lotte and Willi Günthart-Maag where
the "Dr Rudolf Maag Prize" is annually awarded.

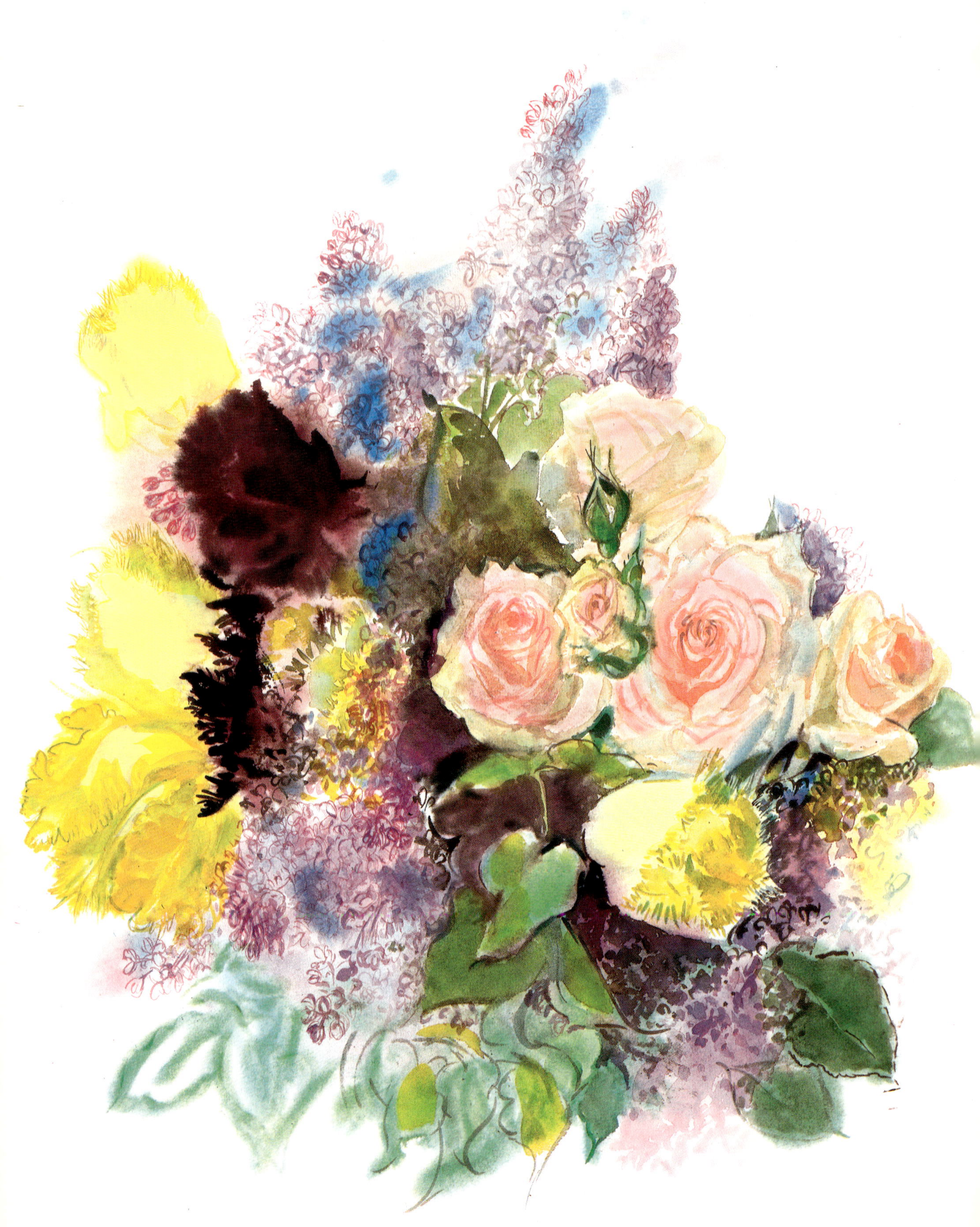

Table of Contents   Page

ISBN number 0-913196-46-0
Printed in Switzerland

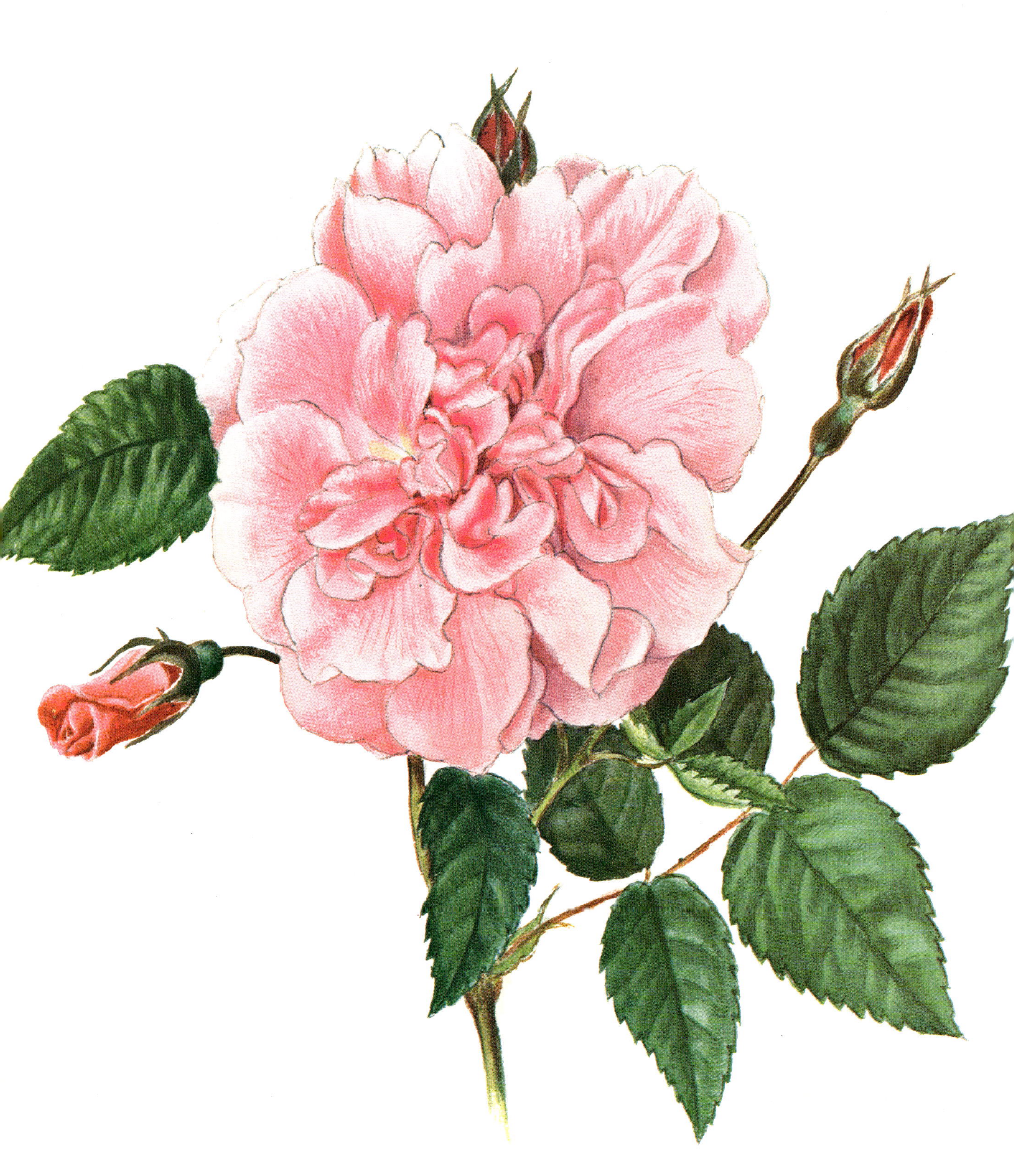

Foreword

Fourteen years ago the late George Lawrence, founding director of the Hunt Institute, had the pleasure of introducing the splendid catalogue that Lotte and Willi Günthart produced for our first exhibition of her work. The drawings, prints and paintings in that retrospective show amply displayed Mrs Günthart's exuberant sensitivity to form, color and light in her graphic celebration of plants, an alliance of feeling and technique that Dr. Lawrence esteemed greatly. Keen empathy informed his foreword to the catalogue, and it exemplified the sort of spontaneous resonance that Mrs Günthart's aesthetic evokes.

The avid response to that earlier exhibition and its now out-of-print catalogue virtually assured another Günthart show at the Institute, and the happy occasion has now arrived. Our second exhibition of Mrs Günthart's work presents a broad selection of her recent water colors. She chose the title herself, but it may be even more apt than she has realized. Phrased to invoke the continuing satisfaction of a full life fully lived, it can equally epitomize her water colors themselves, which seem to be invested with the fullness of life. Their subjects reflect a light that is sometimes glowing, sometimes brilliant, but always essentially golden – the living light remembered from a dappled country garden on a perfect day.

The present show is not retrospective in the usual sense; rather, it augments the more inclusive earlier one. However, this companion volume does offer a comprehensive view of the artist's life and œuvre. Its content ranges far beyond just the catalogue of works now exhibited, providing as well a composite account of activities, experiences, reflections, techniques and achievements, richly illustrated and engagingly glossed. But Mrs Günthart is not one to look backward only; she has also included new scholarly contributions on her beloved roses, continuing her practice of promoting such studies and seeing them into print.

Again as in 1970, the Hunt Institute is most grateful to Lotte and Willi Günthart for lending the artworks for a magnificent show, for unstinted assistance in planning and logistics, and for producing a notable publication especially for the occasion. We are particularly pleased to be publishing the present volume, which is not only a graphic showpiece but also the definitive record of Mrs Günthart's career. We trust, however, that supplements will be required as her golden light lingers.

Robert W. Kiger

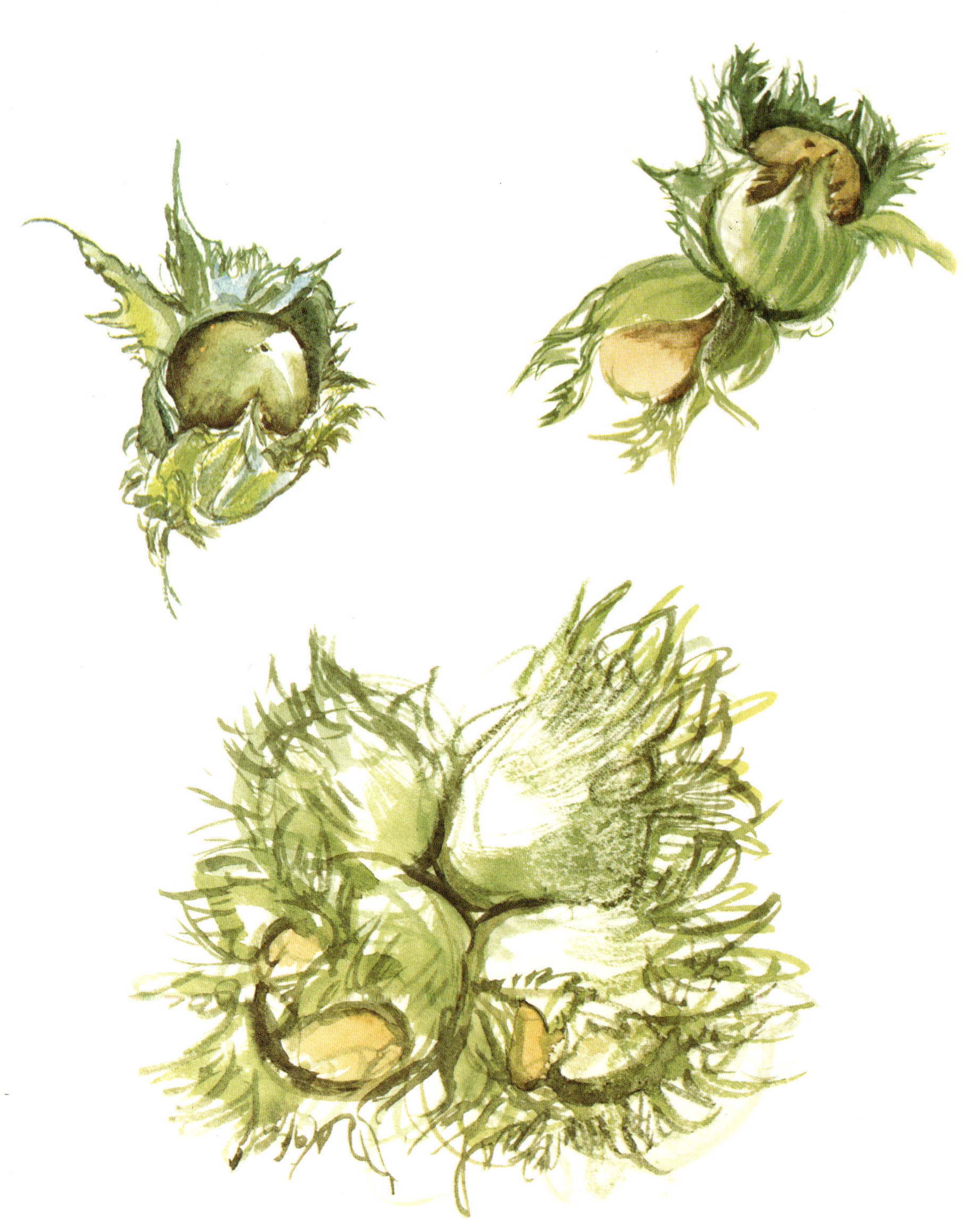

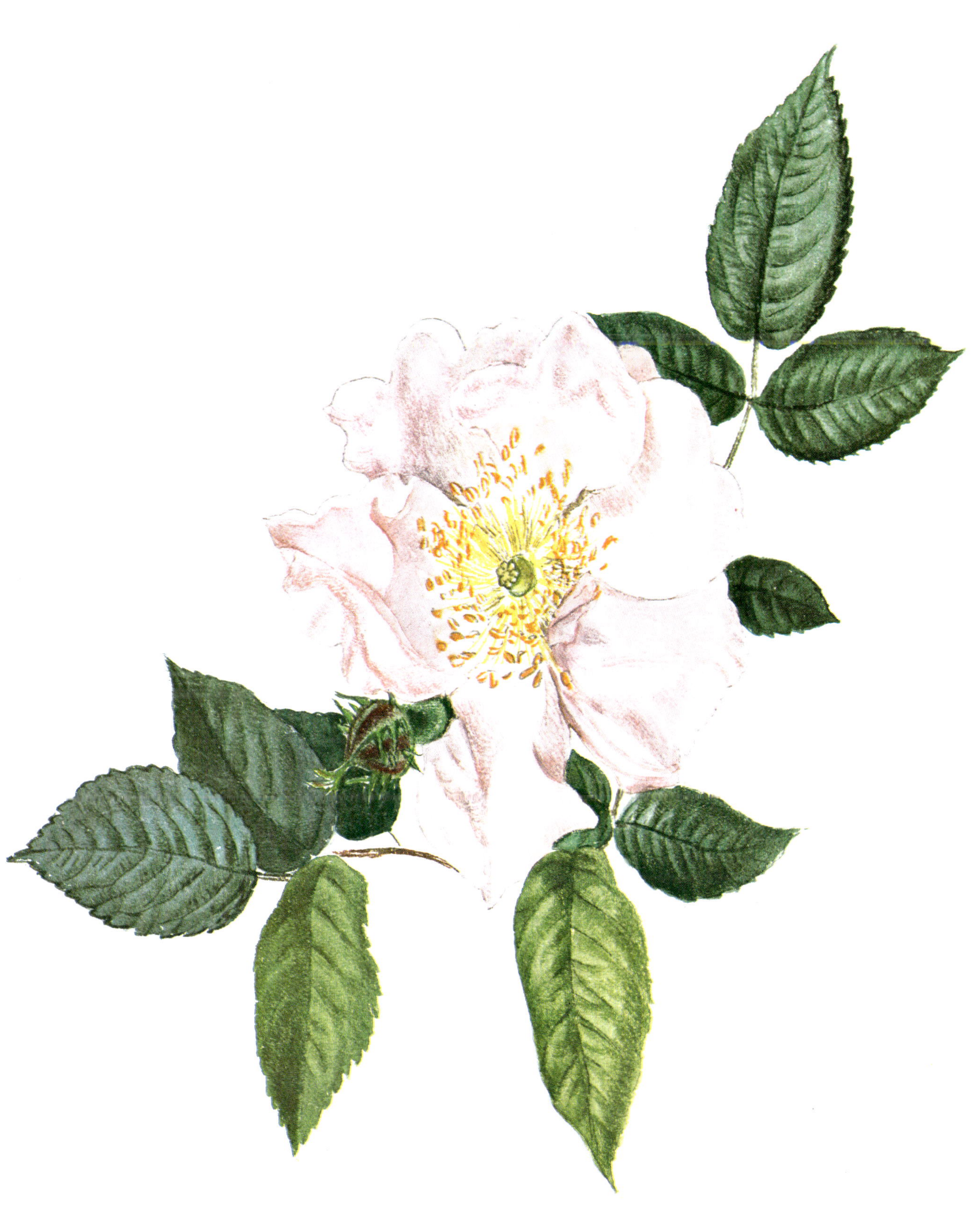

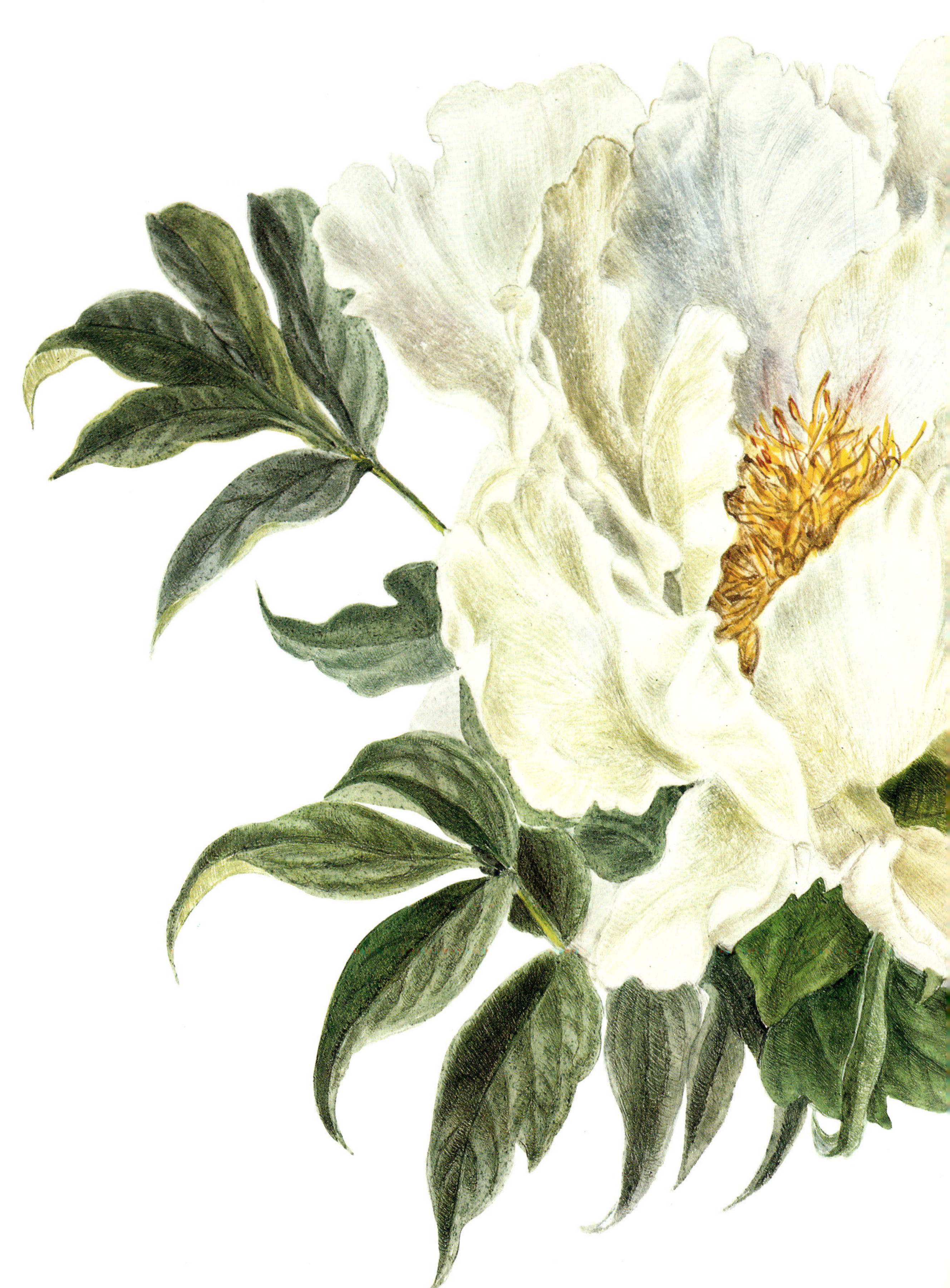

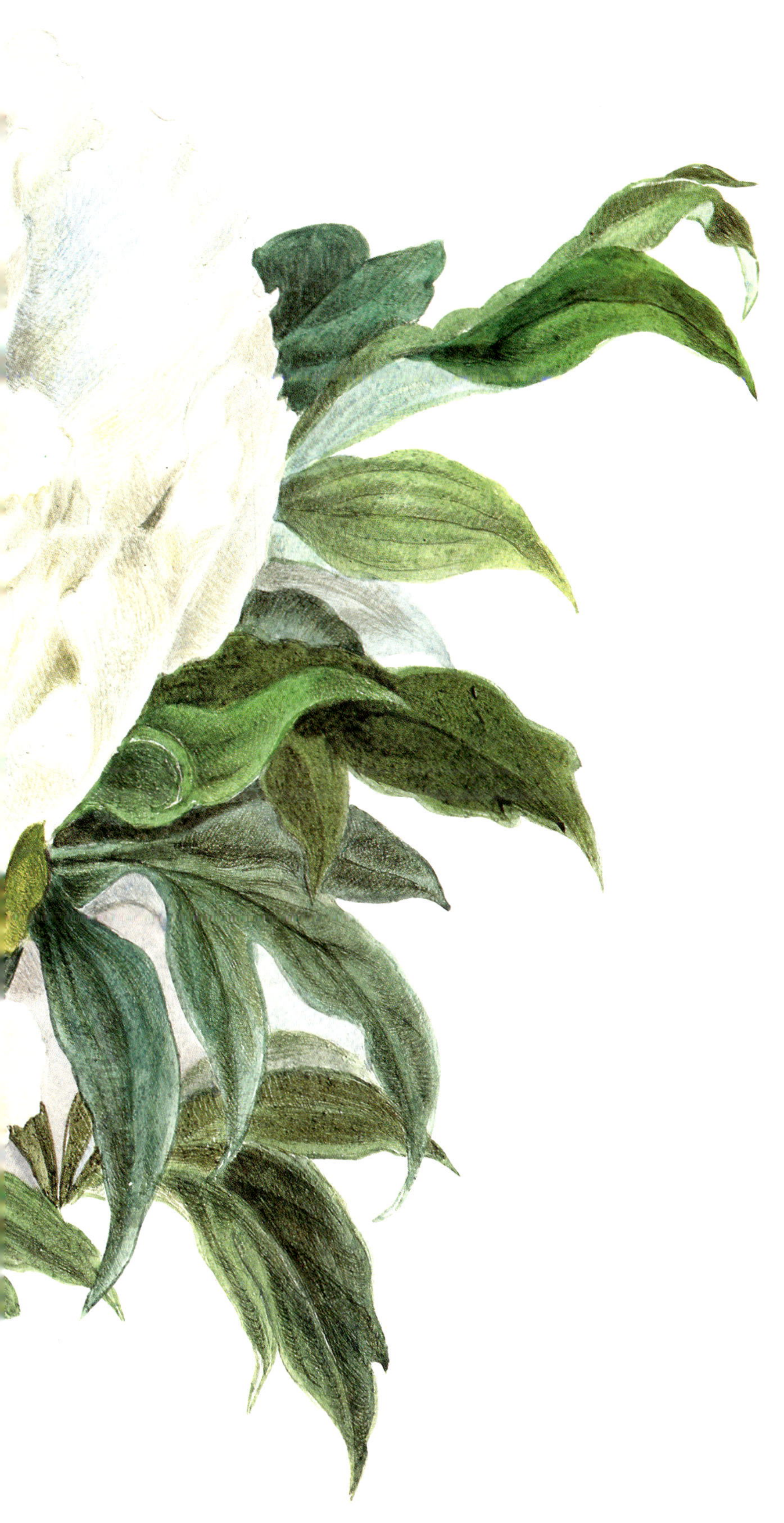

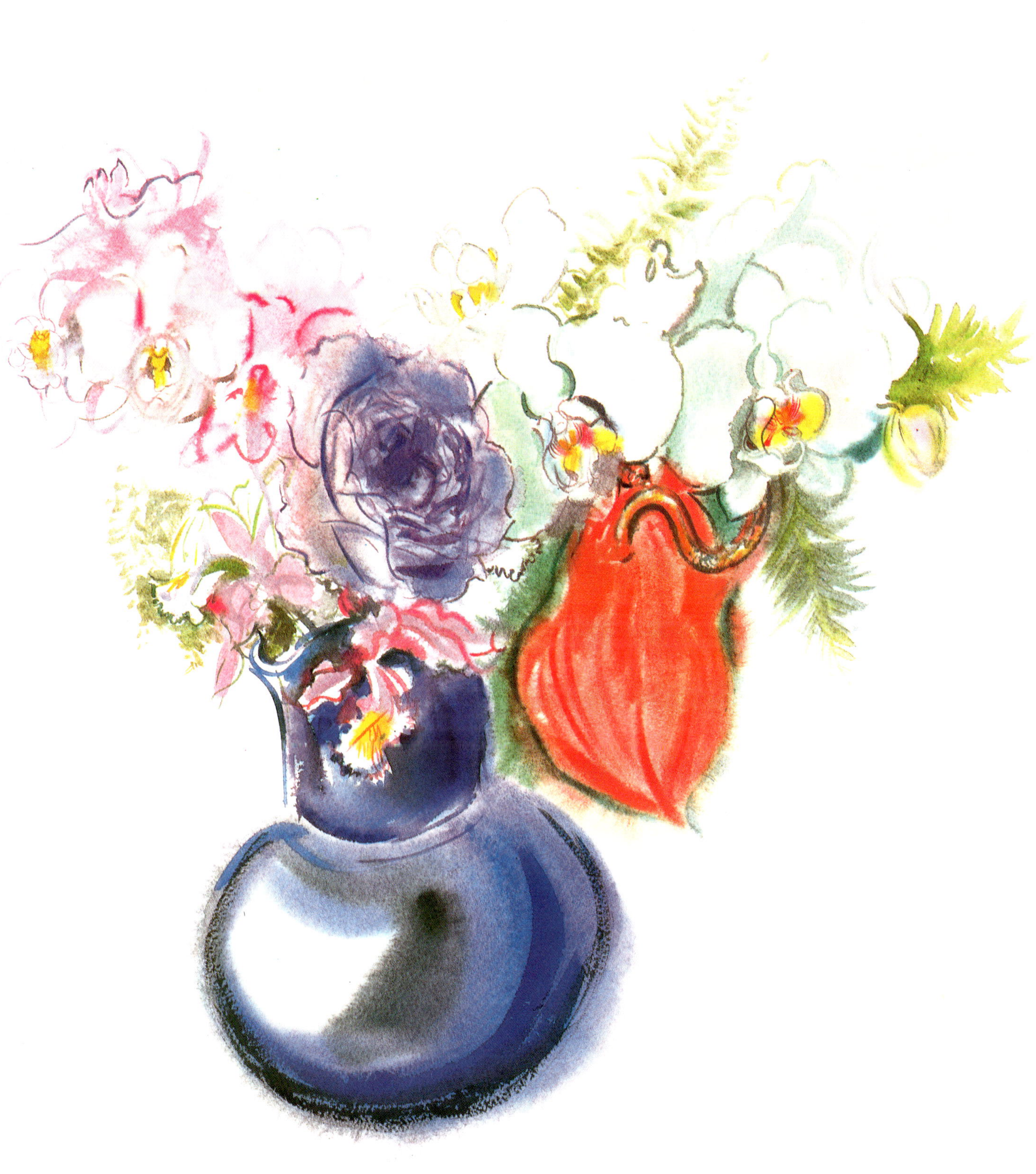

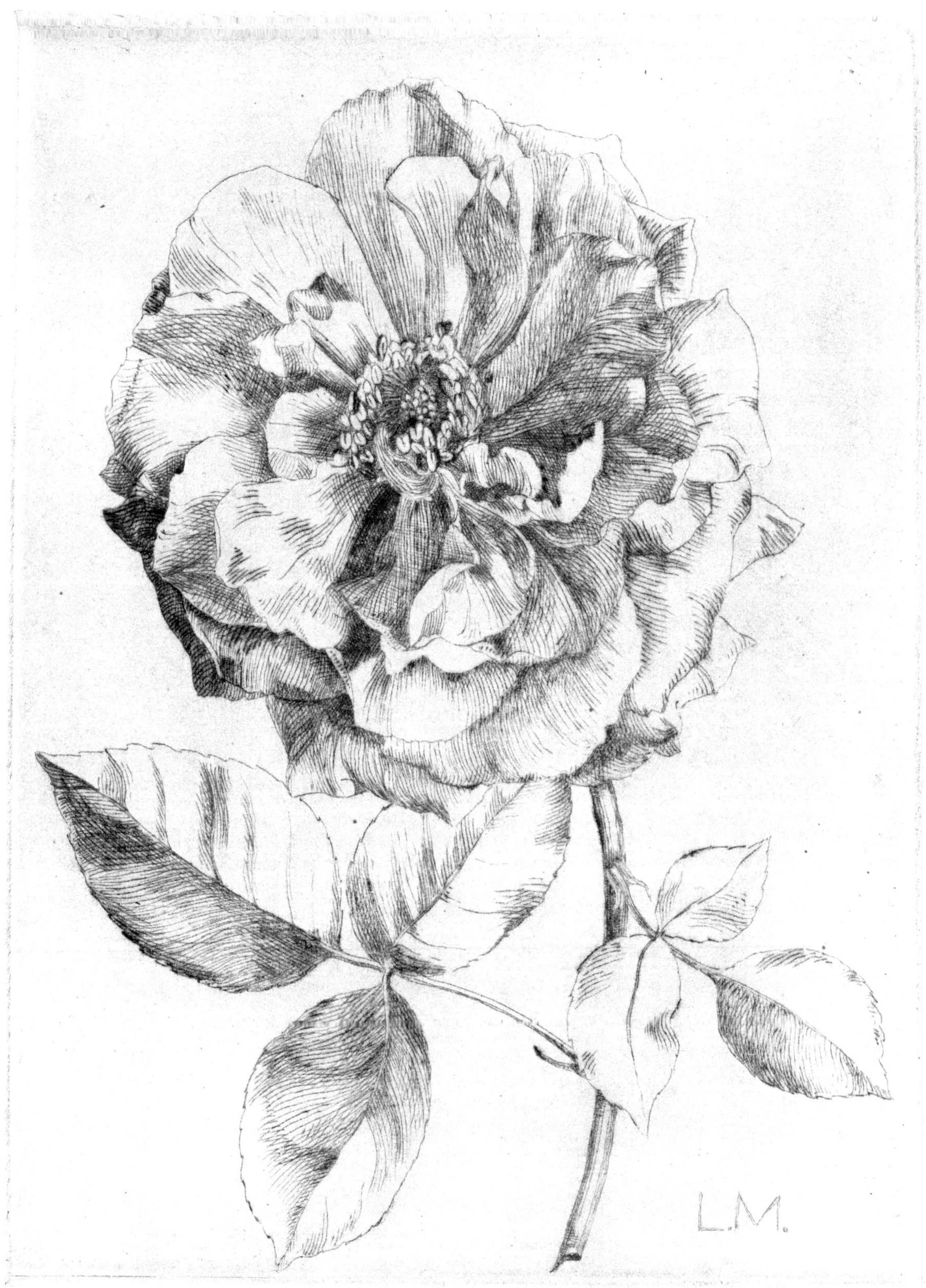
L.M.

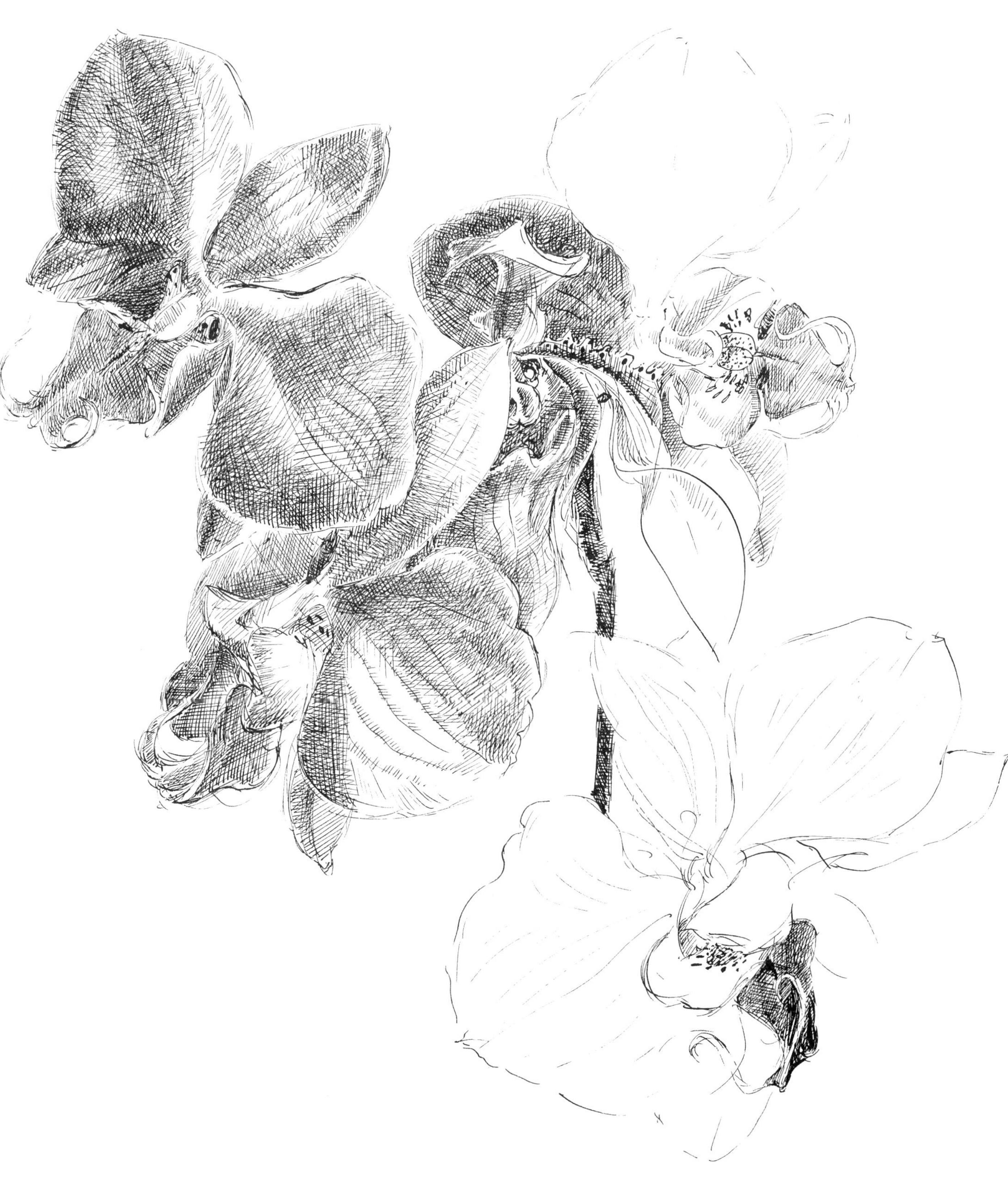

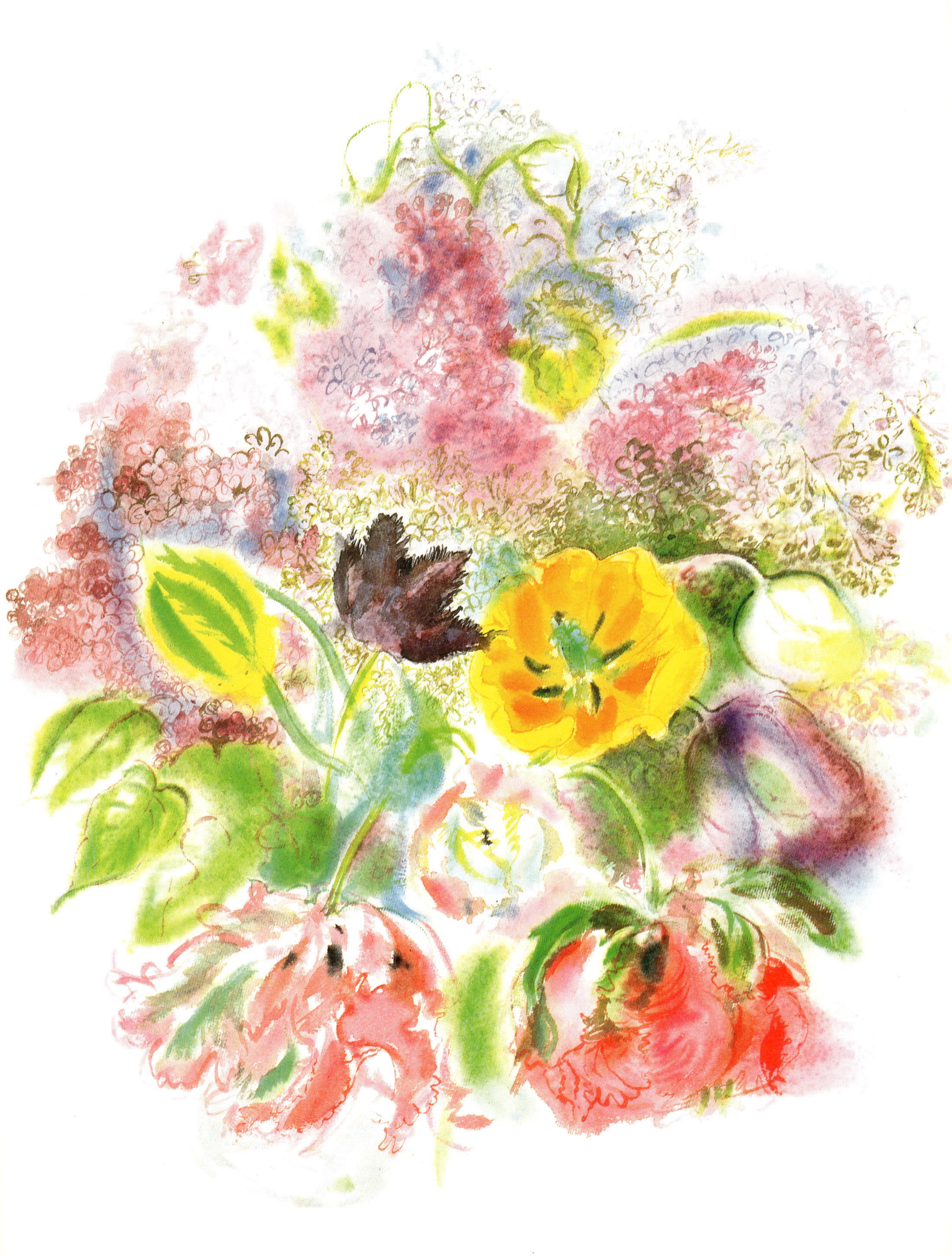

Preface

When you approach Regensberg, where Lotte and Willi Günthart live, you have the feeling that you are leaving reality for the realm of fantasy. The towers and turrets of the village, perched high on the top of a vine-clad hill, give it a fairy-tale appearance, and you would not be entirely surprised if you had to make way for a knight in medieval armour riding out through the ancient gateway to champion the cause of beauty in a philistine world. And sprouting from his helmet you would notice the favour granted him by the châtelaine of Regensberg – a perfect rose.

Such romantic notions are not quickly dispelled by contact with Lotte Günthart in person. She is beautiful, with a faint resemblance to the great French actress Françoise Rosay – Garbo even – with her charmingly accented but fluent English. She is an enchanting hostess: interesting, amusing, warm-hearted, generous. Staying as I once did with my family as her guests for a holiday in the Red Rose House was a magic experience.

In conversation with Lotte over some days I began to realise that this apparently idyllic state of affairs has been achieved at considerable human cost, but not until I read this all-too-brief autobiography did I understand how much pain and struggle had been required to give birth to Lotte's art, and a style of living which has brought almost as much joy to her many friends as her paintings.

As one of her teachers perceived quite early on, Lotte's modesty is so marked that it amounts to a fault. I am glad that at last she has been persuaded to lift the veil just a little – to reveal some of the pains – and the pleasures – which have made her the very remarkable artist and the very rare person she is today.

Richard Baker, OBE
London

Linger golden Light

When I look back on my life, I cannot help thinking of the verse:

"Stone by stone a wall is made,
And each stone must lie square,
Petal by petal a rose unfolds,
And each petal must be fair.
Little by little a faith is built,
Day by day it grows,
Stronger, at last, than a wall of stone,
Lovelier than a rose."

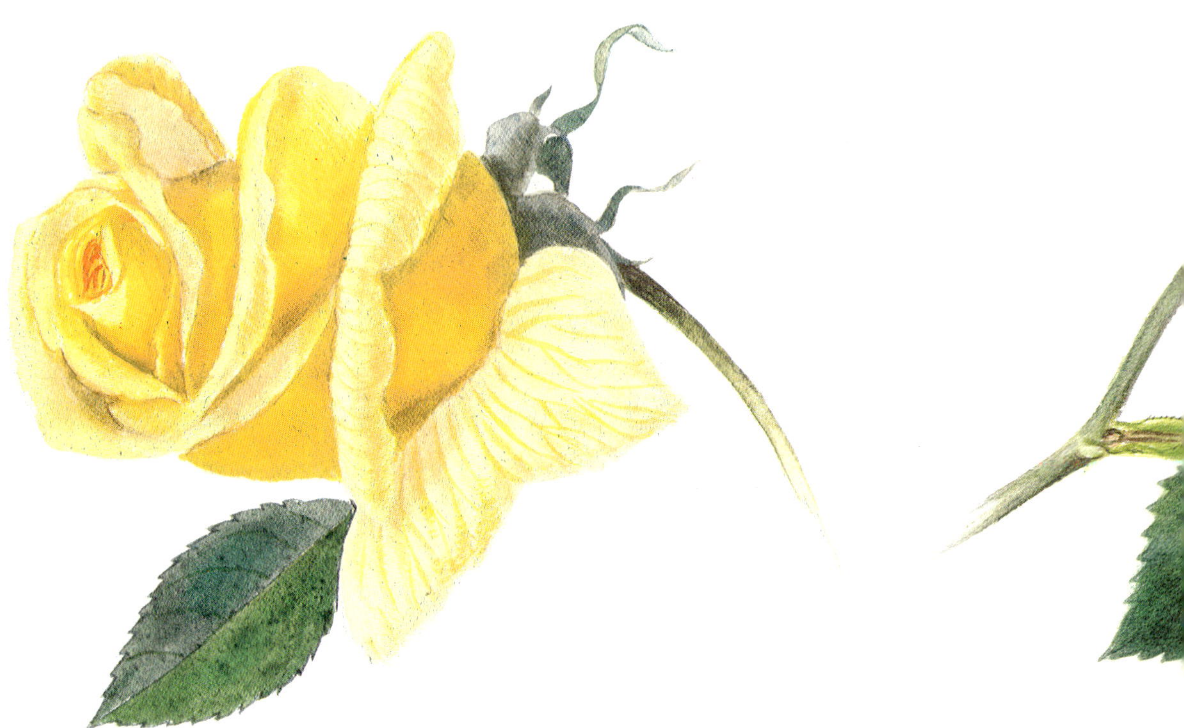

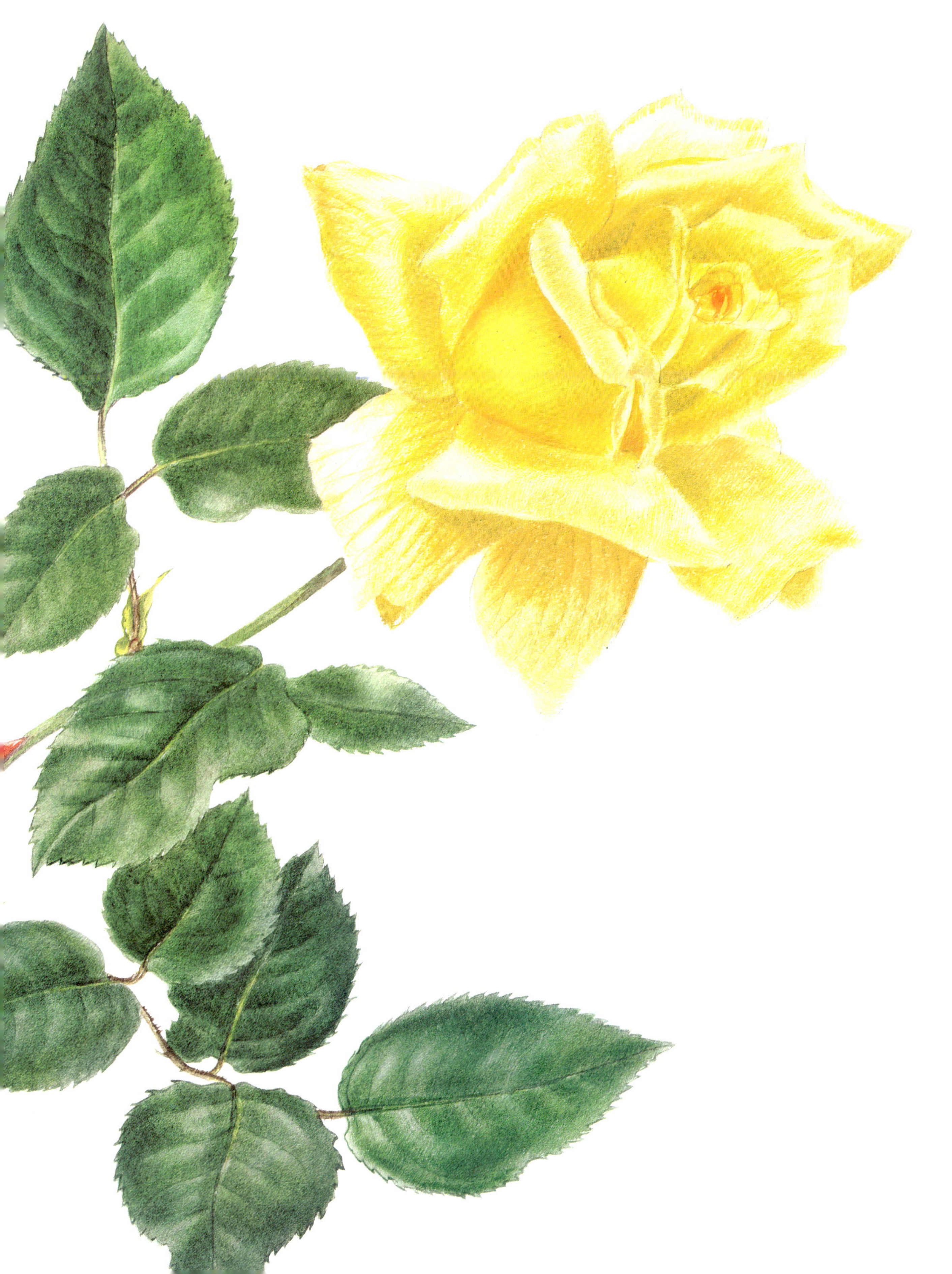

Until I reached the age of five, I was a lively and cheerful child, full of merry ideas, with lots of friends of my own age. My parents lived in a small house in the suburbs of Frankfurt, Germany, near the large factory where my father was employed as a chemical engineer.
A lovely garden surrounded the house, and gravel paths led to the rose clad summer-house whose wood was bleached grey by the sun. In the garden, there was a number of espalier pear, small apple and plum trees, and lots of flowers. Fragrant phlox, larkspurs in all shades of blue, campanulae in various pastel colours, marguerites, and roses everywhere. One of the roses, «Gruss an Teplitz», was dark red and sweetly perfumed; it seemed to bloom continually. This was my father's favourite, and he drew the rose in all stages of growth. He also completed a drawing of his daughter aged two years, with roses like a halo around her head. Elegant silver birches lined the path to the front door. These were my favourite trees, and always reminded me of my mother, with her silver blonde hair. Mother sang folk songs whilst preparing meals in the kitchen, and I loved listening to the lovely melodies. It was astonishing to see how many different things were in our garden; even a small stall for two Toggenburger goats which were sent to us by my Swiss grandfather. The goat milk was intended to save me from being hungry, for it was war-time (1914–1918), and everywhere there were small children dying like flies because they were nourished almost only on black chicory coffee and potatoes, with no butter or milk. My mother learned how to milk, and the dear goats provided so much, that there was enough for me, as well as for many children from the neighbourhood to enjoy this treat. Life at this time was good, and having so many friends made each day something special.
The year 1918 brought the end of the war. Endless lines of soldiers marched down our street, and I pressed my nose flat against the window-pane so that I could see better. Not all of them were on foot; some sat on vehicles, but they all appeared tired, grieved and dirty. They kept singing the same song over and over again "Ich hatt' einen Kameraden…", which ended with the words "We will meet again back home". This song always made me cry; to me it seemed so desperate, and yet so full of hope.
After the air raids, Hans, my friend from next door, and I would hunt for shell splinters which were a prize find. Hans also had a beautiful collection of marbles, large and small, all glistening in many colours. The marbles and the shell splinters were his treasure, yet he gave them all to me when I returned to Switzerland with my parents, who were Swiss, after the war ended.

Whereas the German chemical engineers had had to spend the entire four years of war at the front, my father, the Swiss chemist, had to serve only short spells of military duty for his neutral country. He was, therefore, much envied by his colleagues, because during their absence he had filled vacant posts and was thus promoted to top positions. Those who had been his friends before the war were now embittered and envious enemies. The working conditions became more and more unpleasant for my father, and in the end it was impossible for him to remain in the factory near Frankfurt. With a heavy heart, he decided to return to Switzerland to take over the small chemical factory owned by his father. It was so difficult for me to say good-bye to all my friends, and I left with a very sad heart.

One gloomy November evening, a man and a women with their child arrived at the Swiss border. The customs official checked their passports and said "You may enter the country, but the child must remain here in Germany. She cannot pass the border".

Mother implored with him and tried to make him understand that they could not possibly leave me, a five year old child, alone at night in a strange city. The customs official was stubborn, and repeated, "The parents may enter Switzerland but the child must remain here". Mother was close to desperation, and I shivered with fright. It was cold and wet, and we were all freezing. We returned into German territory, and my parents carefully watched the small customs house. At last the official was relieved from duty, and this proved to be our opportunity for a second chance. Mother, who at that time wore long full skirts, told me to hide underneath her skirt, to try not to move and to generally make myself as invisible as possible. I slipped under and clung to her legs. Father walked closely by and thus we approached the customs house once again. Father presented the passport to the official who sat comfortably inside the warm house, and I was successfully smuggled into Switzerland under my mother's skirt. Late that same evening, we all arrived at grandfather's house where he and my dear grandmother, unfortunately paralysed, as well as father's sister were all waiting to welcome us.

I had never been ill whilst living in the house near Frankfurt, but now I suddenly contracted a bad attack of angina. This irksome illness was to recur time and time again, and I became visibly paler and weaker. I missed my dear lively friends. To me, the Swiss village children seemed unfriendly and proper.

From my earliest childhood, drawing with colours and sketching with pencils had always had a special significance to me. I used to ask for an "encil" because I could not pronounce the word "pencil", and then would immediately begin to draw on an old piece of wrapping

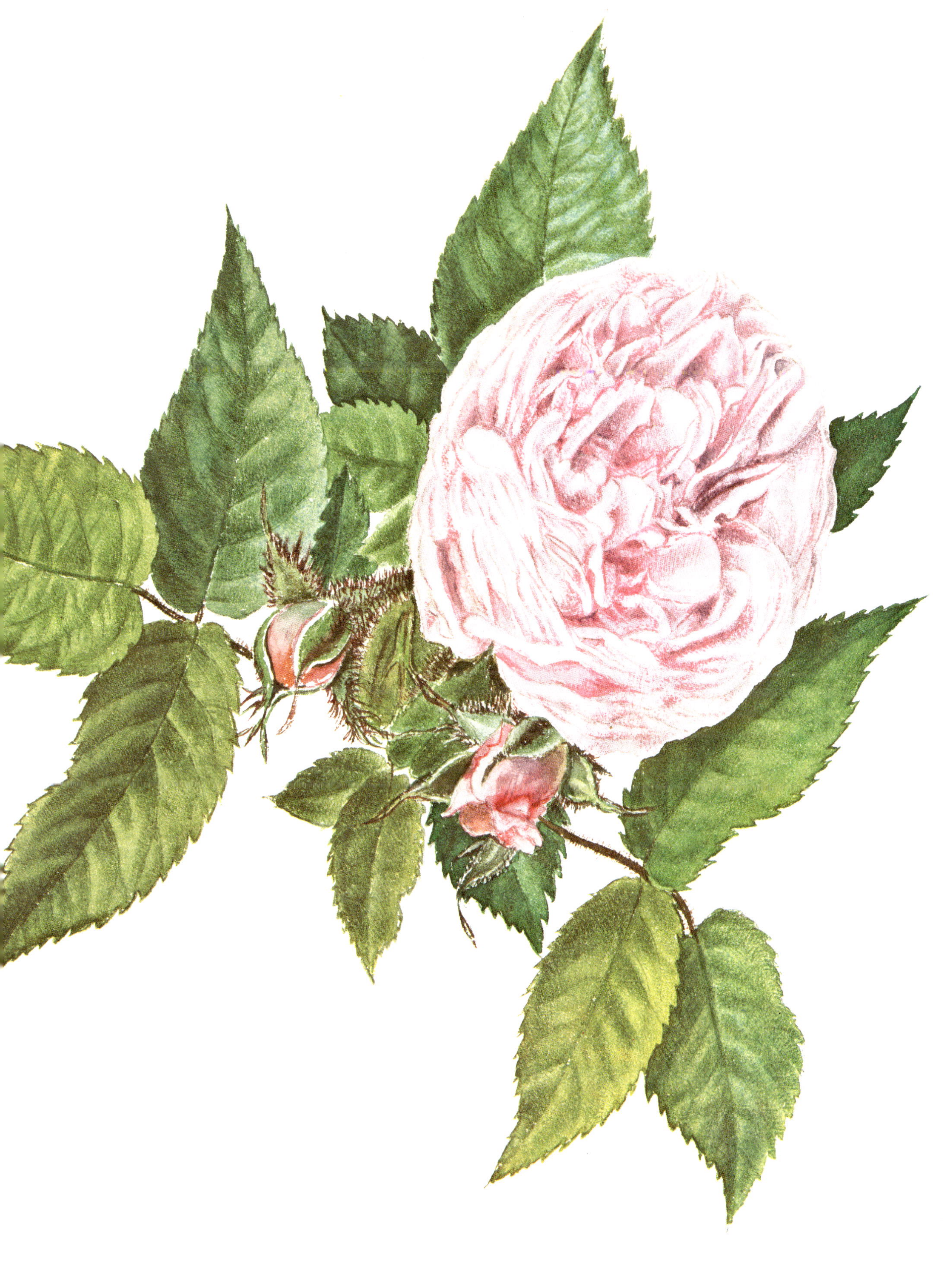

paper, never bothering about dolls. For my second birthday, father gave me a box of coloured pencils, which made me very happy.

Unless I was playing together with children, my entire spare time was taken up with drawing and painting, and later when I was able to read, on books. With this newly acquired ability, I eagerly searched all over the house for any reading matter I could find. Books became my closest friends. In my day-dreams, all sorts of imaginative stories materialized, and sometimes it was difficult to separate fantasy from reality.

Then came school; I came to life again and was happy, and being amongst children I was no longer lonely. The teacher liked me, and I liked him too, and soon became his favourite. My essay was always the longest, twenty pages instead of the few from most other pupils. He often called me to the front of the class, and patting me on the shoulder would say "Listen to what Lotte has written", and he would then read my essay aloud to the class. He also collected my drawings and pinned them to the blackboard in full view.

I was good at drawing, and in the second form had developed my own technique, which was especially popular with the boys. On small rectangles of blotting paper which I had cut from exercise books, I painted flowers, roe deer and fir trees in water colours, and the absorbent paper produced brilliant hues. I framed my paintings with golden-bronze edges or painted the edges black. The boys clamoured after these colourful efforts, and were always willing to part with their treasures in exchange. I soon had a collection of pressed edelweiss, rare birds' feathers, and sometimes even a cherished pen-knife.

When I was eight years old, I read the collected works of Gottfried Keller, starting with "Der grüne Heinrich". After this, I devoured the works by Selma Lagerlöf. I was so fascinated by the novel "Gösta Berling" that I read it five times in the same year. I tried to depict all the figures appearing in this book on my sketching pad, as clearly as my inner eye imagined them to be. Later on, I tried to do same with Dostoevsky's "The Brothers Karamazov" and also with Hamsuns' "Mysteries". The fairy-tales by Hans Christian Andersen, which I have read with great enthusiasm since my first school days, are my constant companion, even today, and I never tire of reading them afresh because each time they enlighten me to a new significance. Since my early childhood, I attempted to illustrate my favourite tales by Andersen. Among these, were "The Mermaid", "The Seven Swans", "The Emperor's New Clothes", and above all, the exquisite jewel "The Snow Queen", with its deep symbolism, wherein the rose, which was also to play a role in my later life, has a specially important part. In proof of my great esteem and admiration for Andersen, I have

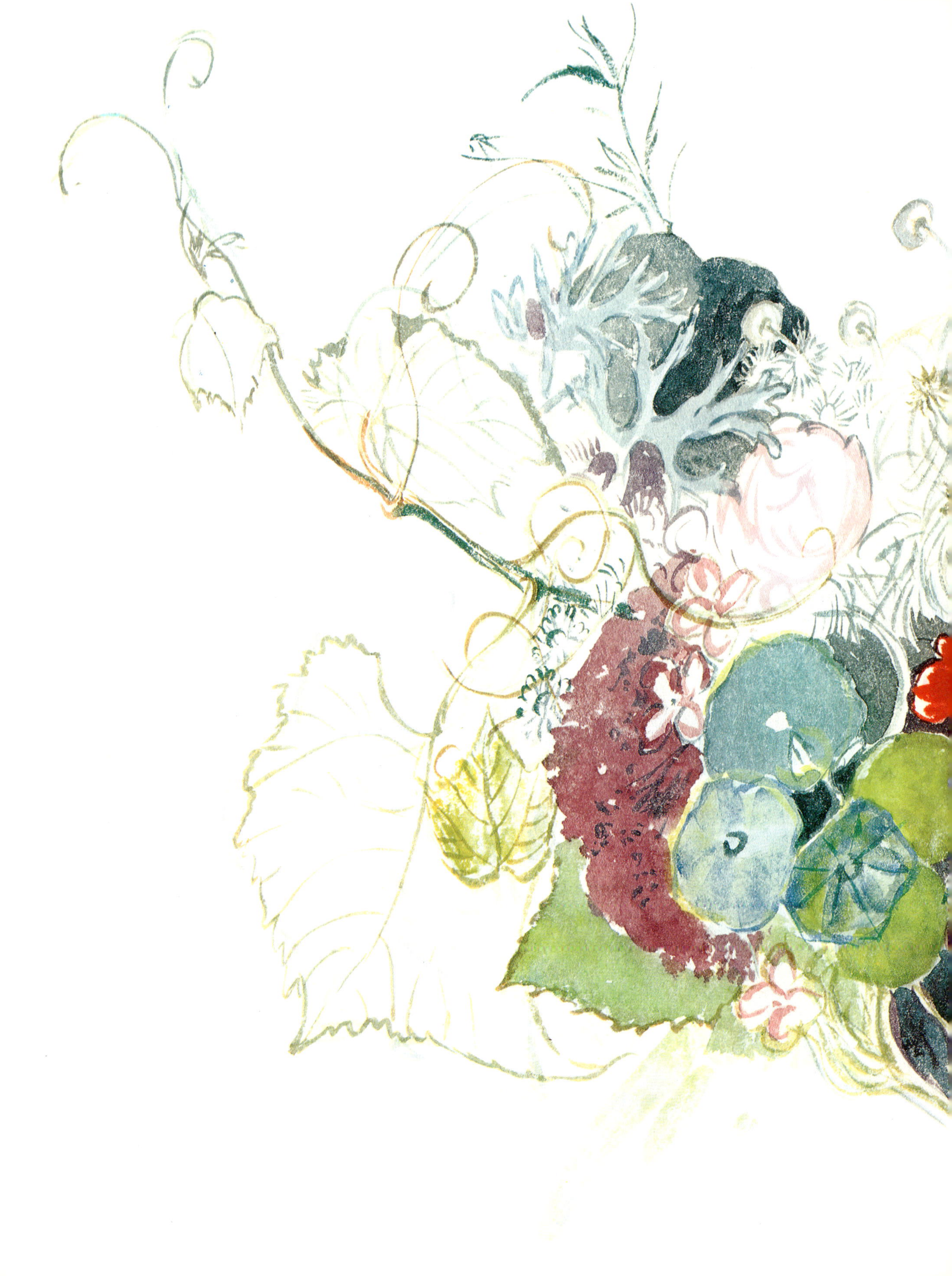

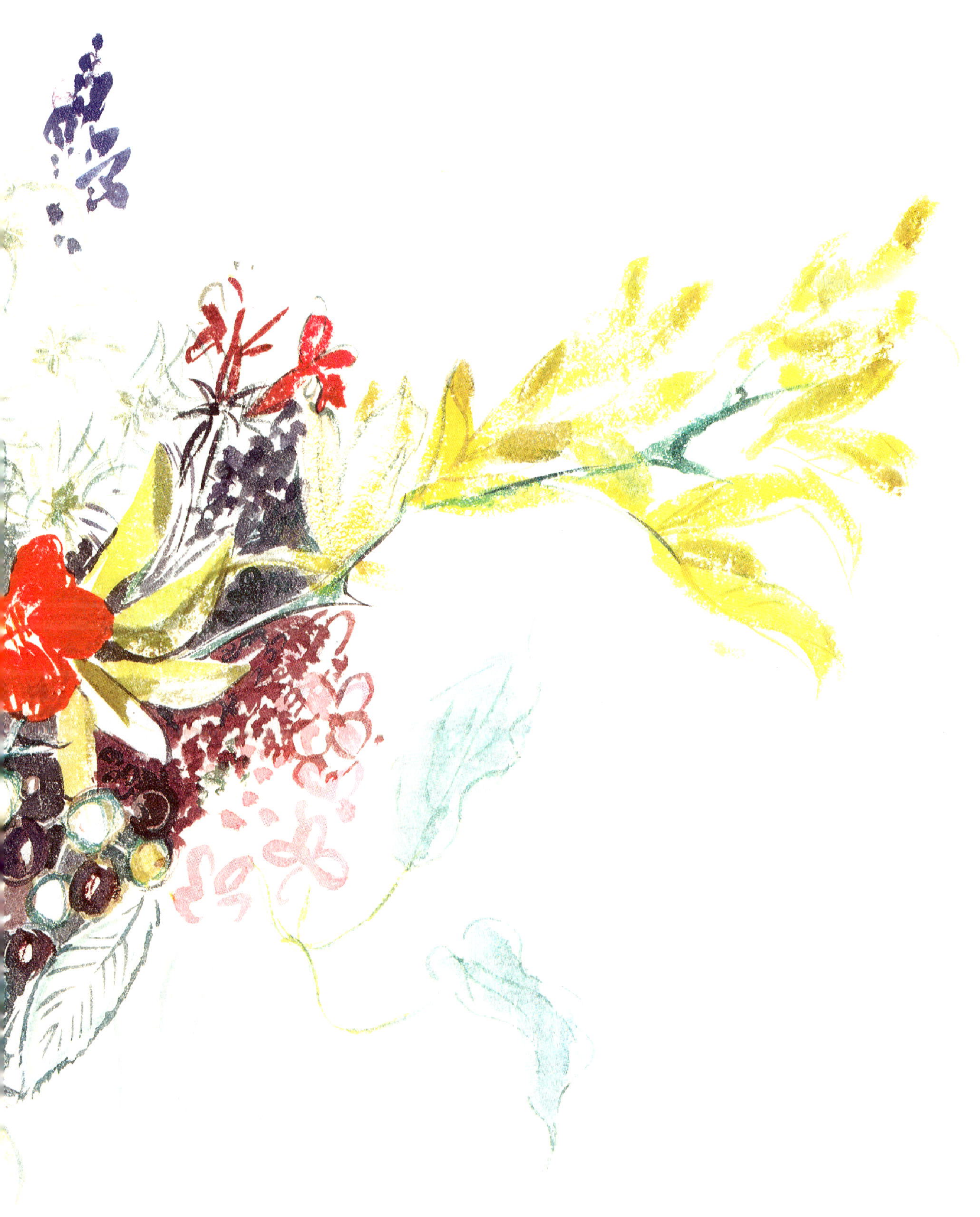

tried for over fifty years to illustrate his works. It was a one-sided admiration, because I was never able to worthily do justice to his great talent, and so almost everything was banished to the waste-paper basket.

In my ninth year, I became acquainted with the painter Waldemar Flaig who lived during the summer months together with his family in the Castle Meersburg on Lake Constance, and in the winter in Berlin. There he knew everyone and everything of importance during the wild twenties; the Reinhardts, Ilse Heims, the Thimigs, the Russian ballerina Tatiana Barbakoff and many other celebrities belonged to his circle of friends. He often said to me "When you are seventeen, I will take you to Berlin and introduce you to all the interesting people – you'll love it". From then on, Berlin was never out of my thoughts for long, and I sensed that one day I would go there.

During many summers, I was allowed to have painting lessons with him. He often warned me from too much mixing, or overpainting, because the colours would become dull and dead. If not handled lightly and carefully, their purity, freshness and glow would otherwise be lost.

Unfortunately, Flaig died when I was seventeen, but I still managed to go to Berlin, even though it was not until I was twenty-one, and I found the city as fascinating as Flaig had told me. Flaig was always full of praise for my sketches and paintings, which of course boosted my morale no end. Under his tuition I made my first nude study in charcoal and ruddle; he could inspire enthusiasm in his pupils.

For some seven years, I had violin lessons, but when I was fourteen I heard Yehudi Menuhin play, after which I vowed never to touch my instrument again. My parents often played piano in duet, Beethoven's 5th for example. I listened enraptured to my mother playing Beethoven's sonatas or Schubert's impromptus. Father preferred to play Beethoven, although in his youth he was very fond of Richard Wagner. He particularly enjoyed playing Gluck's compositions, which he excelled at. Through his virtuosity on the piano, "Iphigenie auf Tauris" and "Reigen seliger Geister" are unforgettable for me.

I was deeply grieved when my mother forbade me to visit father on his death-bed because I knew, that in spite of his condition, he would have wished me to visit him. I went into town that particular morning because I wanted to be alone; there is no better place to be so than amongst the crowds in a busy city. I walked slowly along the path beside the river Limmat, trying to communicate happiness to my beloved father before the final farewell. I felt that he would have wished above all to hear music again, but mother wanted neither grammophone nor radio in the house. I therefore attempted to send him one of his favourite melodies. I concentrated all my powers of imagination and strength on Gluck's music from the "Reigen seliger Geister", until my ears rang with the sounds of a full orchestra. When the enthralling sounds came to an end and the last sweet notes faded, I suddenly realised that the mist had cleared and I was in a busy street filled with people and the confusion of voices. Standing in front of the Fraumünster church, I noticed that the clock on the tower showed just after ten thirty. I drove home to ask mother about father's condition, and she said, "Well, something odd happened about ten thirty this morning". Father was apparently peacefully dozing when all of a sudden he awoke and started to wave his arms to an imaginary concert and then with a sigh, and eyes gleaming with happiness, he said "What a wonderful piece of music that was". I was overjoyed to realise that my final message had reached him. He died shortly after.

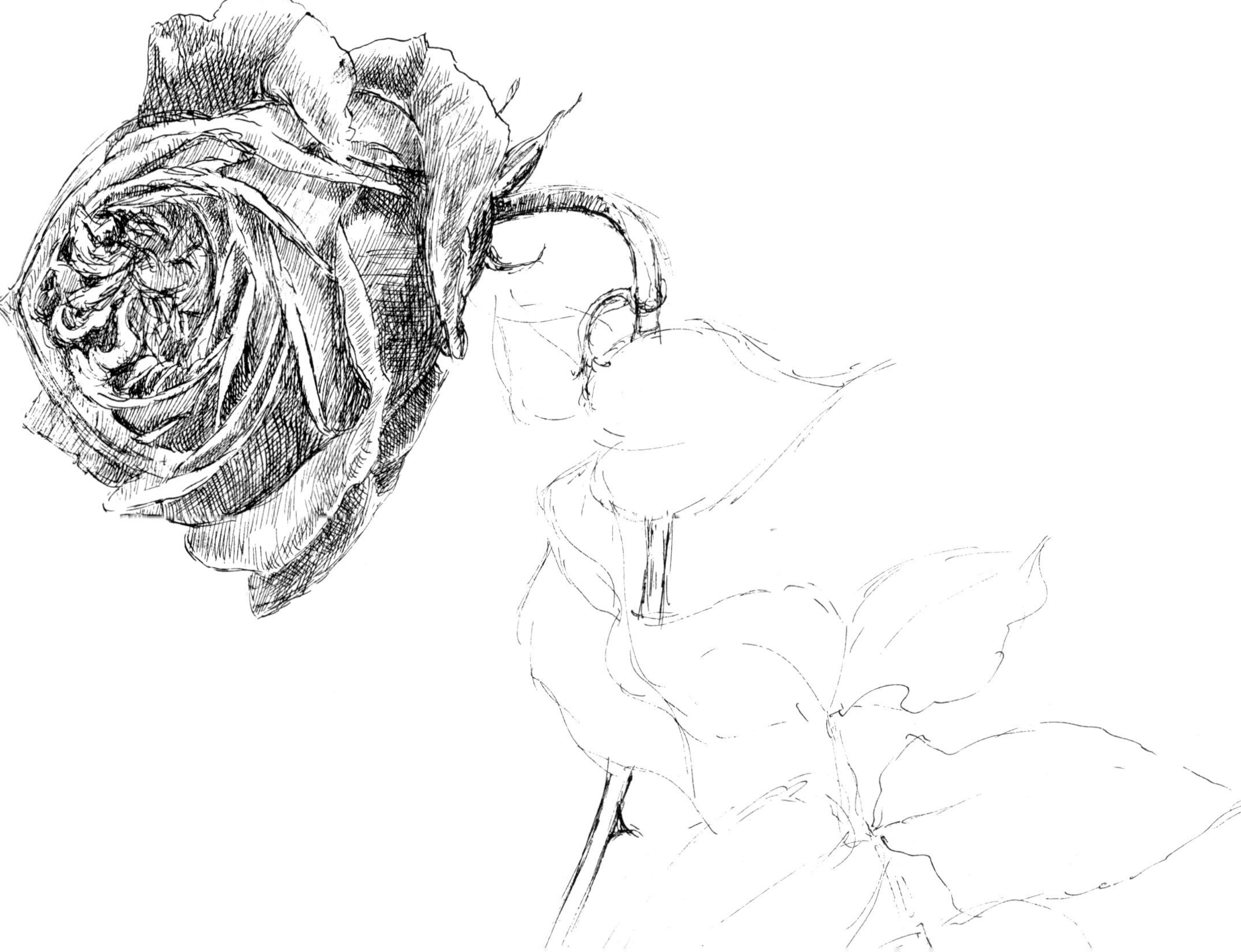

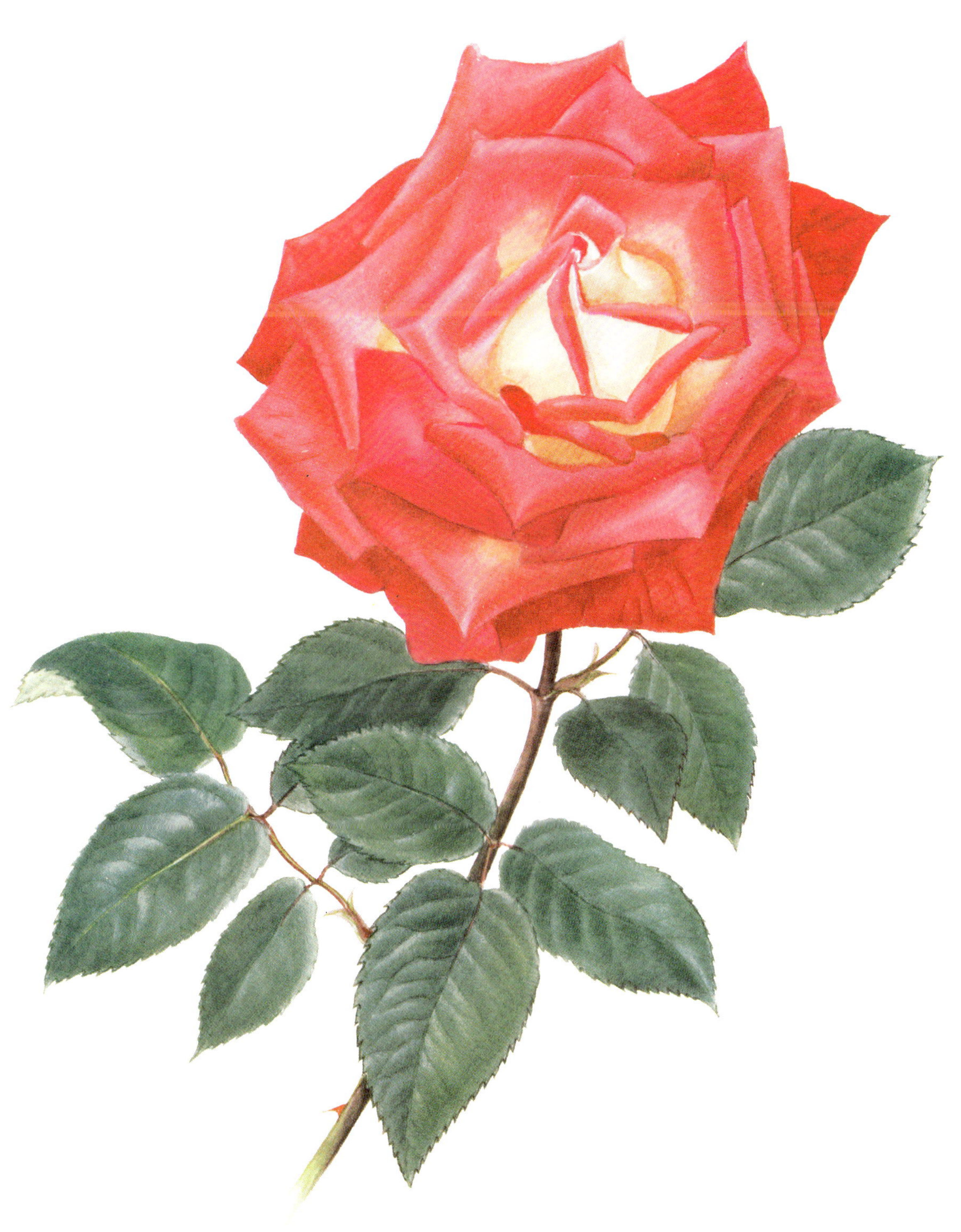

Once a strangely beautiful dream had helped me tremendously in getting over my first and biggest disappointment in love. In this dream, I was walking over gentle hills. It was spring and the sun shone warmly from a pale blue sky, and this warmth penetrated my body like a comforting embracement. I stepped over the lush green meadows, now free of snow, and I felt lightfooted and carefree. The spring flowers were everywhere, purple violets, pale yellow primroses, white anemones, dark blue enzian and red and golden auricula. The whole pasture seemed to be a carpet of blossoms. Then I heard music; the wonderful chorus of St. Matthew's Passion by Johann Sebastian Bach, and a voice sang the words "Choose your own way, and have no fear of that which torments your heart. He who shows the way to the clouds and wind will guide you on your path". Waking up, I felt content and happier than I had been for a long time. I wonder whoever could have sent me this musical message.

Aged nineteen, I made a second visit to London. This time it was not only to learn the English language, but to study various subjects at the Central School of Arts and Crafts. This included fashion design, drawing and cutting, as well as the design of material and wallpaper. The school was enormous; a city within itself. However, I did not profit as much there as I had done in Paris. Probably, im my enthusiasm, I had enrolled for too many subjects at once. Mrs Cochrane, the couture teacher impressed me very much; she was brisk and lively, and had an open mind for anything new and beautiful.

Why this pleasant lady chose me to collect for the German Jewish students expelled by Hitler will always baffle me. It was December 1933, extremely cold with thick fog in London. My English was still not too good, and I implored her not to send me, a foreigner, out on to the streets of London to collect for the campaign. Never before in my life had I done anything like it, let alone in a foreign language and in a city unknown to me. I assured her that I would probably not be able to sell a single badge, and that it would all be pure luck.

All my persuasion was in vain; she remained steadfast and I was allocated an area near the church of St. Martin's in the Fields. The following day, a sandwich board was hung around my neck on which all the badges which I was supposed to sell were neatly arranged in rows. A large tin was thrust into my hand, into which the pennies and shillings would hopefully be donated. Thus equipped, I took up my position outside this famous church. I kept thinking to myself about what I should say, and probably looked rather bashful standing closely to the church railings at a bus-stop. Only one person noticed me standing

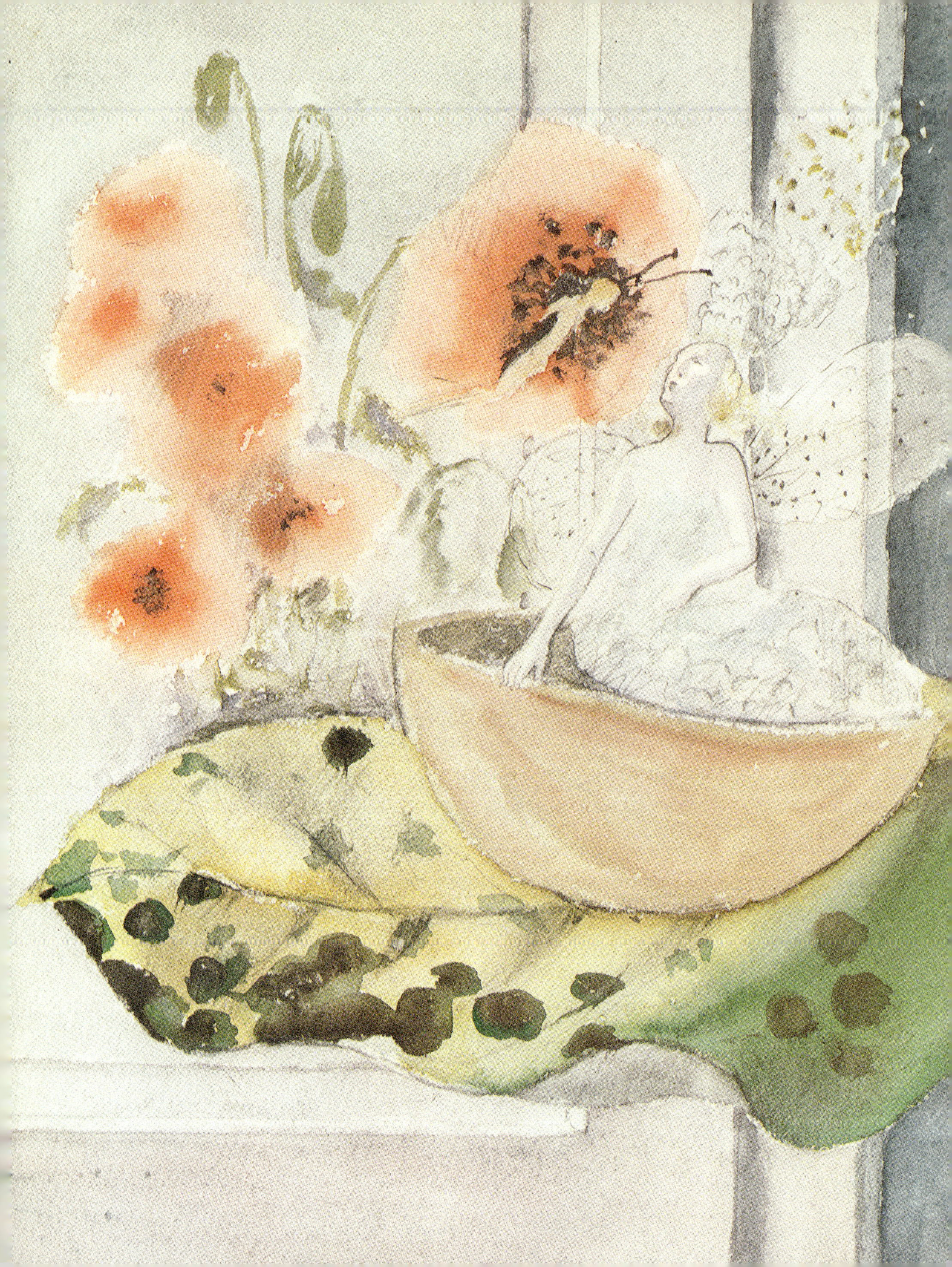

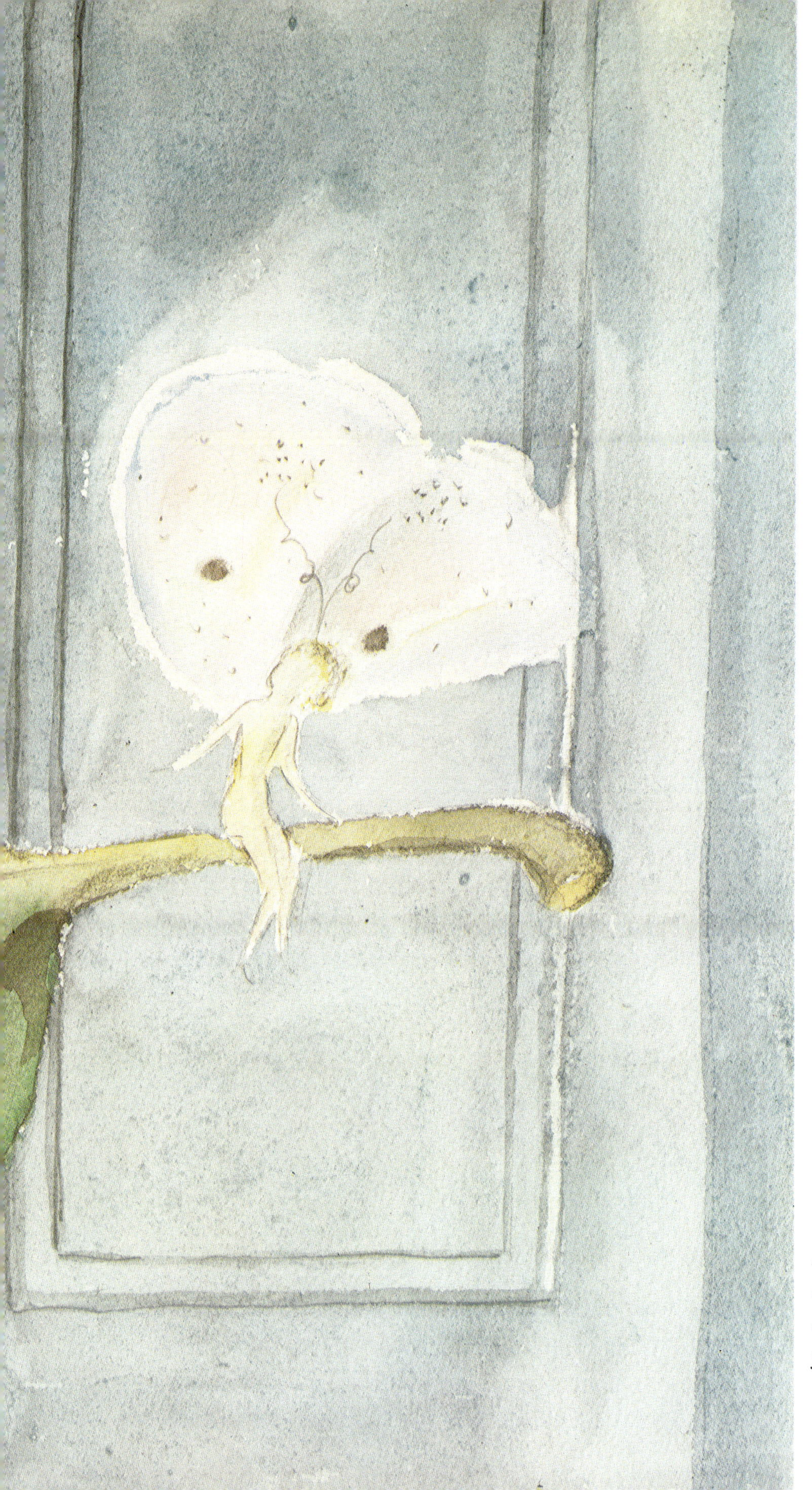

An understandable diversion from painting plant diseases. I was seventeen years old.

there, and after his enquiry as to the cause of the collection, I repeated my carefully rehearsed lines. At this he stormed off, shouting that he would never donate to the Jews and that as far as he cared, they could look after themselves. The heavy Christmas traffic had caused some traffic jams, and a bus came to a standstill. The driver, who had probably observed me for some time, called out also asking about the cause of the collection. After repeating my lines again, he said "What an ungrateful task you have, and if you stay shyly hidden away at the back of the pavement you'll not sell a single badge by tonight".
I thought this most likely. He asked for my tin and gave me all his halfpennies, and shook it with an impressive rattle. "Look", he said, "this is how to do it. Shake it as loudly as you can and give the passers by a big smile, especially to the men, they always have a soft heart for a pretty girl". Suddenly the traffic started moving again, and my kind benefactor drove away calling "Good luck". Following his instructions, I approached the nearest person, and holding the tin under his nose, sold a badge in no time. From then on, everything was easy, and soon the tin was full of coins. Most people were friendly, giving without even asking the cause. Contrary to what the bus-driver had told me, the only really unpleasant people were in fact, men. One gave me a stiff lecture on why I, as a foreigner, was collecting for German Jewish students. I did not have an answer to give him in my basic English. Well, why was I doing it? Another said that he did not like the Jews anyway and he did not care what Hitler did with them. Yet another said that nobody helped him when he was in trouble, and that all the Jews were interested in was money. According to him, they had more than enough and should collect amongst themselves. A middle-aged man enquired about the cause, at first rather rudely, mentioning that I was not even able to speak the language properly. Then, with a sudden smile, he pushed a one pound note into the tin and said "That's for your lovely face". With no more ado, he removed all the remaining badges and left me with my task finished, just as I had begun to enjoy myself. Now and again, interesting people had stopped for a chat. On the church steps, I met a father and mother with their two sons, all blonde and blue-eyed. They spoke to me in the purest High German, and I discovered that they were a German Jewish family that had emigrated. They were very kind and affectionate to me, and generously filled my tin to the brim. Upon leaving, the father turned to me and very ceremoniously said "One day God will reward you for this", at which I automatically gave him a smile, thinking it was just a nice thing which he had said. However, his expression was serious and he again repeated "Believe me, God will bless you for what you are doing here for us, even in years to come".

His solemnity made a deep impression on my soul and strangely moved me, and I had no other choice but to believe his words.

I gained a great deal from visiting the various galleries in London. The Tate Gallery, housing many paintings by Turner, one of my favourites, interested me particularly. The longer I remained in London, the more I became fascinated by this beautiful city. On arriving, it had appeared to be dull and conservative, but as time progressed it completely captivated my heart, and made a lifelong impression on me.

The crisis of the depression during "the thirties" was by no means over when during 1936–1938 I attended the Berlin Art School. In our house, as likewise in many others, thriftiness was the order of the day. Although people looked upon me as the only daughter of well-to-do parents, I knew, as an "insider", that supporting our company was as dangerous as a mountaineering expedition, and that collapse and bankruptcy were possible at any time. Professor Karrer, who was awarded the Nobel Prize, and a close friend of my father, considered it an insane idea to attempt such an undertaking without outside financial backing during those difficult years.

In those times, bankruptcy would have been a tremendous disgrace, and in my dreams I often saw how people pointed with their finger at my father, and I awoke bathed in perspiration.

When I was sixteen, I overheard how the mayor of our village said to father "Well, Dr Maag, now we can raise our hats to you again". This was after an extremely difficult period during which the company actually managed to show a slight profit.

Under these circumstances, on arriving at the railway station in Berlin at eight o'clock in the morning, I went to the information office for assistance with my lodging, and from the large selection of furnished rooms available, it was quite natural that I chose the cheapest. It was a dark and narrow room, overlooking a bleak yard, bare of any vegetation. The furniture consisted of a small cupboard, table, chair and narrow bed. This bed had no resemblance to the flat and comfortable surface which it should have been, and before going to sleep, I had to try and arrange my body around the hard lumps. The room cost 35 Marks per month, this included breakfast and a weekly bath. The bathroom was inconveniently situated at the other end of the apartment, and so I had to pass through the landlady's rooms to reach it.

Father was much against my enthusiasm for Berlin. However, from 1933 he placed the highest obstacles in my path and attempted to dissuade me from going. When I returned

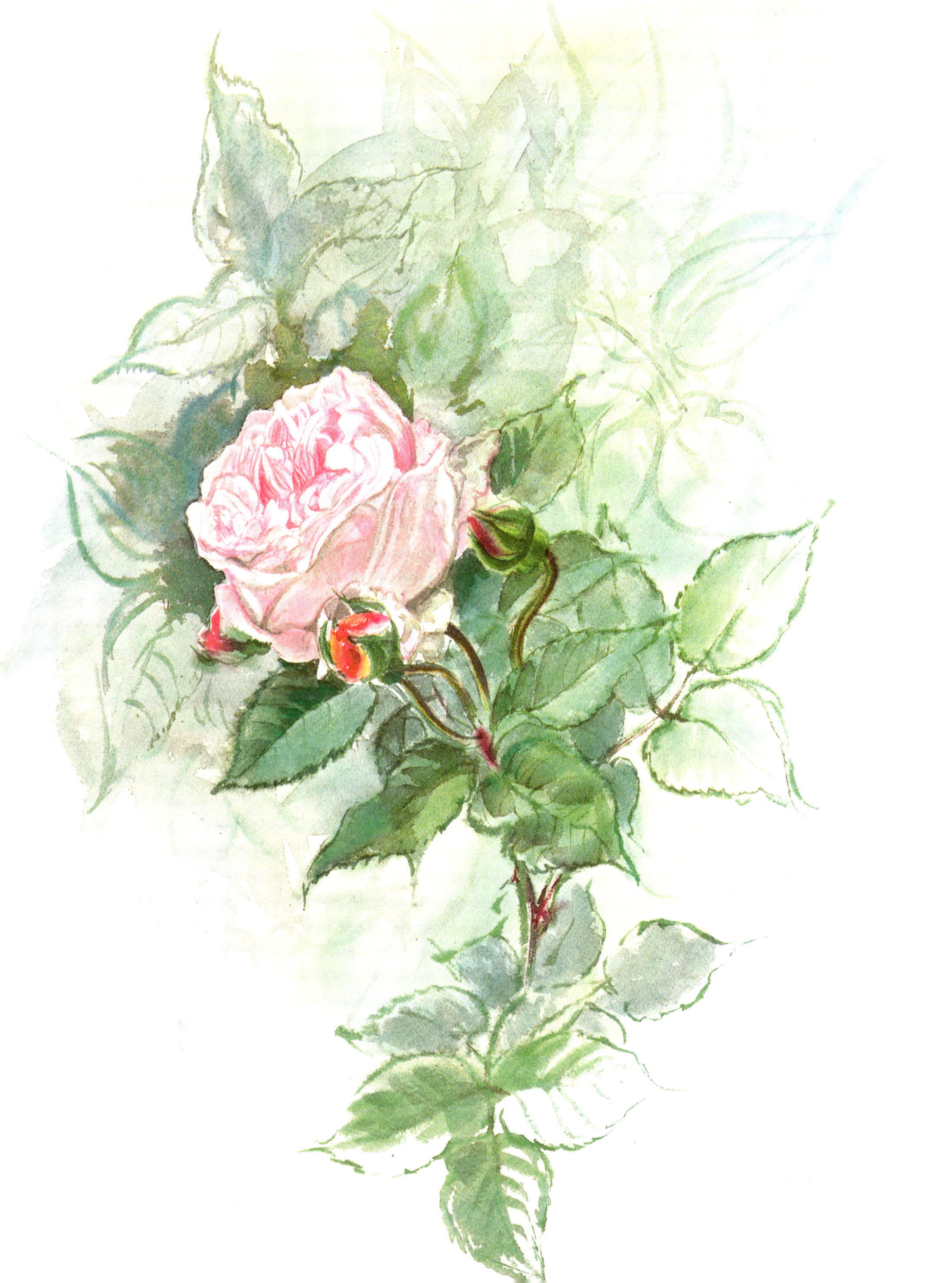

home shortly before my 21st birthday after completing my apprenticeship and studies in Paris, I was still determined to go to Berlin, and argued that I lacked a thorough German educational background, which should have been my foundation before studying in either London or Paris, and father was very upset on hearing this. He tried everything to redirect my thoughts and to advise me against going to Berlin. The man, whose business always came first and had hardly taken time for a holiday, suddenly decided to have a three-week vacation in Florence, travelling via Milan, Ravenna, Mantua, Padua and Pisa.

It was just after Easter, a beautiful time of the year, and the countryside was transformed into one lovely garden. Florence is a unique city, as everyone who has been there well knows, and father tried to convince me that it was the most enticing and ideal city to study art. He showed me everything. We walked, queued, admired, walked and stood again, all day long. It was almost a miracle that we found time to eat and sleep, because when father was excited about anything he was oblivious to the outside world. "Isn't it fantastic?", he asked, time and time again. "The architecture, these statues and paintings, aren't they magnificent?" And then, "… and the beautiful landscape; it's paradise". I put up with his "paradise" for three weeks, and all the time had only one thought in mind, Berlin; if only I could have been there. Today I am amazed that so much beauty could have passed in front of my eyes without registering the slightest impression. My poor father went to so much trouble, all in vain, because as soon as we arrived back home, I immediately asked "When may I go to Berlin? I have already lost three valuable working weeks by going to Italy". Father was shocked that I spoke of our educational trip as a waste of time, but resigned himself to my stubborness.

At the beginning of May, I went to Berlin, and I felt as though a childhood dream was about to come true. Thirteen years had passed by since Flaig had told me about this fascinating city. My father, as a young student, had also spent one year in Berlin, but he almost hated the city and had never felt at home. He found the people rude, snobbish, arrogant and sarcastic. The Berliners I soon met appeared lively, humorous and quick-witted. I interpreted their so-called brashness as a kind of armour to protect their warm and vulnerable nature from being mis-used.

I remained three years in Berlin and the longer I stayed, the closer the people of this city became to me. Even the poorest were able to smile and joke, and I never once met an embittered person. They even joked about their hardship and poverty, and I have never known a more courageous people than the Berliners. Some thirty years later, for the first

42

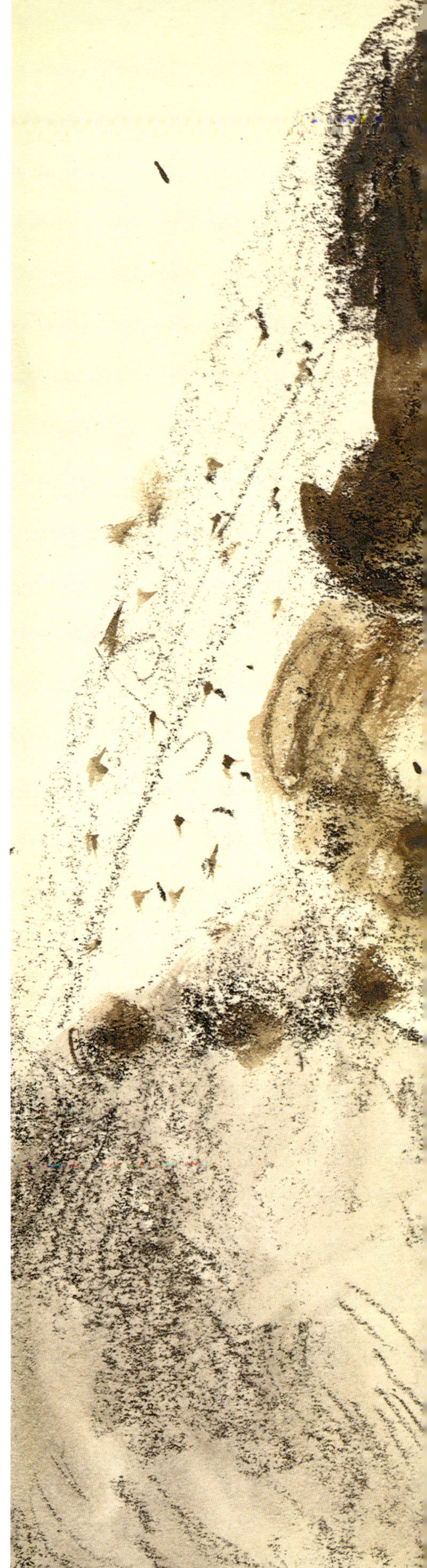

An early sketch of a self-portrait. Berlin 1938.

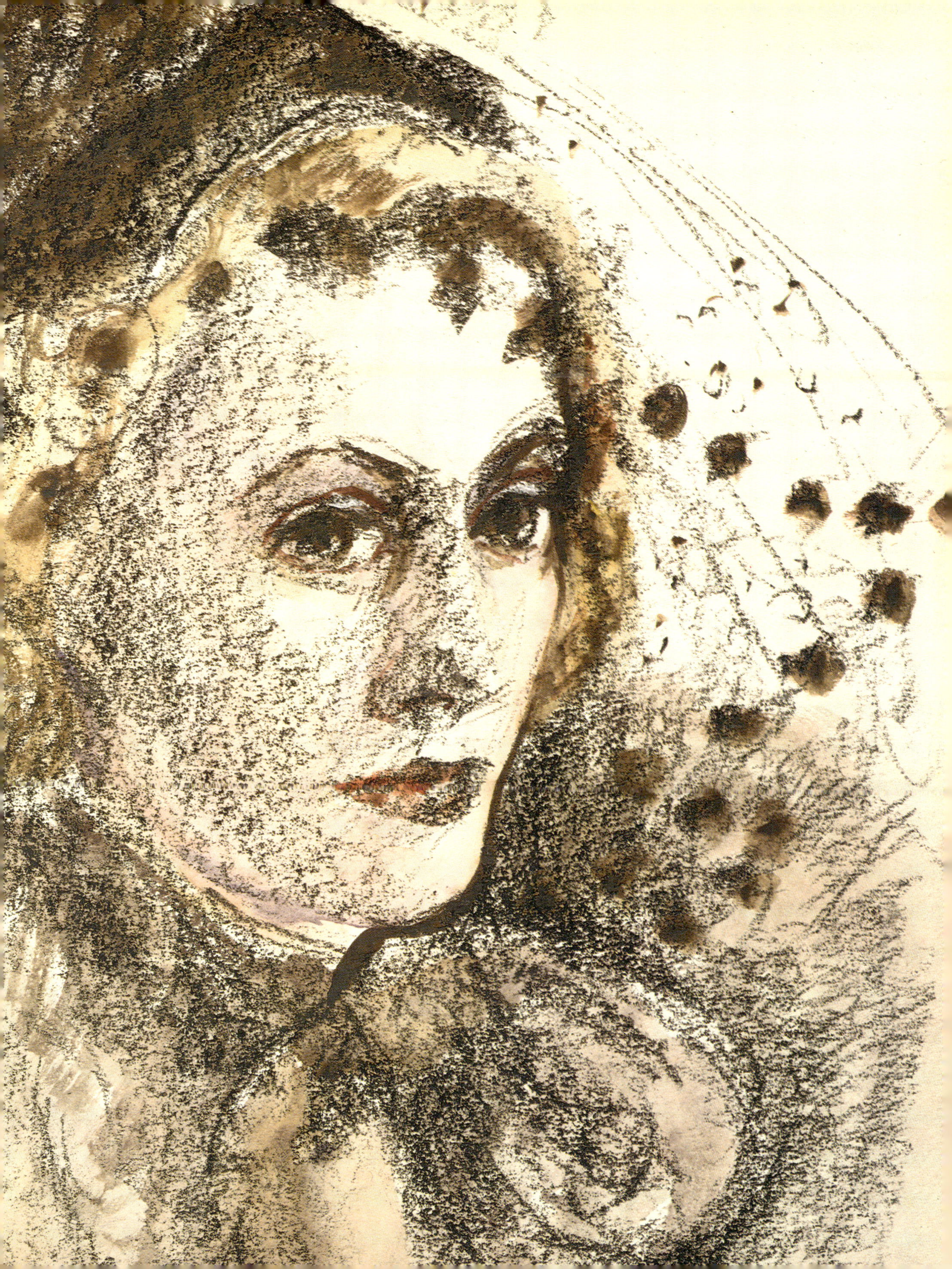

time in America, I found the New Yorkers to be a close comparison with their dauntless and patient acceptance of life. Strangely, New York itself reminds me more than any other city I know of Berlin, even though apparently so different. Only the severe harshness radiated on a cold winter day by the city of New York, and which always gave me a feeling of uncanniness and anticipation, was never given me by Berlin.

Life in Berlin was very inexpensive, and the school fees were my biggest outlay. Means of transport was on foot, or by fourth class rail for a longer journey. At that time, there were still four classes. A student's ticket from Berlin to the Swiss border cost me eighteen Marks. I also found out that I could buy a portion of lentil soup from the outside counter at Woolworths for fifteen Pfennig which one ate standing on the street. Soup with a sausage in it cost thirty Pfennig, too expensive for me. So, several lunchtimes each week found me eating my lentil soup amongst beggars in front of Woolworths. I ate my evening meal in my room, and this was usually a "Schrippen", which was two small bread rolls costing only five Pfennig, butter and meat paste, and a cup of tea which I was allowed to make in my landlady's kitchen.

Breakfast was usually another "Schrippen", butter and jam, and a cup of coffee made from coffee grains. On Sundays, the landlady used fresh grains, but then used them again every day till the next Sunday, and so the drink became weaker and weaker as the days passed. The whole house smelt of camphor, cabbage and floor polish, a strange scent indeed. These circumstances never bothered me. I was happy and carefree as never before in all my life, and I even slept soundly on my uncomfortable bed. I was able to attend the Academy of Art, the teachers were excellent and interesting, and I felt as though my work was slowly but surely improving. Professor G. Ulrich taught me several different painting techniques including dry-point engraving; the latter I found to be fascinating. Even as a child I had always enjoyed working and any tasks given me had filled me with satisfaction and contentment. At home, I had never been praised for my work, and so the sincere and warm compliments from my various teachers, such as Léger, Bissière, Severini, John Farleigh and Professor G. Ulrich, were wonderful and made me extremely pleased. My student days in Paris and London were full of happiness and completely absorbing. When Severini of the Academie Ranson first examined one of my two-minute pen and ink studies from the nude, I was eighteen at the time, which I had made with fast and sure strokes, he exclaimed "Mais c'est formidable, c'est un Matisse, un jeune Picasso". During my farewell visit to Léger after one year of studying under him at the Académie de la Grande Chaumière in

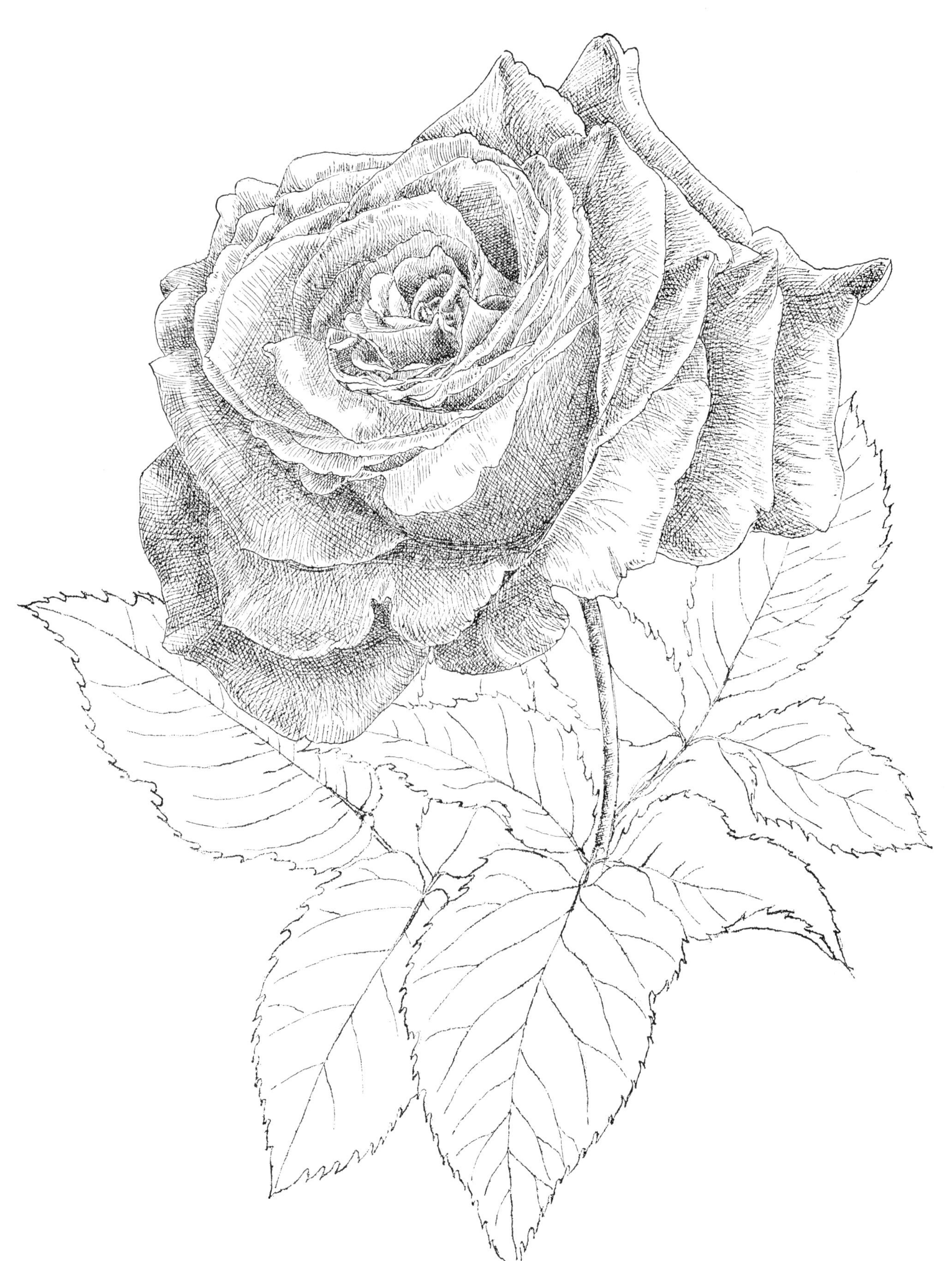

Paris, he told me "Vous auriez sûrement du succès, vous êtes très douée, vous avez de la persévérance et vous avez travaillée pendant cette année ici plus qu'un étudiant de la médecine à la Sorbonne". I remarked that his last statement was very much exaggerated, to which he indignantly replied that my greatest handicap was my modesty. Nonetheless, this compliment from such a great artist was a tremendous accomplishment.

Artists constantly question themselves as to the meaning of their work, and sometimes reach a point of despair. Such moments only dominate until a slight glimmer of hope is seen on the horizon, and only then one can realise that the years of hardship and toil have brought progress along a never ending path, upon which one is never completely satisfied with ones capabilities and achievements until death. It is a never ending search, always for the unknown, and an everlasting learning. Possibly this is why artists remain so youthful even though they become older the same as other mortals. Their work is never finished, and an artist cannot and is rarely able to be unproductive and rest on his laurels. A flame within the soul seems to drive one constantly towards new creations and work; a wonderful experience, but sometimes also torment. The imagination gives no peace until the paintings are born on paper; like a child in a mother's womb awaiting its birth. Whilst I was studying in Berlin I met Hans, a tall, dark and handsome man. He had studied history, and since this was one of my interests, we were never lost for words. We had the same taste in music too, and went to many of the magnificent concerts held by the Berlin Philharmonic Orchestra. On Sundays, we took long walks through the "Grunewald". It was early spring, and in every respect a wonderful time of the year. We planned to marry, and with much enthusiasm I immediately started to search for a suitable three-room apartment into which we could move at the end of the summer. I eventually found a charming home on Lake Lietzen; the balcony had a view to the park and the lake, and the price was not too high.

During the summer holidays, Hans stayed for three weeks at my parents house. Towards the end, father and Hans went to a restaurant for a long discussion, and both returned in silence and looking very pale. Father had tried to persuade Hans to join our company, but Hans had adamantly refused, stating that this was not his profession. He was a historian and loved his work.

Hans returned to Berlin. Unfortunately, I had a bad attack of angina and had to remain at home. Unhappy months followed; my parents were strongly opposed to the marriage, and by autumn, worn out from the illness and depressed by the tense situation at home, I sent

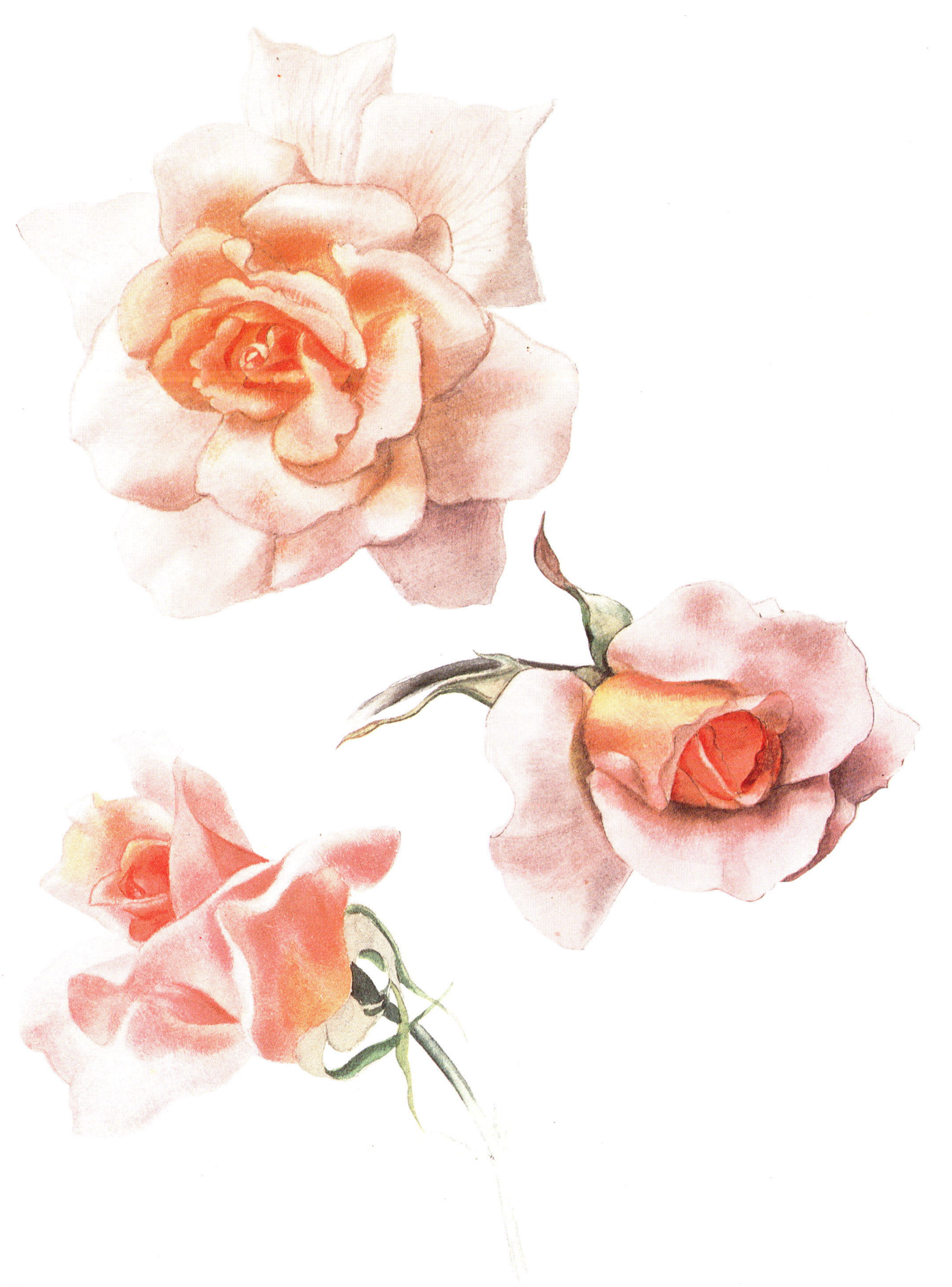

a farewell letter to Hans. I no longer wanted or cared for anything anymore, and my work alone kept my head above water.

Time passed, and I became fully occupied with our company's preparations for the Swiss Exposition to be held in 1939. I painted an outsize pear, grapes and an apple, all made of plaster of Paris, and which were depicted with disease and scab, and also an enlarged vegetable bed of tomatoes, red and white cabbages, leeks, etc… which had been cut out of cardboard. This required a great deal of space, and I was able to use the studio belonging to a friend who was an advertising artist, and work together with two young commercial artists. I painted an extremely realistic looking scab on the enormous apple. Father came daily to control my work, and I had to remove this scab with turpentine because he did not approve of it. The second scab, the third and fourth neither found favour under father's scathing eye, and meek as a lamb, again and again I wiped them off with the help of a great quantity of turpentine without the slightest grumble. When father was again full of criticism for my fifth attempt, I realised that the two commercial artists had downed their work and were staring at us full of contempt. I had no explanation for their behaviour, and it was not until father had left, that the uproar broke out. "There can only be one such patient angel as you in the whole world. It's unbelievable how he treats you. The scab is absolutely fantastic, so realistic, it's mean…" They continued in this manner, and only at their firm insistence did I agree to leave the fifth edition of the scab on the apple. Father came the next day, and his only comment was that it was much better now. However, as a result of using so much turpentine to rub out the perpetual scab on the apple, I had an ugly eczema on my right hand. The doctor consulted confirmed that the eczema was from turpentine, and forbade any further use. Luckily, the oil painting on the giant plaster grapes, pear and apple was finished and I was able to work on the other paintings with my right hand bandaged. I was commissioned by Willi Günthart, who I became acquainted with at this time, to do various paintings for the Swiss Exposition to be held in 1939.

He was my first employer; himself already established and well known as a commercial artist with influential clients. He had his own large studio and many employees. With my first earnings, I bought a radio, which gave me a lot of pleasure. The unforgettable "Landi" was opened, and at the end of this memorable exposition which bound many different Swiss people together in a strangely unique way, war was declared in Europe.

Painting was out of the question. I had to take over the duties of the men in our company

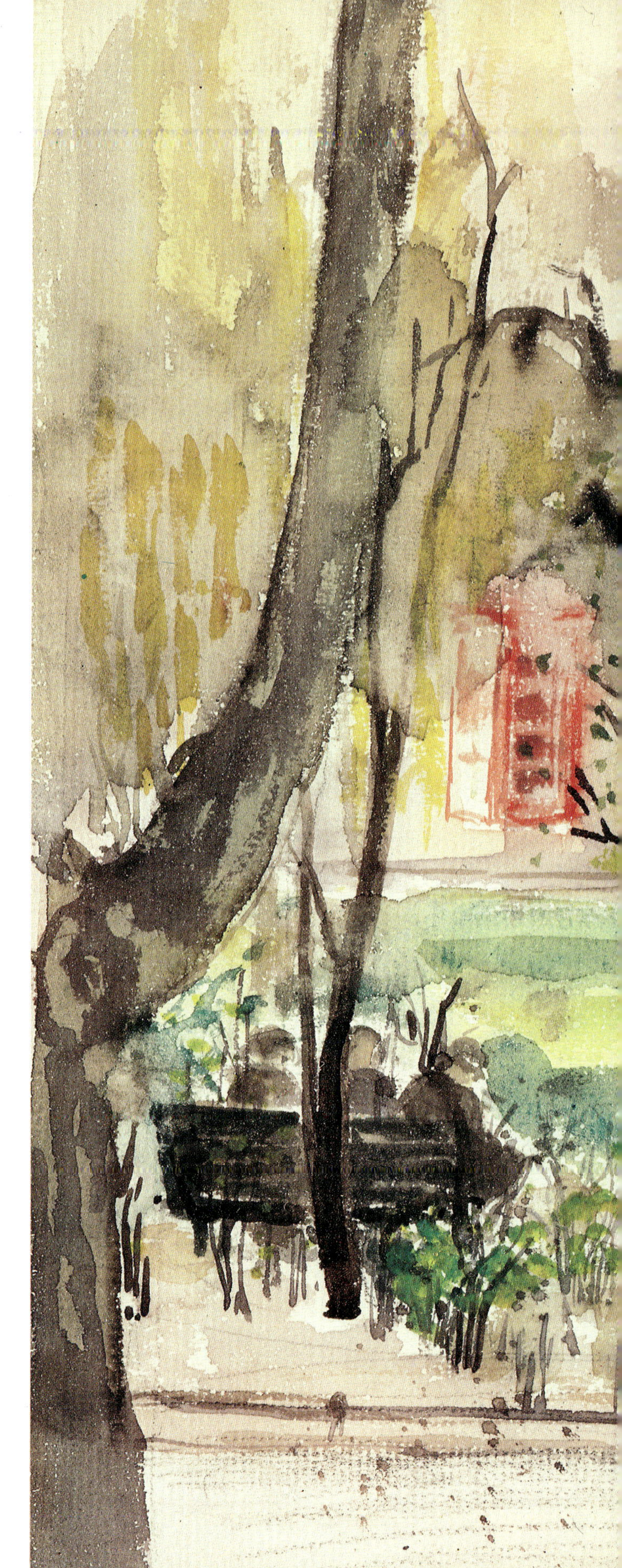

View of the "Stubenrauchplatz" in Berlin, 1937.

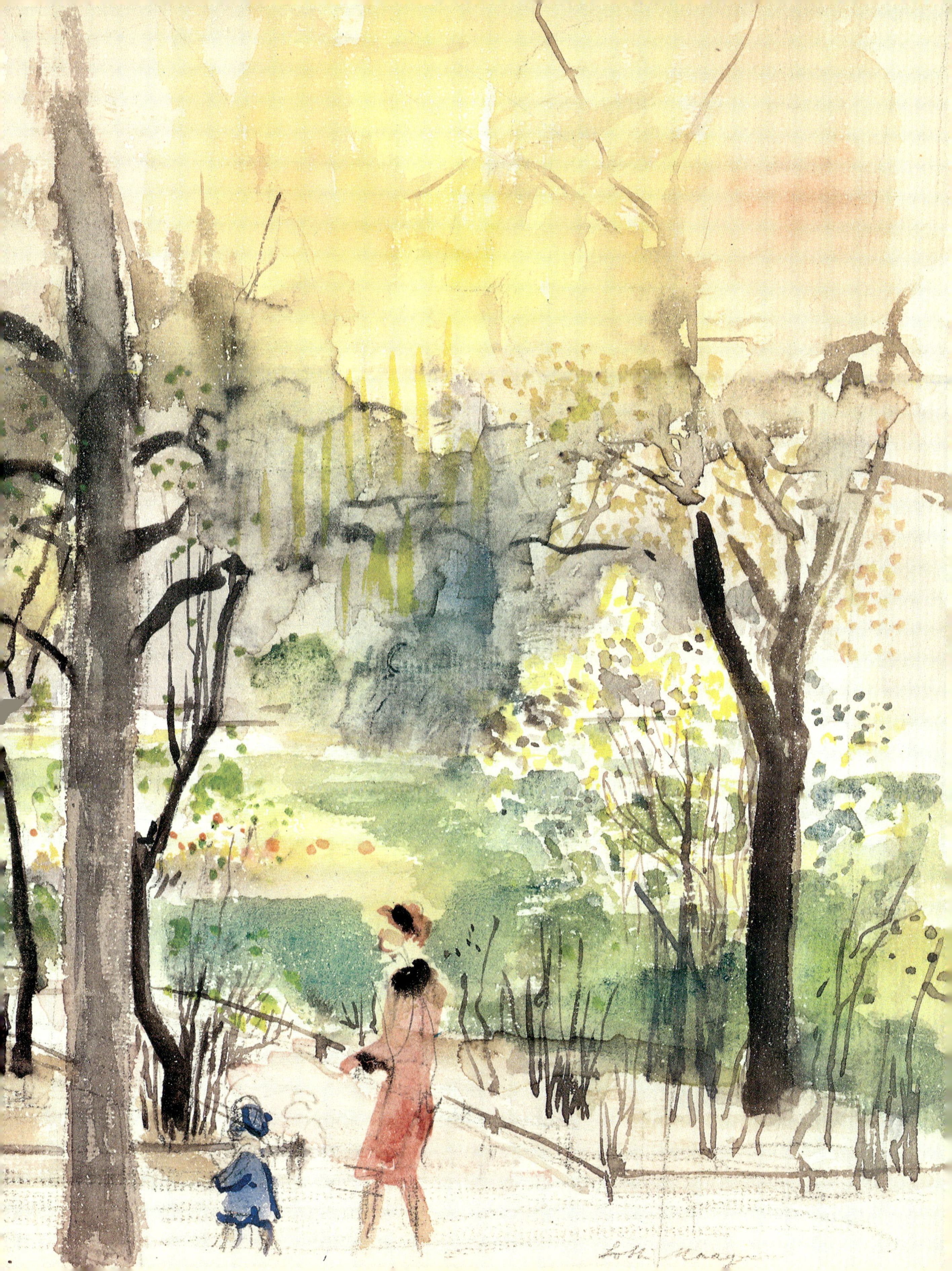

who had been called-up for military service. My mornings were taken up with spraying the greenhouse plants with various insecticides which I had mixed, weighing every ingredient exactly because otherwise the plants would have been scorched. From one thirty in the afternoon until six in the evening, my time was spent pulling up innumerable weeds in the gardens.

My poor mother was confined to her bed from 1940 till 1941, virtually paralysed with a severe attack of rheumatism. At the end of the summer in 1941, Ernst George Ruegg, the affectionate Swiss painter and poet visited us. He asked me what paintings I had made in the meantime, but mother replied that this was no time for painting, because it was war, and that I had to replace the absent men. On hearing this, the usually so sweet tempered man became very emphatic, almost angry, something which we had never witnessed before, and said to my parents, "Don't you realise it's a crime what you're doing, keeping your daughter from her profession? Don't you know that she has a talent amounting to genius? Anyone can weed the gardens, cook and clean, or do any other menial tasks, but what your daughter can do, that is very rare. You are burying a jewel in the sand, yes, it's infamous, a disgrace, such a waste of talent". He continued in this manner, until my parents became almost afraid, but after his visit and temperamental outburst, they gave me more time to paint again. During this time, so precious because it was newly won, I painted my most beautiful garden pictures.

Willi Günthart was jokingly nicknamed "the foal" by his client of the time, Dr Fritz Wahlen who was a Professor for Plant Cultivation, and for whom I also painted a frieze in tempera of wild flowers for the Swiss Exposition.

Willi belonged, without doubt, to the equestrian circle, and as a lieutenant during the war spent most of his time on horseback. He had two mares, named Eva and Antoinette, and we spent many a fine day together riding across fields, and through the woods.

Christa, our youngest daughter, has inherited his love of horses, likewise her own children aged twelve and ten years.

When Christa was seven, we went to see the touching film "Crin Blanc". She sat on my left, and a small boy of about six years with black curly hair sat on my right hand side. Christa soon realised that the wonderful place where the boy and his horse are happy ever after, was actually death. She was quiet throughout the film, and only when the lights came on again did I notice that the front of her coat was damp with the tears which had silently rolled down her cheeks at the end of this wonderful but sad film. We left the cinema and the small boy clutched me with his hot and sticky hand, and imploringly asked me, "It's true, isn't it, no one can harm them anymore?" His dark eyes looked so full of fear, that I reassured him that they had arrived safely in the happy land. He even followed us to the tram, although he lived in the opposite direction. It was as if he had to rid himself of an inner fear and could only do so by talking to someone. At last he said goodbye, and Christa said "The boy and his horse both drowned in the sea and that poor boy did not want to believe it". "Yes, Christa", was all I said.

There was still plenty of snow in the mountains in the first few days of March 1942, but it was sunny and warm, and we planned to meet for a skiing weekend in Gstaad where Willi was stationed for military service. He came to meet me at the railway station riding his light-footed and snorting mare. The following day we made a ski-tour to the Rinderberg, and ate our lunch sitting on a tree trunk close to the summit of the mountain. The sky was a deep blue, the snow was melting in the heat of the midday sun, and the rays conjured a carpet of diamonds in the snow. I was sitting next to Willi, and suddenly I knew that a moment of such perfect bliss occurs very rarely in a lifetime. This was happiness. It cannot be purchased. Such rare precious moments of felicity can not be forced. They are never to be found in a cheerful, noisy crowd. Neither are they with you when you are spoilt with beautiful presents. Happiness reveals itself only in a gentle peaceful way, when you are together with the one you love and trust, surrounded by beautiful nature. As soon as plans begin to be formed, and wishes become apparent to be fulfilled for oneself, the family and for ones profession, then it departs as silently as it came, sad and disappointed; sometimes never to return if one cannot again become a modest and unassuming vagabond.

Our wedding in August 1942 was very quiet, and we were married by a priest who was a friend of Willi's, in my parent's house. Father decorated the rooms with the soft pale red "Mme Jules Boucher" roses from his vast rosary. Instead of an extravagant wedding feast and dowry for his daughter, he made a generous gift to each of his employees. My parents considered that it was unrefined to compile a list of wedding presents, and so we began our married life with nothing. In some respects this was ideal, because we were able to collect one lovely piece after the other, and some ten years later, we were more or less well furnished with oak furniture which was suited to our house. Our first eight years were spent in a three-roomed apartment in the Enge Park, one of the nicest quarters of Zürich. Our daugther Lotte Lisa Katharina was born there in 1944. She was the child we had both

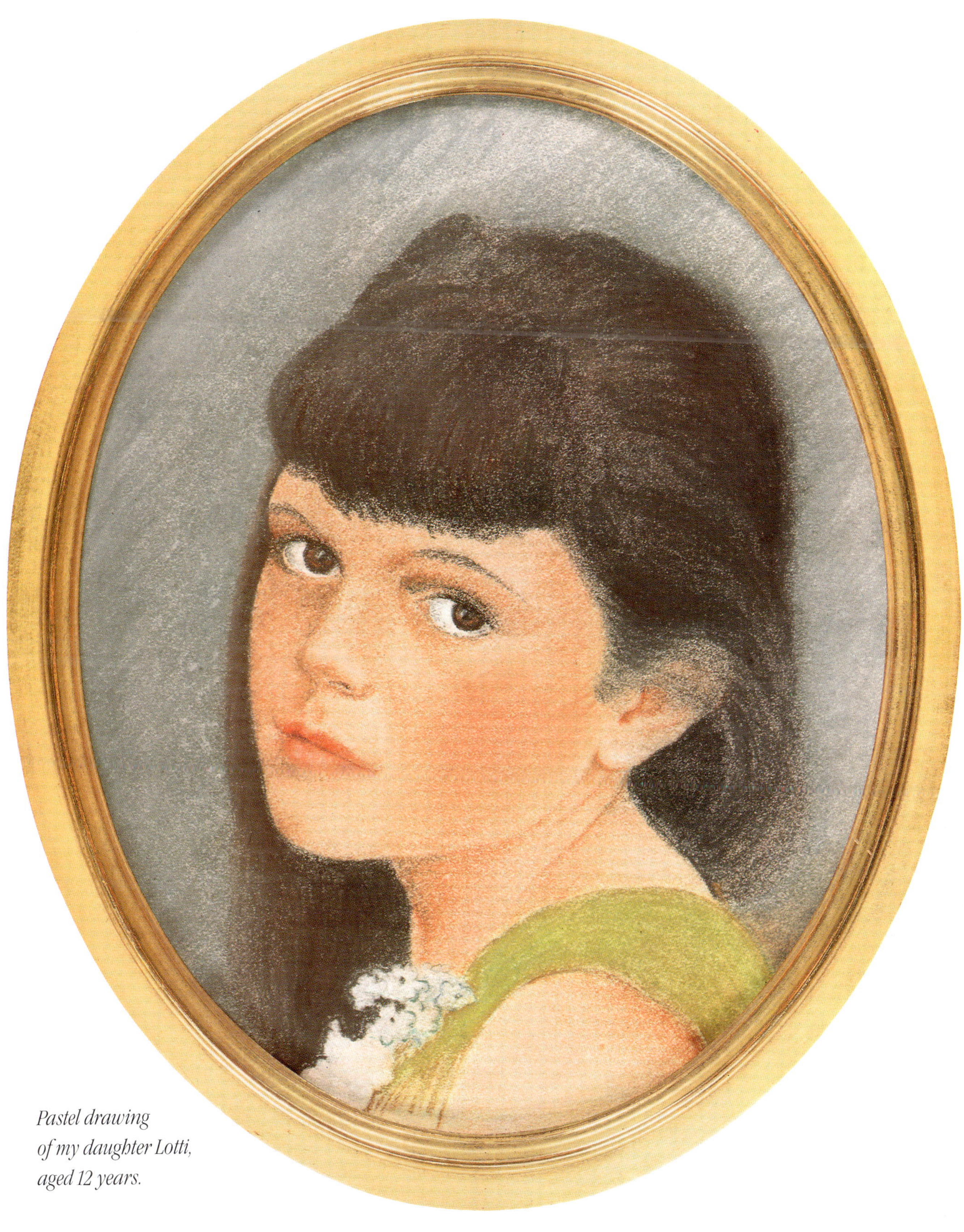

*Pastel drawing
of my daughter Lotti,
aged 12 years.*

longed for; I had often dreamed of a pale complexioned girl with chestnut hair and hazel eyes, and for the card announcing the birth of the baby, I sketched an almost open chestnut bud. The eight pound baby girl actually developed into a red haired beauty with pale skin and large hazel eyes. She became an actress in New York, married and became the mother of a daughter and a son. Our second child, also a daughter, was born in 1948. Lilli Christina grew up into a lovely dark blonde girl, charming and good natured. She later attended business school, married at a young age, and had a son and a daugther.

She is the angel of the Red Rose House, and corresponds all over the world with the many guests of our small "hotel" in the English, French or German language. Both of the two-room apartments are constantly reserved.

During my pregnancy, I illustrated several books and also composed the advertising brochures for our company.

After the birth of Christa, I was ill for a long time, and became so thin that often people I knew would say to me on the street "It's good to be slim, but you are so thin it looks terrible. Have you got cancer?"

In 1950, my father bought the Engelfried House from a friend of my mother's in Regensberg at a good price. I would have preferred to remain in Zürich; the eight hundred year old house appeared frighteningly large and in need of repair. I remarked that it would be more suitable for a family with a dozen children instead of Willi, myself and the two small girls. Nobody else had wanted to purchase the house, and when we moved in, after nine months of necessary renovations, many people poked fun at us, and thought we could have well afforded to build a nice detached house, and not to have to live in such a ruin. One of our company's employees told me that his wife would never have moved in there even if ten horses had pulled her.

This house, which I so disliked at the beginning, slowly grew on me, and I fell in love with it. I found it more and more livable in, and I am now dreading the day when we will have to leave this wonderful house. It is very big, and quite impractical; the bedrooms on the first floor, kitchen, lounge and dining rooms as well as the so-called "knights room" on the second, and my studio on the third floor. In summer we take our meals in the rose pergola.

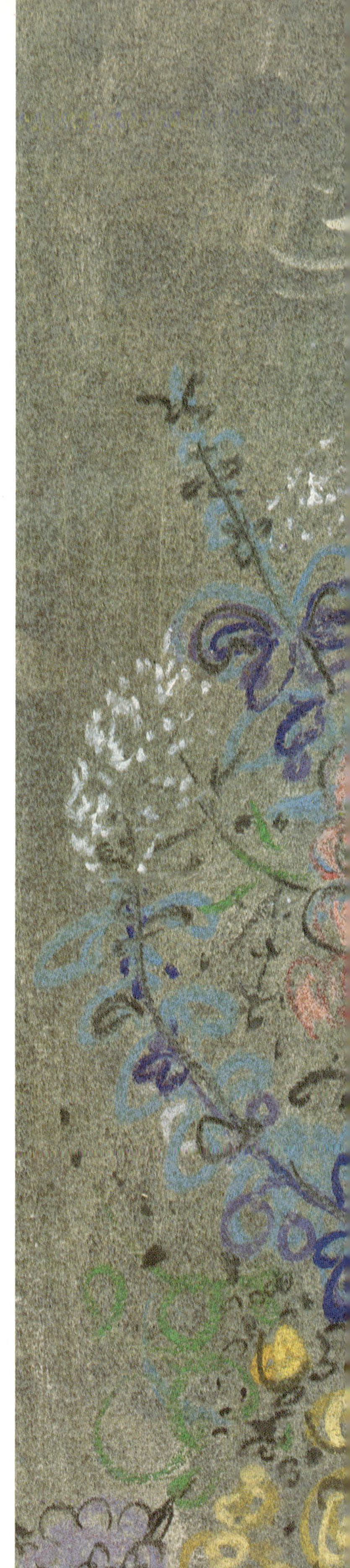

Pastel drawing of my daughter Christa, 1953.

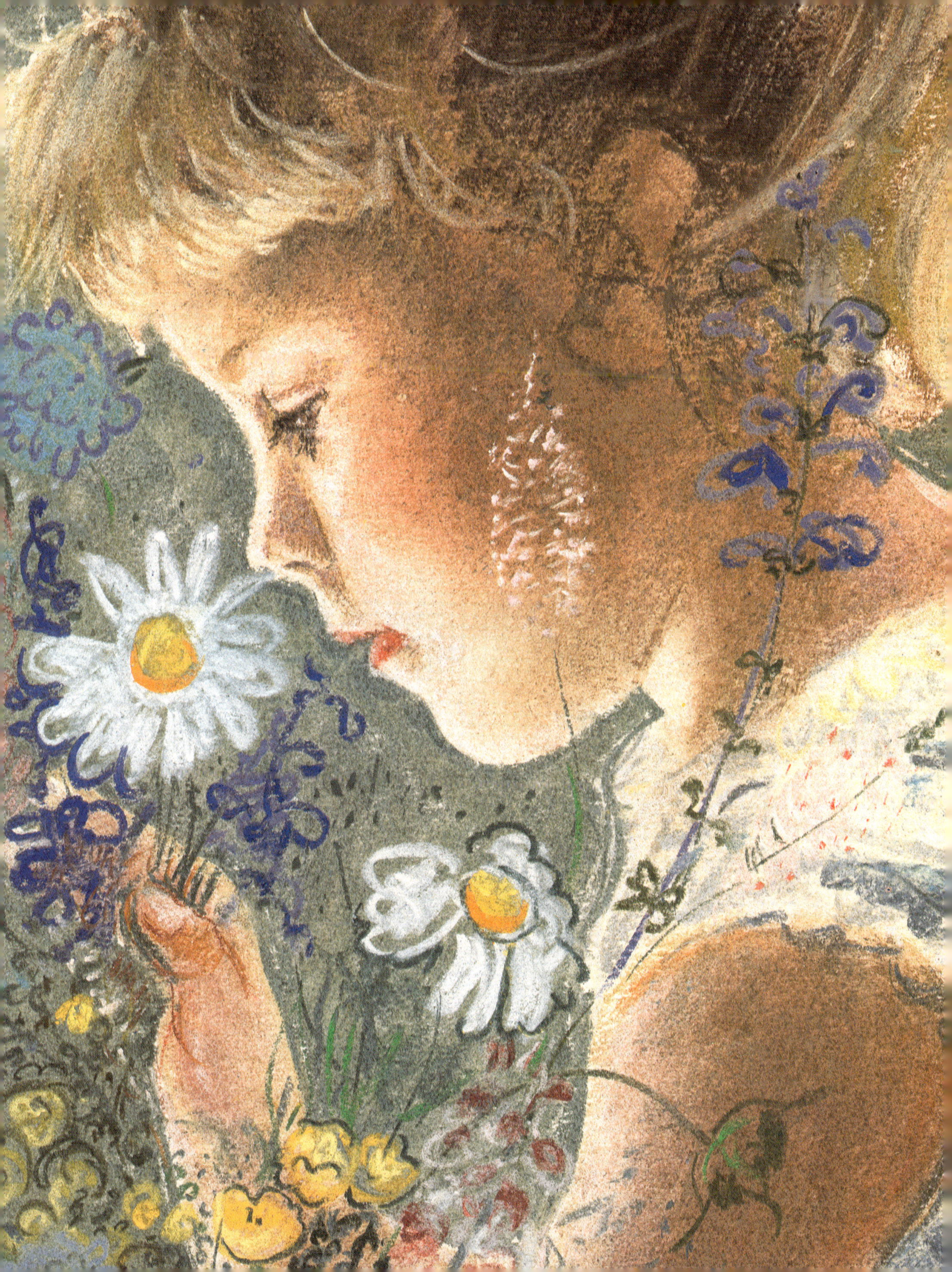

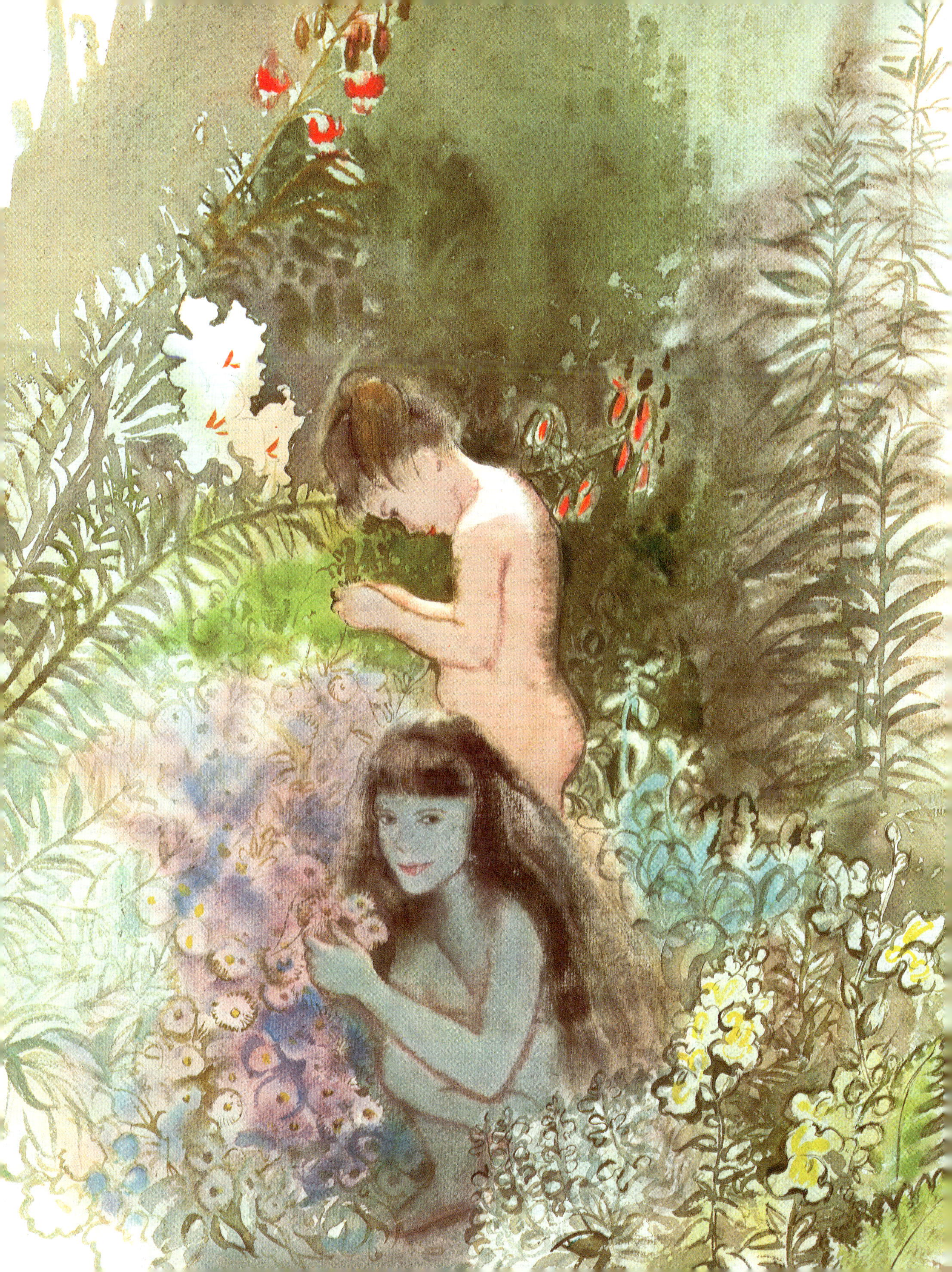

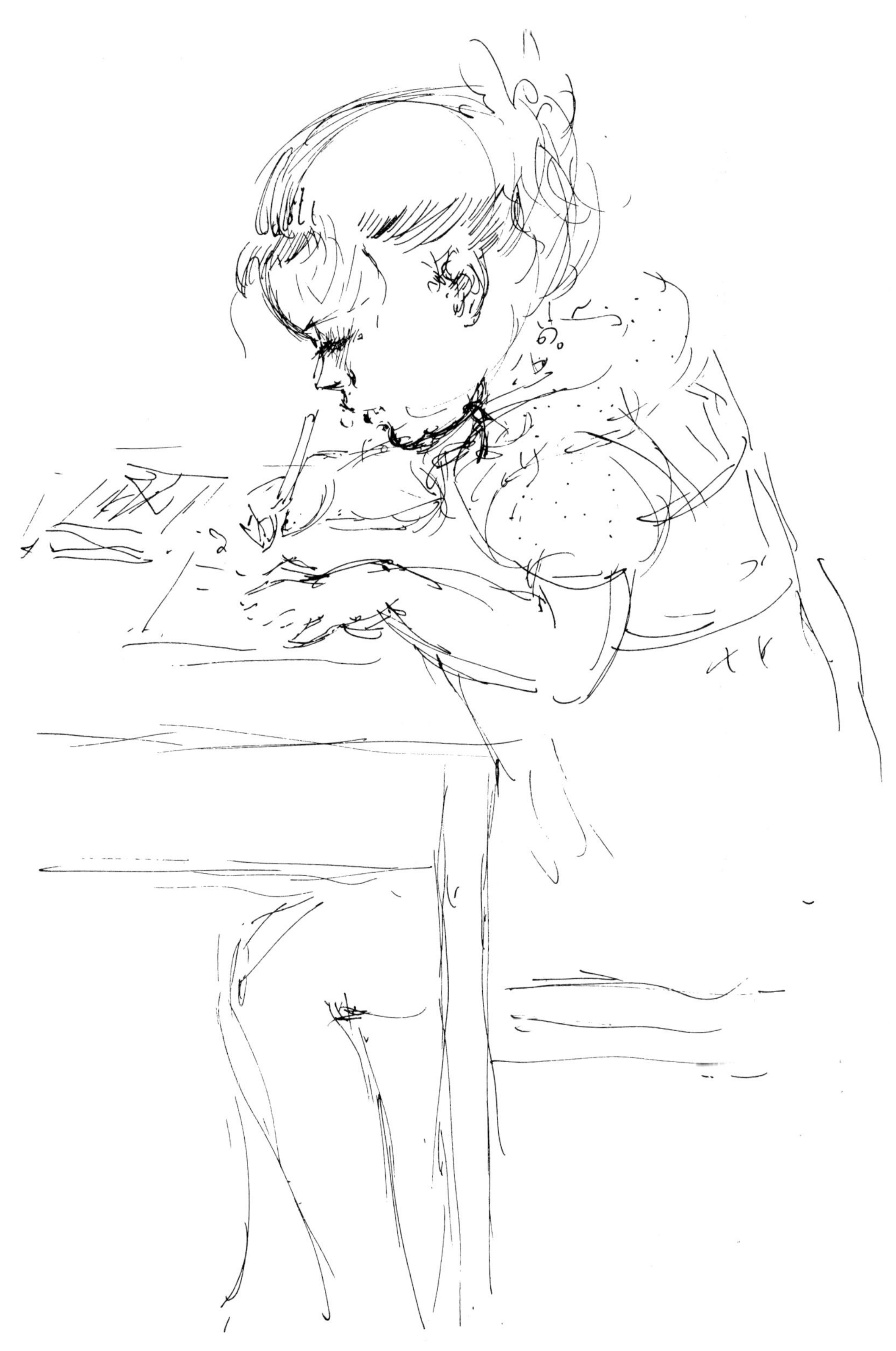

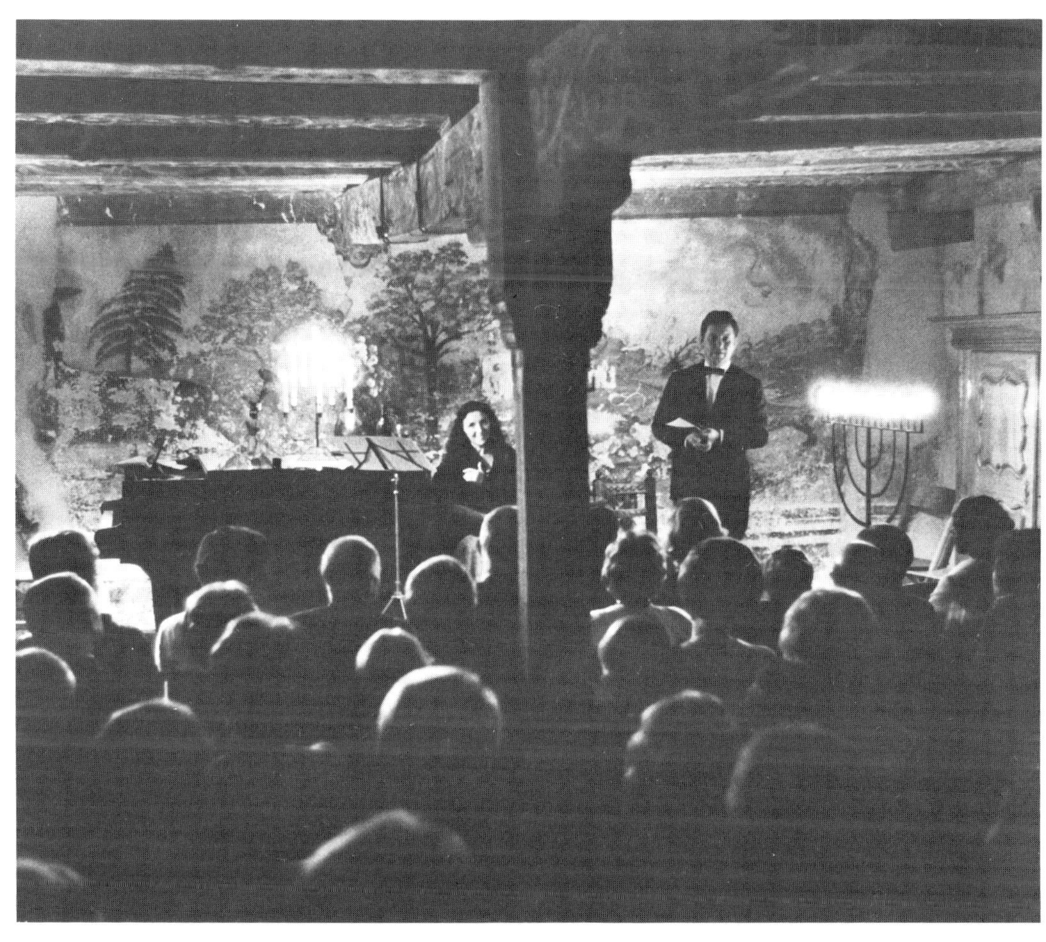

Richard Baker during a sketch performed in the "knights room", Engelfried House, Regensberg. Also present was Princesse Zouïna Benhalla.

A few years ago, during a visit from Richard Baker, the well-known BBC London broadcaster, together with his wife and two sons, I served the meal in the rose pergola. There was a special menu for the boys, and they helped me to carry everything up and down, after which one of them said "Do you know you have just climbed 780 steps?" He had counted them all, something which I had never thought to do over all the years.

When the children were young, Engelfried House was the favourite playground for all the children in Regensberg, because at that time there was no kindergarten. We often had a dozen or more small, wild guests running all over both house and garden.
Before our daughters attended school, I devoted my whole time to their upbringing and during those years made no paintings except for a few small portraits of children.
Every evening I used to sit at the bedside of our children for an hour or so, to tell them a fairy story, or to sing a favourite lullaby together. Before they went to sleep, we said a short prayer. For me, prayer is not asking for things, it is the grateful acknowledgement of all that God has already done; it is saying thank-you.
These childhood prayers, in which nothing was asked for, probably explains why both our daughters affectionately bade us goodnight for many years thanking for the lovely day. "What are they thanking for?", I once asked Willi, and he replied "Be pleased that they are so loving and grateful. That they know how to say thank you, even for a normal day when they haven't received any presents". Yes, I was happy with these children filled with so much love and goodness, and I hoped above all, that in later life, their innocent charm would not be abused.
I am very lucky that I have had the same home-help since thirty-four years. During the first years when the children were small, she gave me tremendous support, which was very comforting, especially since after Christa's birth I was ill for some years. She spoiled me like no nurse could have done, which certainly aided my recovery. I was grateful that she continued to help me even after her marriage, even though only in the mornings, because she now had her own household to manage, for she is one of the nicest and trustworthy people that I know. It is a wonderfully comforting situation for me, that my endless disarray, countless notes, sketches, and the preparations for a coming exhibition or future publication, will not be tidied up. I would never find anything, whereas in my disorder, I can find things with an almost clairvoyant sureness.

23 December, 1963

<u>Private</u>

Dear Herr Rathgeb,

  I am indeed obliged to you for sending me the beautiful book of rose pictures, which I am glad to have in my possession. Pray accept my thanks and my good wishes.

    Yours sincerely,

     Winston S. Churchill

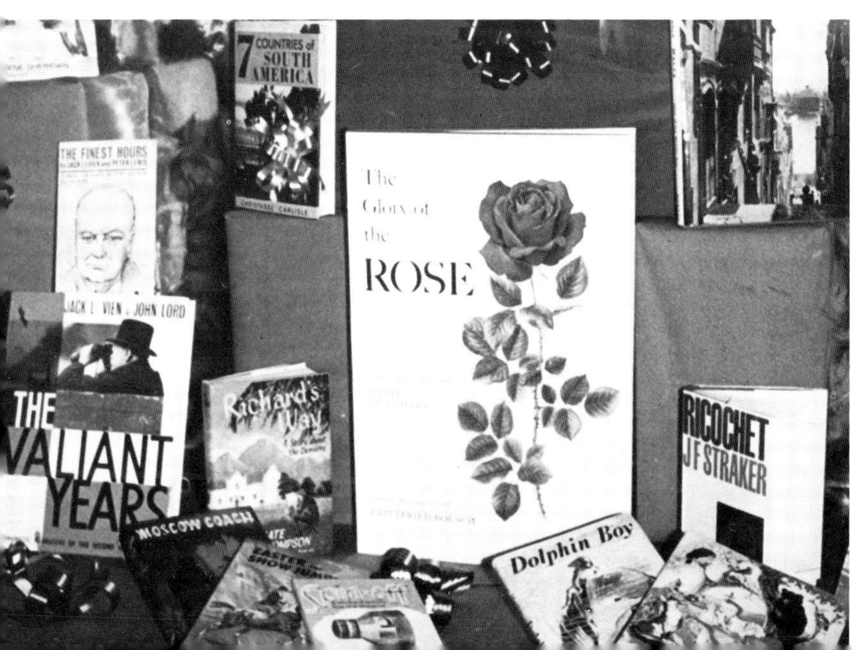

A book-shop window in London.

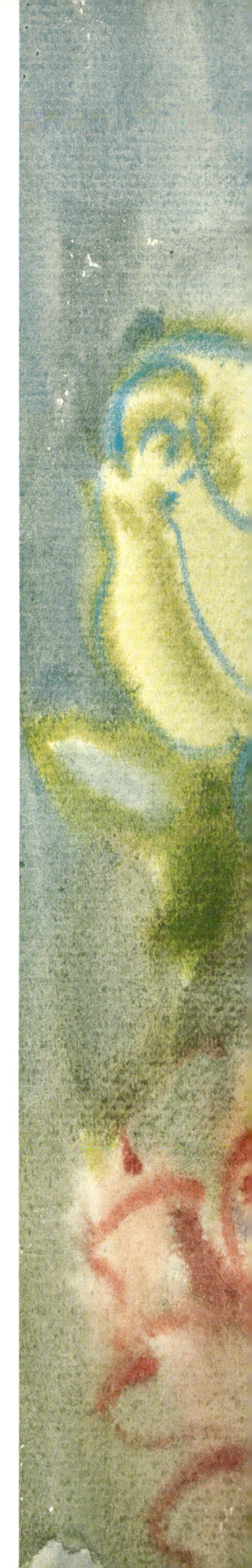

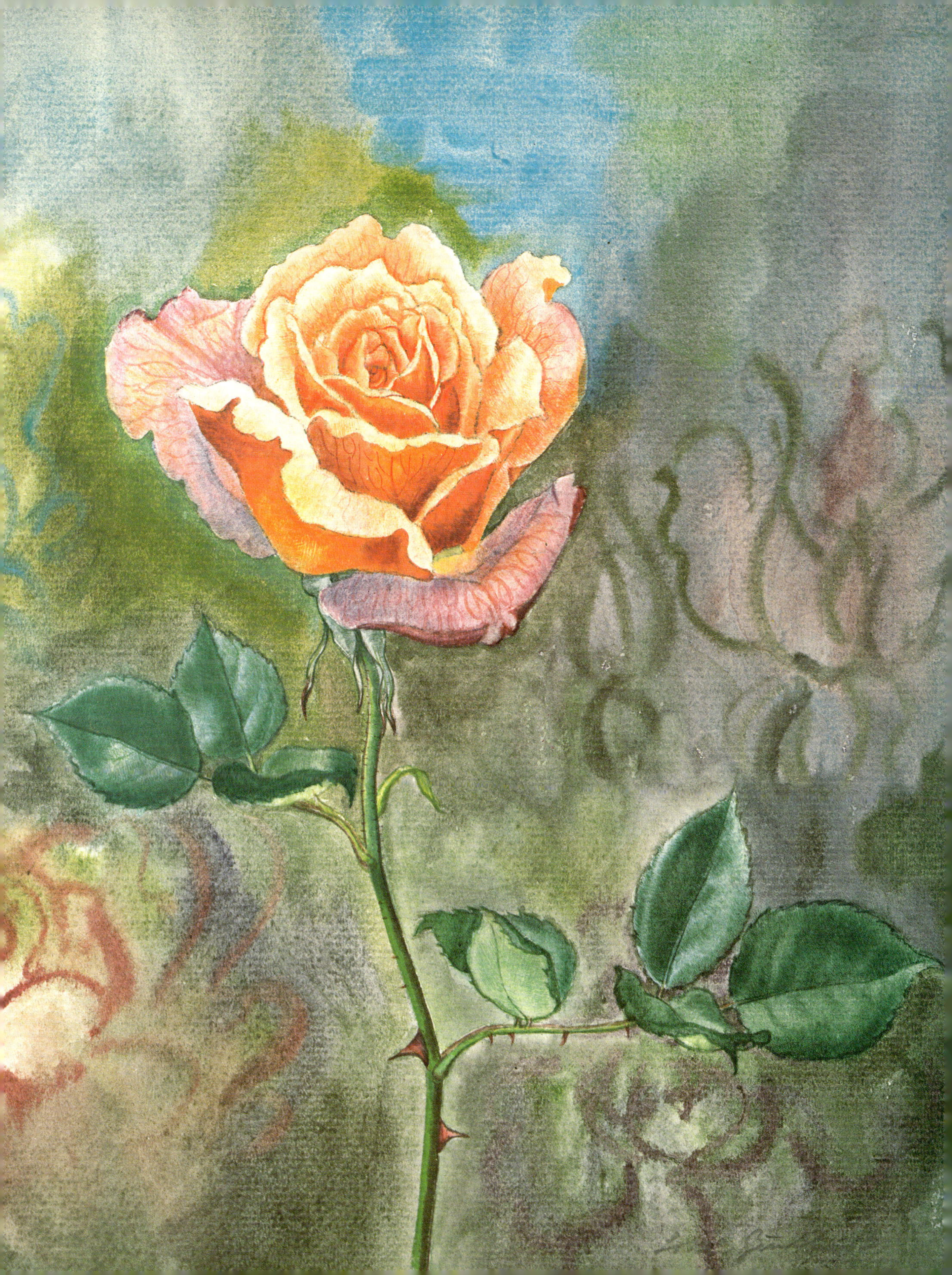

The glorious summer of 1947 when I was expecting my second child was not a happy year for me. My husband decided, in order to help my father who had increasingly approached him with his business problems, to give up his studio in Zürich to work as a partner in father's company. Over the years, Willi had built up a fine reputation as a commercial artist and advertising agent, and had a first-class and large clientele. He loved his profession, and had learned everything involved with it. From the beginning, he had appeared suited to this profession, and had taken to it with a natural ability; it was his life and vocation. I therefore used every argument I could think of to discourage him from this step, but it was of no use. Only a few years ago, Willi confided in me that he had never for one moment imagined that the problems he would face would be so tremendous.

It is true to say that in most large companies, there is always a group of people who are never in agreement with the owner, partly due to jealousy or partly due to the destructiveness which is in many people. For us, it was similar to an obstacle race.

As soon as Willi had a new idea or made a discovery, it was opposed by all and sundry. In 1958, Professor Alfred Studer, a friend of Willi's who worked for a large Swiss company as Head of Medical Research, arranged that his company would submit various substances for biological evaluation and development to our laboratories. I was keenly interested that the project would be a success, and repeatedly asked Willi if the experiments with the new molecules had begun. Each time my question was abruptly answered, negatively as far as I could make out. There was always some problem. It then became apparent that some of the employees had entered into an intrigue to destroy as soon as possible the connection with this other extremely correct and financially strong company. I did not relent, and continued to question, and this project cost me many a sleepless night. A whole year passed by, and at long last to my relief, Professor P., Head of Chemical Research of this company, enquired about the progress made on evaluation of their substances. When he discovered that our scientists had not commenced experimenting, he told us in plain terms his opinion of this incompetence, and even considered withdrawing the substances to submit them to a more efficient company. Willi, by now angered by the reproach of the professor, and my impatience which had reached boiling point, and with the support of his friend who had originally arranged the whole business, energetically ordered the persons responsible to immediately carry out the experiments. This took effect, and the project commenced without delay, after a year of opposition from all sides.

2 Oct — 5 Oct '81

Once again we have come to this lovely & picturesque city of Regensburg which is so full of Habsburg history. It has been a wonderful visit & we are immensely grateful for all the kindness & the welcome afforded to us by Willi & Lotte, Christa & Eugen. Our love goes too to Frank & Katia & we are taking home a very fine picture which Katia drew for us, with Frank. We now look forward to the days when _we_ can _welcome_ _you_ to London & in the meantime our love remains with you all & we say again thank you enormously we shall not forget.

Ian Bowater
& Ursula

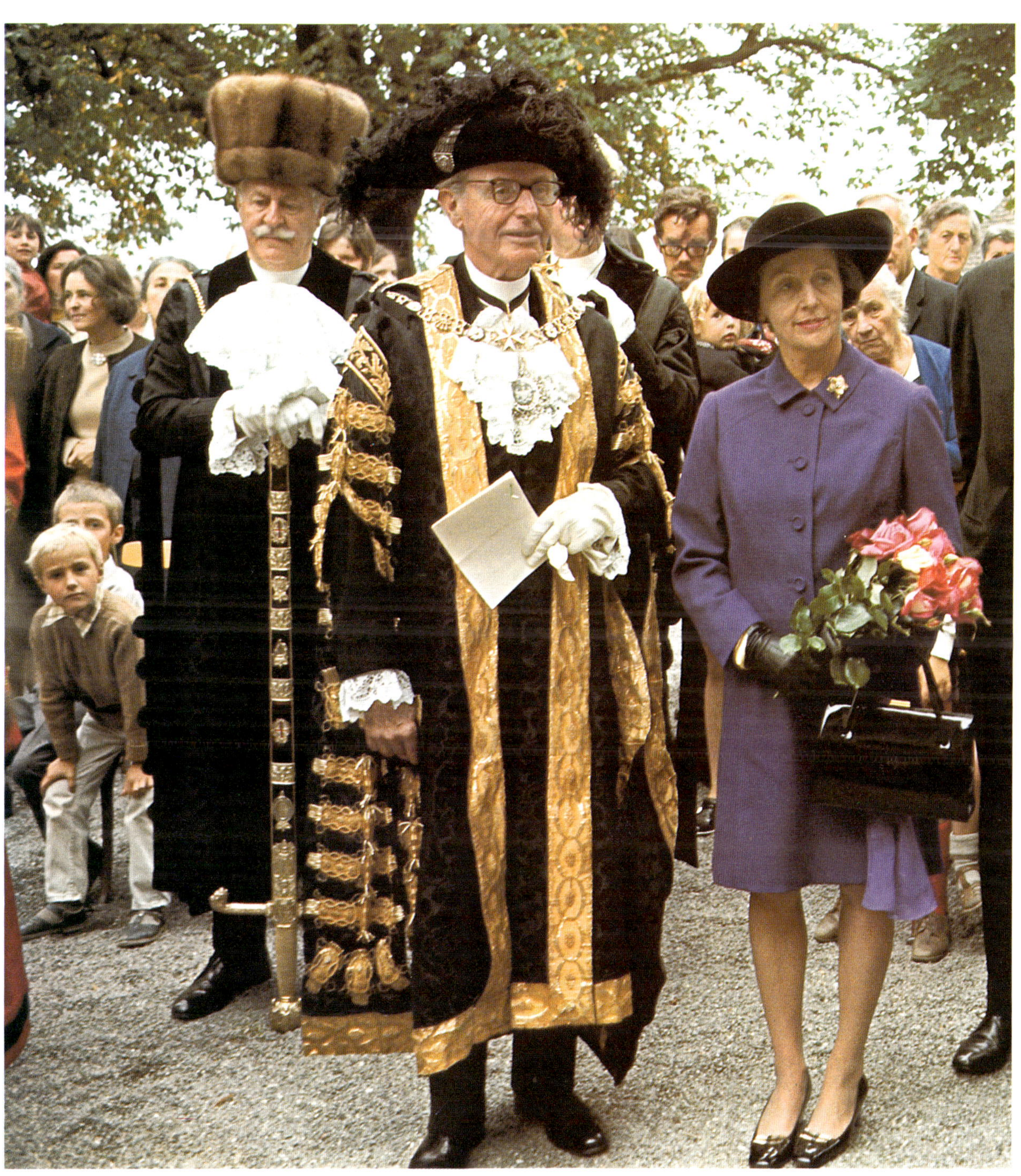

The official visit to Regensberg in 1970 by the Lord Mayor of London, Sir Ian Bowater, and his wife Lady Ursula.

This nerve shattering existence inspired me with the idea that we must, at all costs, strengthen our position; to have a platform on which we could stand in difficult times, and which would enable us to overcome the opposition, alone against the many. Even if Willi was not able to do this, I was determined to do so for myself, and I was convinced that it would help us both, but especially Willi within the company. We were both talented, willing, not unintelligent, but far too modest. This characteristic, strengthened even more by my parents, who were always able to put us in the background, would bring about our ruin, and we would never progress in life, this was certain.

It was all up to me, I had to become "famous".

I soon realised that my free-hand impressionistic water colours which I preferred to the "rose portraits", would never find the wide acceptance of the general public. This was confirmed when I was commissioned in 1954 and 1955 to illustrate two rose calendars for a Zürich company. Both calendars achieved immediate success; the response from all sides was overwhelming and spontaneous. I was now determined to gather my own laurels in this way, and decided to bring out a book with forty life size paintings, of particularly beautiful roses. First of all I had to paint these life size rose pictures, and this was no easy task. From now on I was compelled to spend at least fifty hours each week, painting every day from early morning until dusk.

Eighty different species of hybrid tea roses and over two hundred old shrub roses are blooming in our garden.

They are all my models, because I paint only living roses, nor should I want to do otherwise. Needless to say, it would be much simpler to paint from a photograph; the rose would keep still and never change, and I could paint at leisure.

To paint a living rose, full concentration, patience and stamina are required. There are roses which drive me almost to despair, with their sheer restlessness and mobility. Some open and close their petals within an hour.

I always have symptoms of stage fright when beginning a new painting which requires extreme accuracy, and I doubt my own ability.

When I go to my garden in the early hours of the morning to select the most beautiful rose, still fresh with the dew, from the several hundred to choose from, as my subject for that day, I hope to be able to transfer its grace and elegance, and even the perfume, on to paper with my brush and paints.

In the summer of 1959, I began to paint the first roses for my large rose book, and by

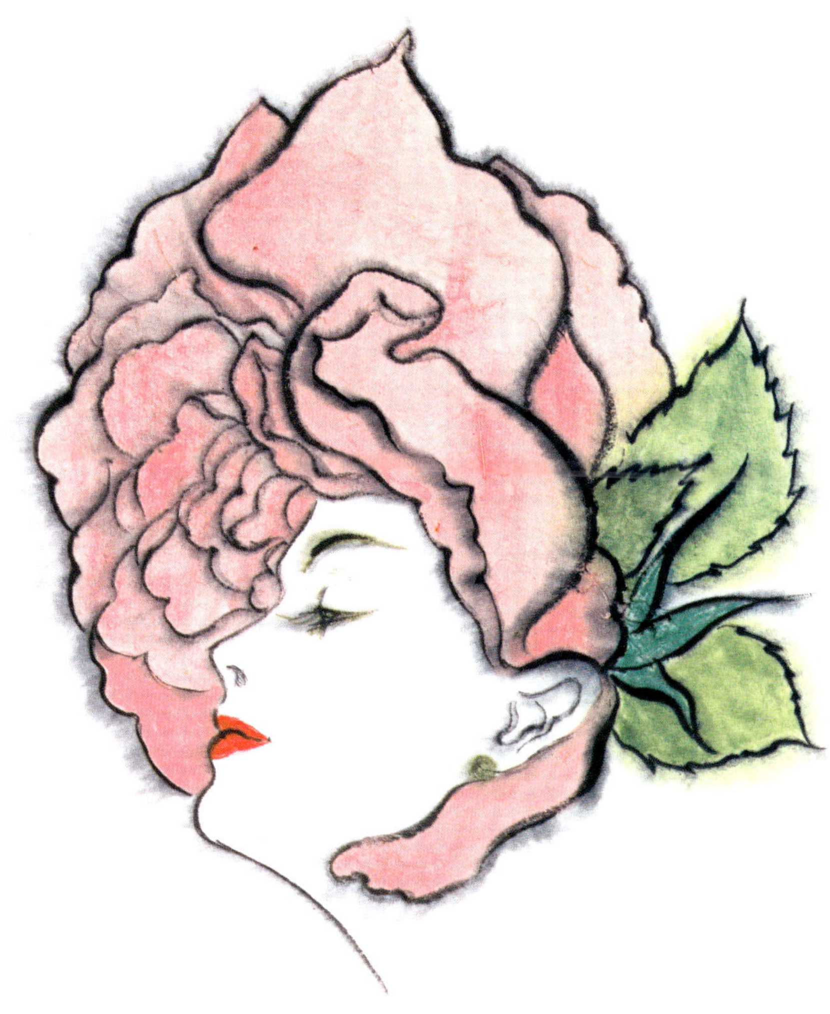

*An illustration from the book "La femme,
le poète, et la rose".*

November 1962, all the pages were printed, bound and accompanied by text, introduction and preface. The books were presented on the counters of numerous book shops, just in time to be bought for Christmas presents. The book, to which we gave the title "Vom Ruhm der Rose" was surprisingly successful, and became a best seller amongst its kind. Many experts on the subject had warned us of the great expense due to size and extravagance of this book. They advised us to make it a smaller size, and to have only half the number of prints because the risk of trying to sell such an expensive book would be too high. Against all expectations, the book sold very well, and the criticisms in the press were excellent. Sometimes, trouble or unfortunate situations have positive results, and only through them we find ourselves on the right path. On recollection of long periods of

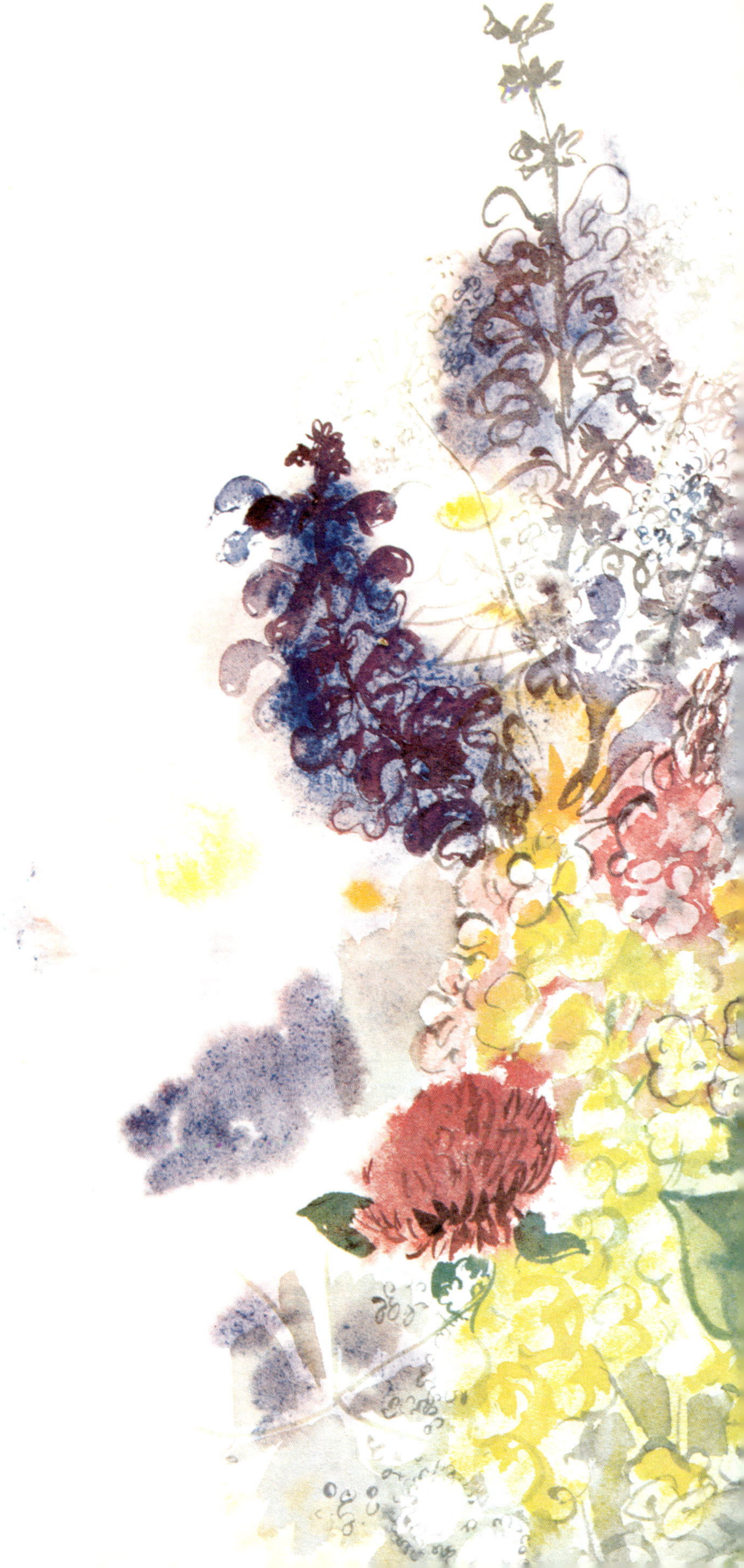

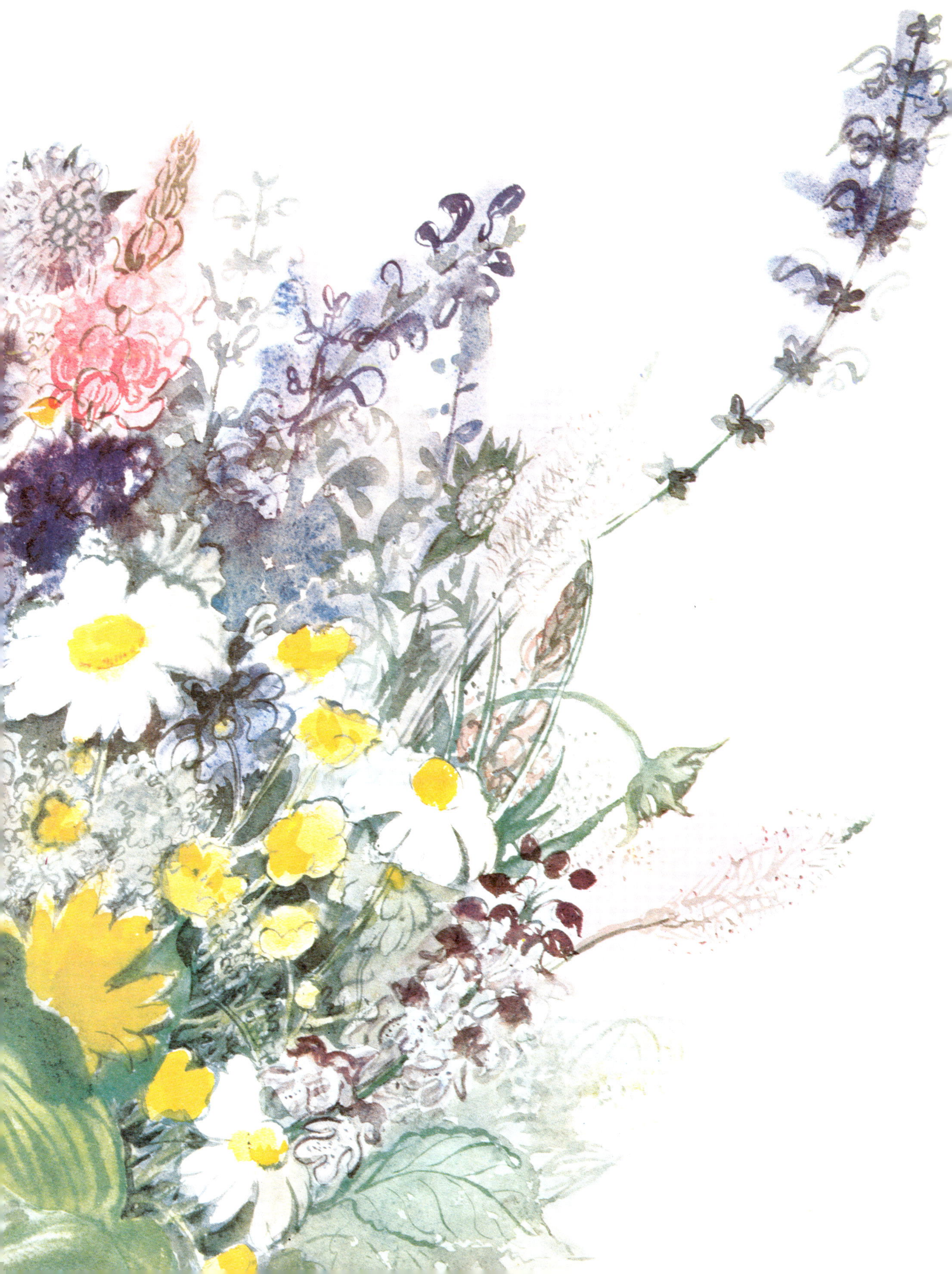

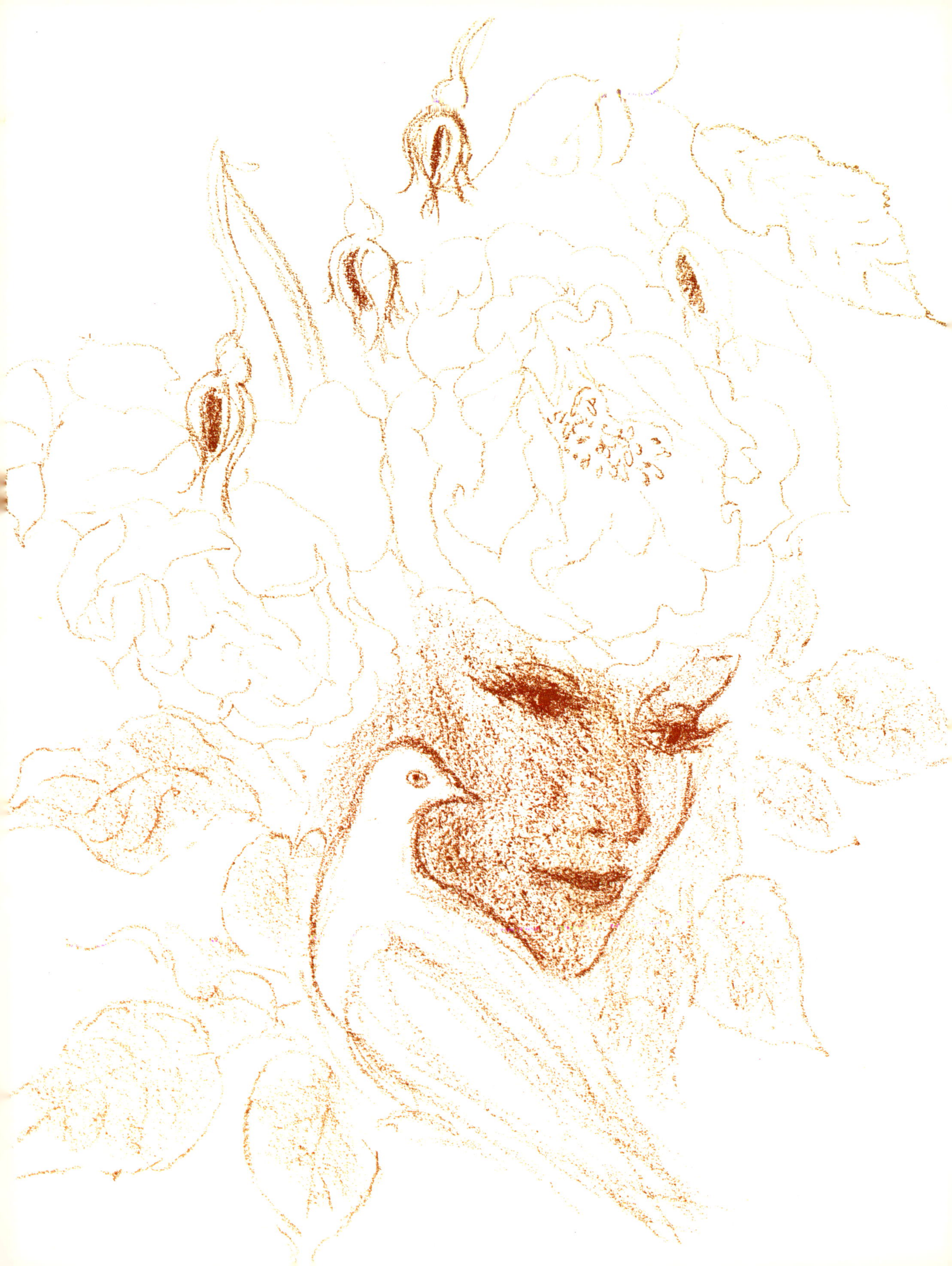

my life, it seems as though an invisible hand has frequently guided me in the right direction. It was often the opposite direction to which I would have chosen, and sometimes full of pain, but now, when looking back, everything seems to have miraculously fallen into place and in some way or other to be connected.

When our daughters attended High School, I arranged concert evenings, sometimes every month, in our "knights room", with its Steinway grand piano. The house became full of life, and the musicians enjoyed performing under such circumstances; the perfect acoustics, the lovely surroundings, and these evenings gave me much pleasure. We often had more than a hundred guests, and then the house no longer appeared too large, but fulfilled its purpose admirably.

We not only held concert evenings; in between we presented lectures or a small play, and Hubert Gravereaux once gave an unforgettable performance.

Hubert, the well-known Parisian actor and poet, is the grandson of the founder of the unique rose gardens in Paris, "La Bagatelle" and "L'Hay les Roses". He has inherited the love of roses from his famous grandfather, and together we decided to compose two books, "A l'heure de l'amour et des roses" and "La femme, le poète et la rose".

Hubert chose great poems from French literature, as well as including some of his own compositions. To celebrate publication, Hubert arranged a large, and festive party in his house. Unfortunately, these attractive books, which were enhanced by sketches and water colours which I had made, were soon unobtainable and out of print.

Hubert also organised a monthly soirée, which was very amusing and stimulating; actors read poems, a young and undiscovered "talent" sang sad songs accompanied by the strings of a guitar, and a curious mixture of society met together. Eccentrics, ladies of disrepute, no doubt, fat and unkempt women, strikingly beautiful young things, a highly elegant marchioness or countess and other top socialites, ladies' men and mens' ladies, "clochards" and long haired pale youths with melancholy eyes; they were all there. All nationalities were apparent, with skins of all colours. In short, it was a real zoo, and anything but boring.

The preparations for our concert evenings were enjoyable. I decorated the rooms with lots of bouquets, and lit seventy-nine candles which I placed everywhere, and the candle-light, together with the beautiful flower arrangements, endowed the house with a fairy tale atmosphere.

An illustration from the book "A l'heure de l'amour et des roses". Printed in 1968.

Our guests were very nice people, and after the concerts we would often all go to the nearby inn called "zur Krone", together with the musicians, and chat till the small hours of the morning on every possible subject.

Later on, when my work for the rose books occupied so much time, we decided to hold the concerts only twice yearly, instead of almost every month.

The summer of 1963 was rich with festivities for me. In June, the rose garden in Lyon named "Parc de la Tête d'Or", was opened with much celebration, and I received an invitation from the mayor, M. Pradel, to participate in the banquet and the following tour of the park. Many guests were invited to this gala dinner, and the culinary art of France had to show its best face. We admired the beautiful women at the table of honour; amongst those present the Begum Yve, Aga Khan, and Princess Grace of Monaco. After the banquet, the gates of the park were ceremoniously opened for the first guests, and in the evening we were entertained by a fantastic display of coloured fountains, accompanied by music. During the same summer, I was invited by the rose grower Jean Gaujard from Feyzin, which is near Lyon, to select a rose which would bear my name. I was so thrilled and honoured with this gift, and the night before my visit to him I almost could not sleep with the excitement. That my name would be immortalized with a rose, was certainly an overwhelming experience for me. There were about twenty people; acquaintances from Lyon, a few rose friends from Switzerland, and the very sympathetic Gaujard family. To be in the position to make a choice is sometimes very tortuous, and I searched, hesitated and compared. Everyone was full of advice, and each pointed to their favourite which they would have chosen. Jean Gaujard showed me a pale red, semi-double bloom with an elegant long bud. Monsieur Victor Hauser considered a perfumed, dark red to be the best, and Willi was in favour of a pink rose. In the meantime, I had found "my" rose.

A magnificent specimen; with large ruby red blooms, and the hundred or more petals were growing like a spiral from the thick, round bud. It seemed to glow with happiness, and looked so vigorous and healthy. It had the round and full shape of the old centifolia rose, with shiny leaves and strong thorns. I do not like the thornless roses. They all asked if it had a perfume, and I replied that to me it was like a red burgundy, Aloxe-Corton, my favourite wine. However, since everyone has their own individual senses of smell, taste, sight, and so on, most find that my rose has only a slight perfume, if at all, and never manage to detect the bouquet of wine. Only the husband of Amy Vanderbilt; incidentally, Amy had written America's most famous cookery book, amongst other activities,

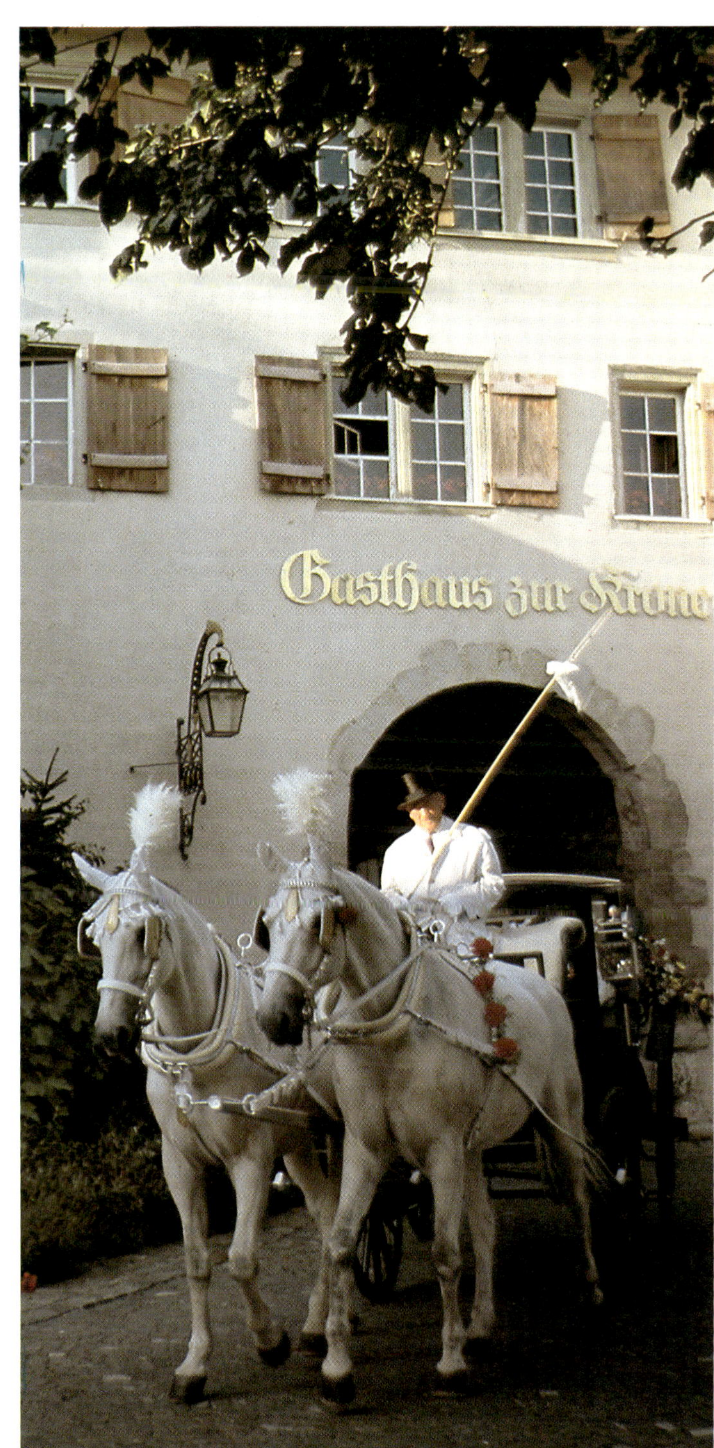

Restaurant "Zur Krone".
As Joseph Wechsberg wrote in the Gourmet
Magazine, New York, March 1979, Regensberg
has one of the finest restaurants outside
France. The rooms also house a permanent exhibition of "Ciba-Brillant" and "Granolithos® "
by Lotte Günthart.
Prints of works by P. J. Redouté, made in
collaboration with the Hunt Library, Pittsburgh,
are also exhibited.

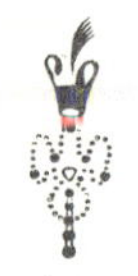

20 Juin 1983.

à Madame Lotte Gunthart.

Madame,

J'ai été infiniment touchée de recevoir, si gracieusement, votre magnifique livre: "La Noblesse de la Rose." lors de mon passage à Regensberg, et vous remercie bien sincèrement de cette très délicate attention.

J'ai admiré longuement la beauté de vos roses, je les trouve plus belles que celles de Redouté!. et de tout cœur je vous félicite pour votre très grand talent. et, également d'avoir pu sauver cet adorable petit village. si poétique avec ses cascades de roses. Un moment inoubliable! Merci —

Bien sincèrement Yve aga khan

Letter received from the Begum Yve, Aga Khan, a great lover of flowers, who has one of the most beautiful gardens on the Riviera in the South of France.

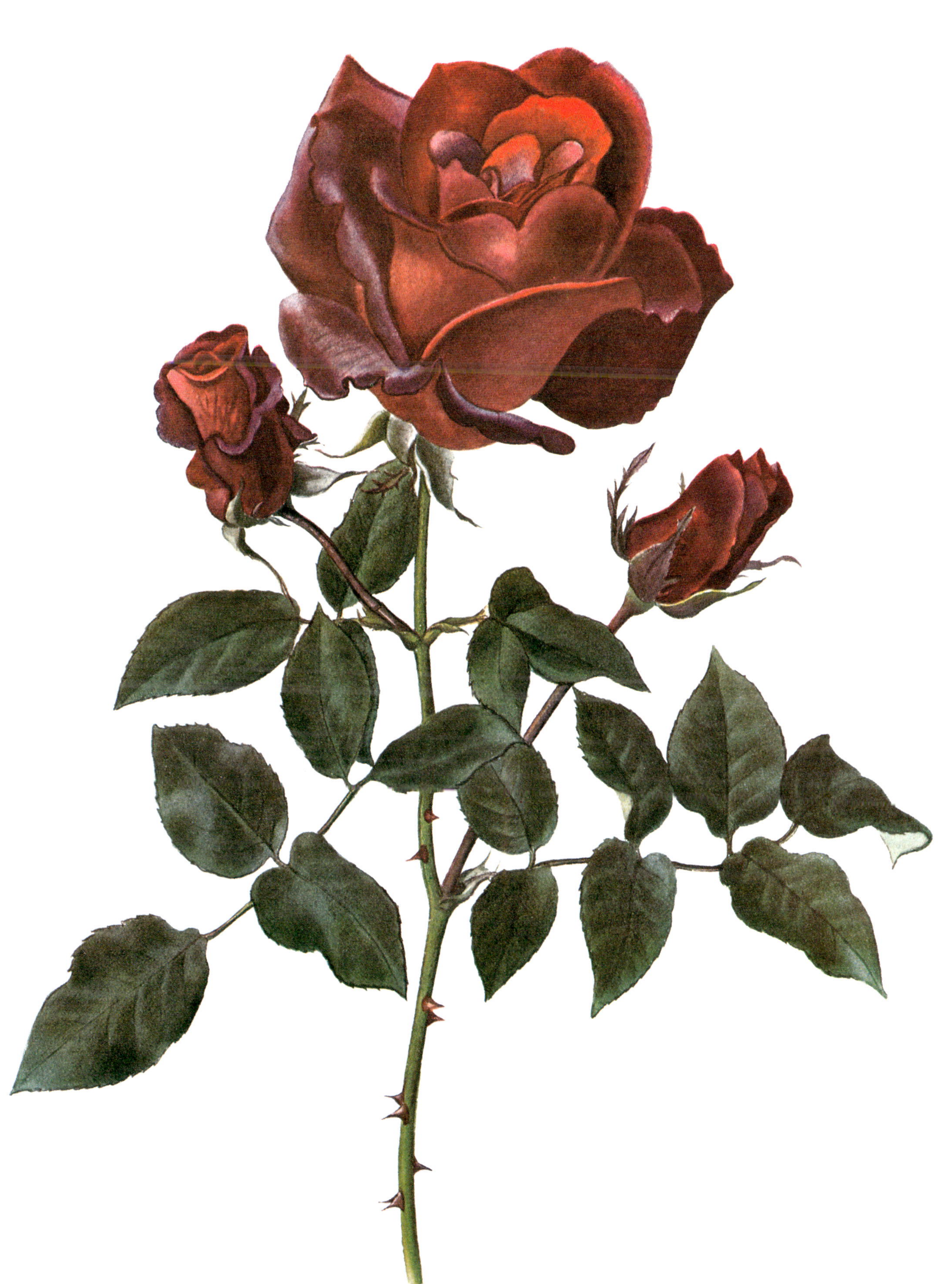

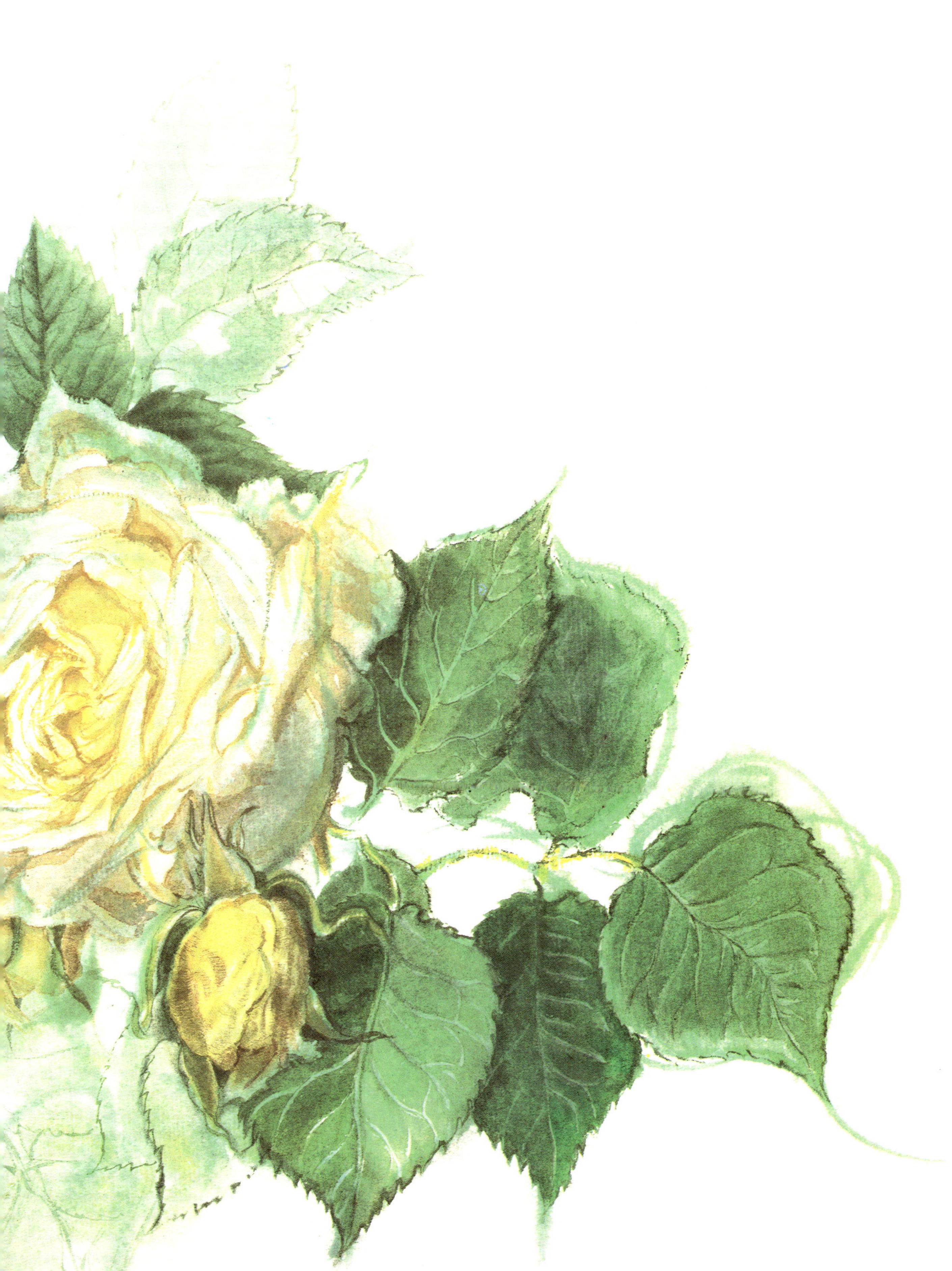

spontaneously exclaimed when he sniffed my rose, that he could detect the smell of red burgundy. He was an expert on that subject, after all, his wife was a cordon bleu. Amy and her husband were once our guests on a lovely summer evening for a small dinner in the garden. I had prepared the meal all on my own, and she found everything so much to her taste, that she made notes and later described the dinner in the "Ladies Home Journal", as "Lotte Günthart's special recipe, liver morsels Zürich style". I love cooking, because it is such a complete relaxation for me from painting, and often exchange recipes with other amateur cooks. But now I have diverted from the Lotte Günthart Rose to Amy Vanderbilt, who also had a rose named after her. It is a beautiful, pale violet variety with a fragrant perfume.

There was loud applause and lots of joy when I resolutely made my final choice. Before this, several people had made a wager that Willi would be able to persuade me to change my mind and select the pink rose, in which case it would have been "Madame Willi Günthart", but this was not to be, and my rose would be "Madame Lotti Günthart".

The festive midday lunch was held in the park belonging to the Chazey Castle, surrounded by hundreds of lovely roses, and the evening meal, which lasted for many hours, was held in the picturesque old town of Pérouge, which like Regensberg is situated on the top of a hill, and is just as old. It was a wonderful day, and the evening and night were like a fairy tale. We had to ascend a narrow, winding staircase by candle-light to reach the mediaeval chamber which was complete with a four poster bed, and a balcony like in Romeo and Juliet, and which was to be our room.

Several months after this eventful "rose christening" I received a letter from Jean Gaujard to say that seedling number 257, which I had selected, was unfortunately not one of his, but had been bred by the Armstrong Nurseries, in California, whose representative he was in France, and if I would consider choosing another rose. But the ruby red rose of a hundred petals was love at first sight for me, and I did not want to change my decision.

I wrote a letter to Mr Armstrong and received a charming reply. He was delighted that one of his creations would bear my name, especially so because during the three years in which he had grown this rose in his own garden, it had become the firm favourite of his wife.

I had made the perfect choice.

He invited me to come to Los Angeles, to participate in the festive rose christening and to hold an exhibition of my paintings, and I happily accepted this invitation.

"Lotte Günthart" was therefore christened twice, this time in California in September 1964.

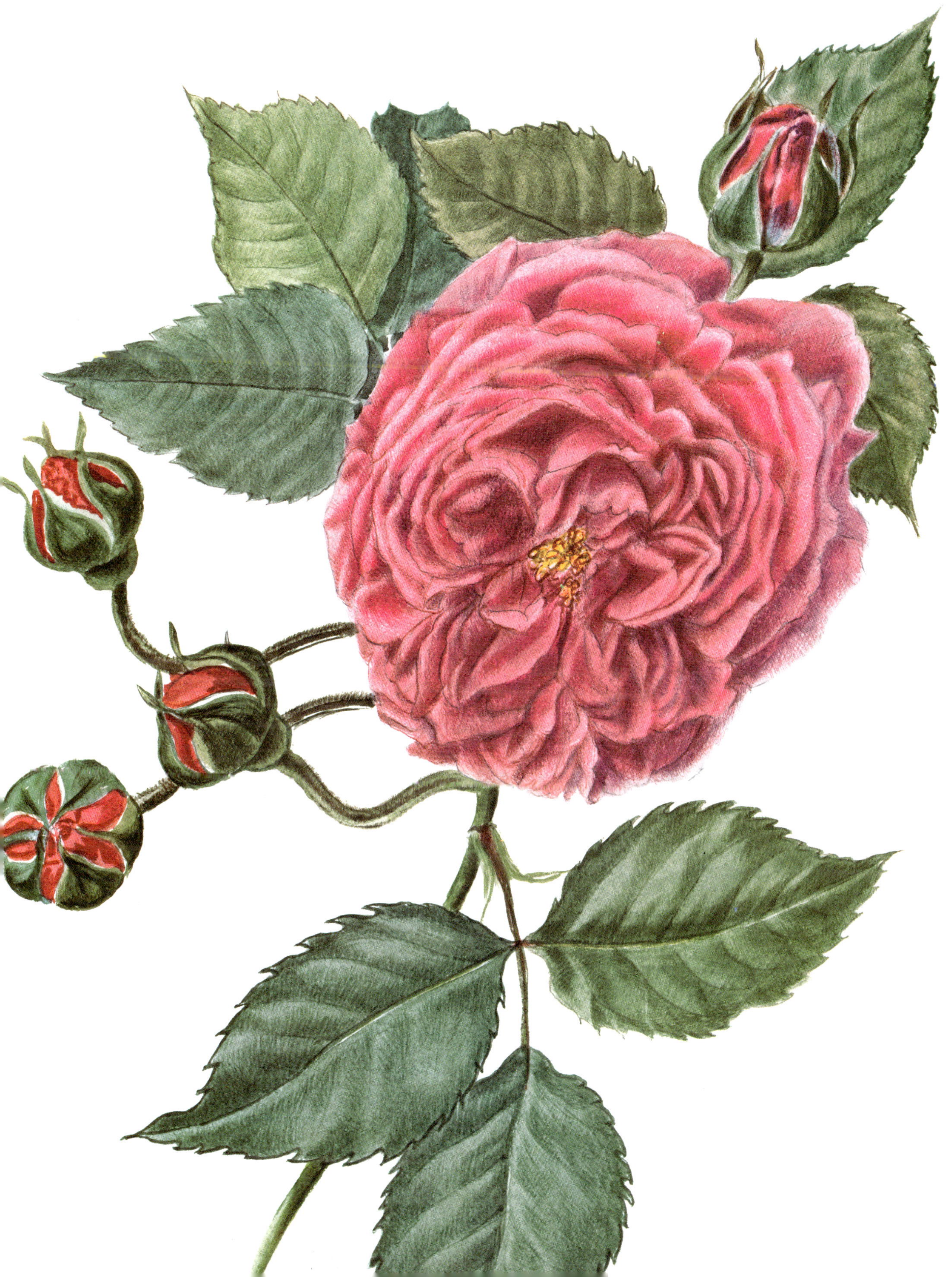

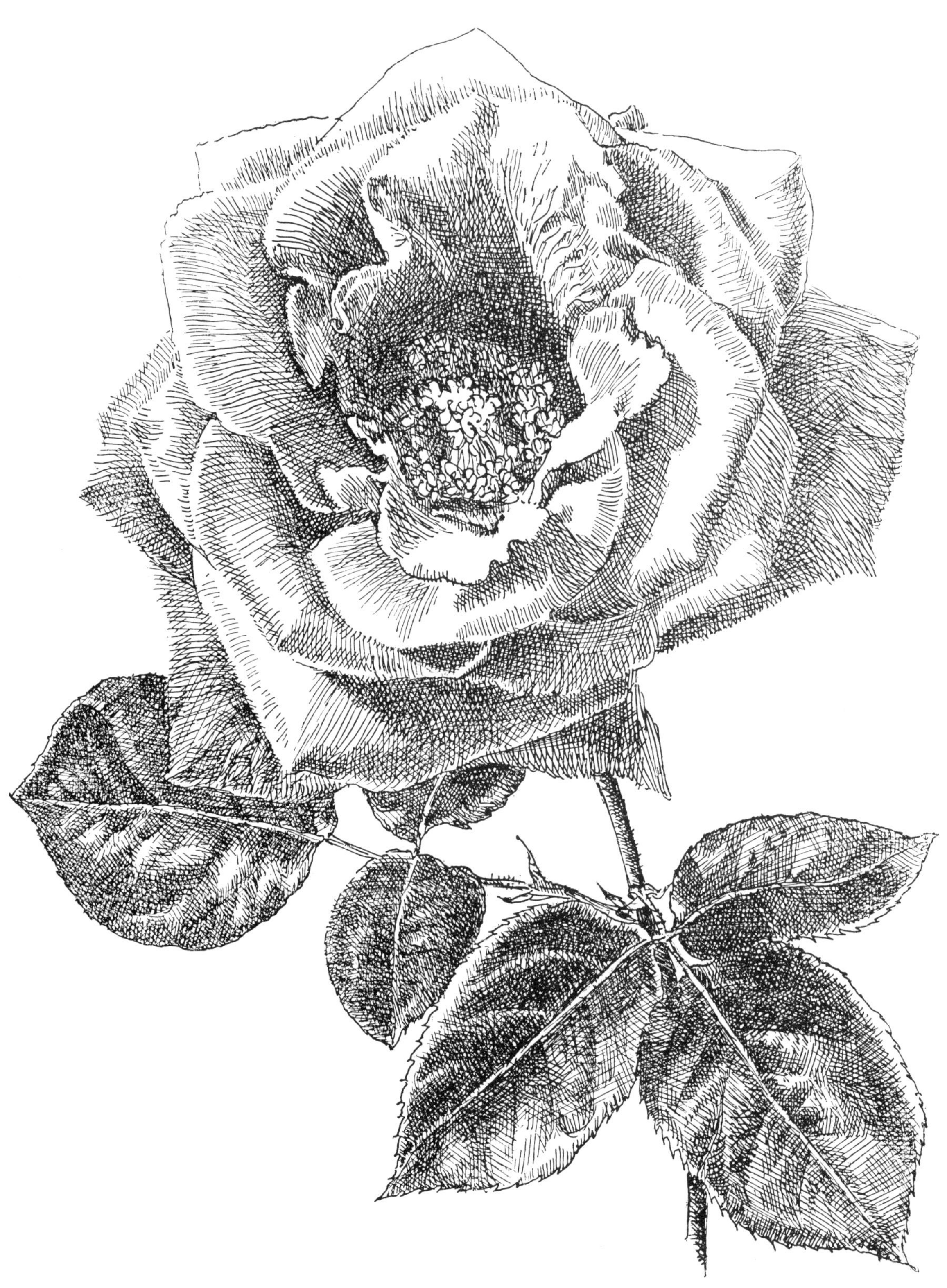

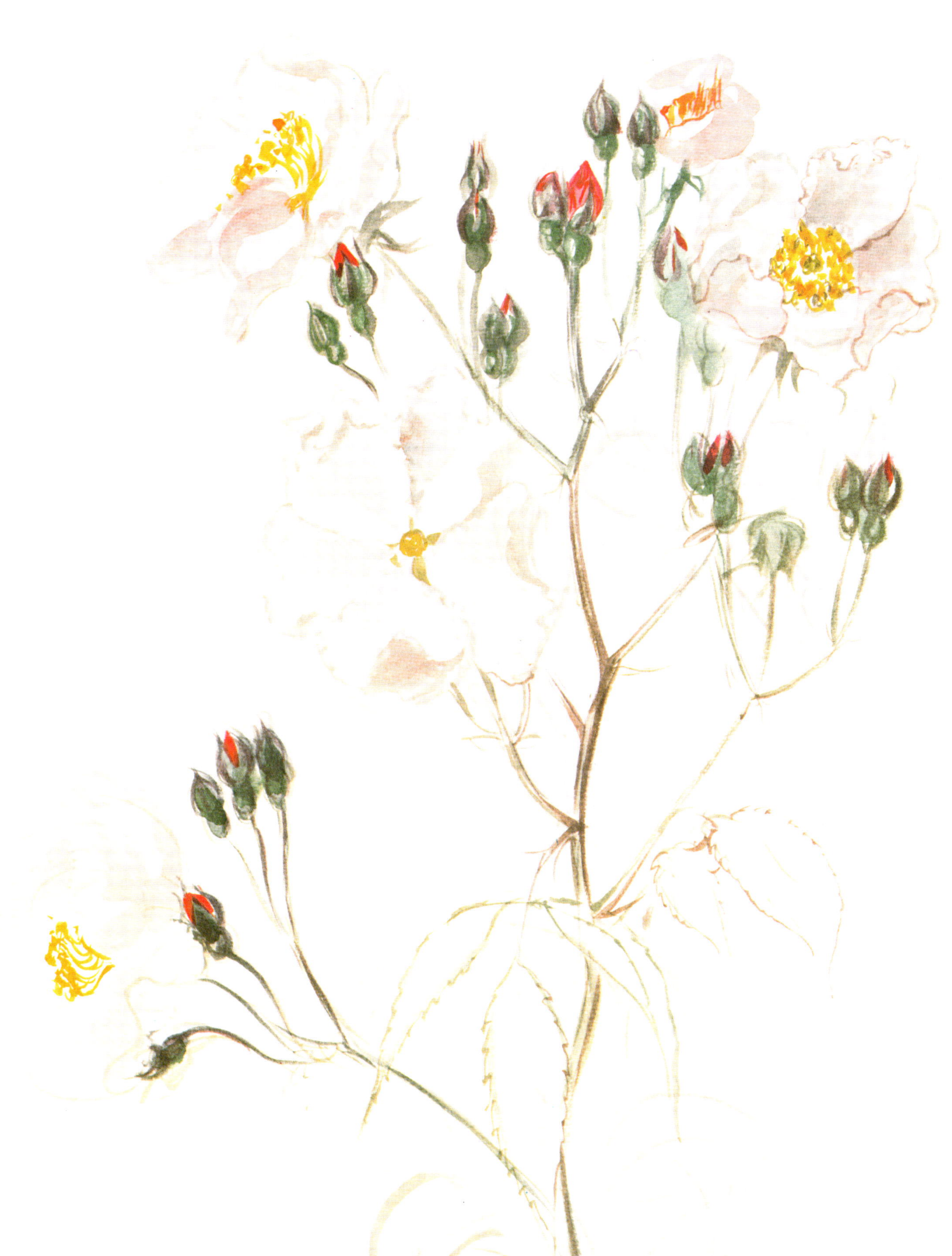

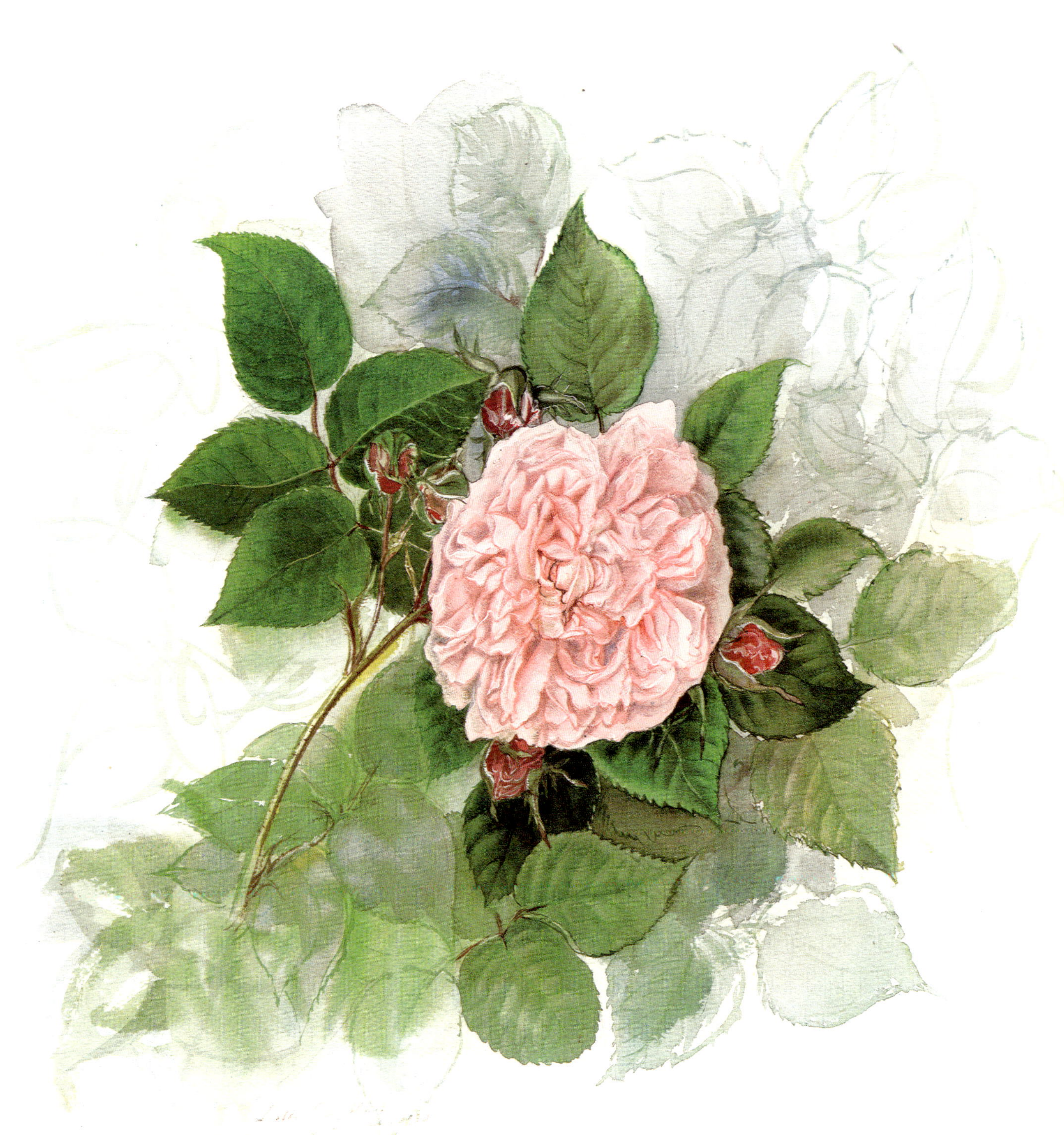

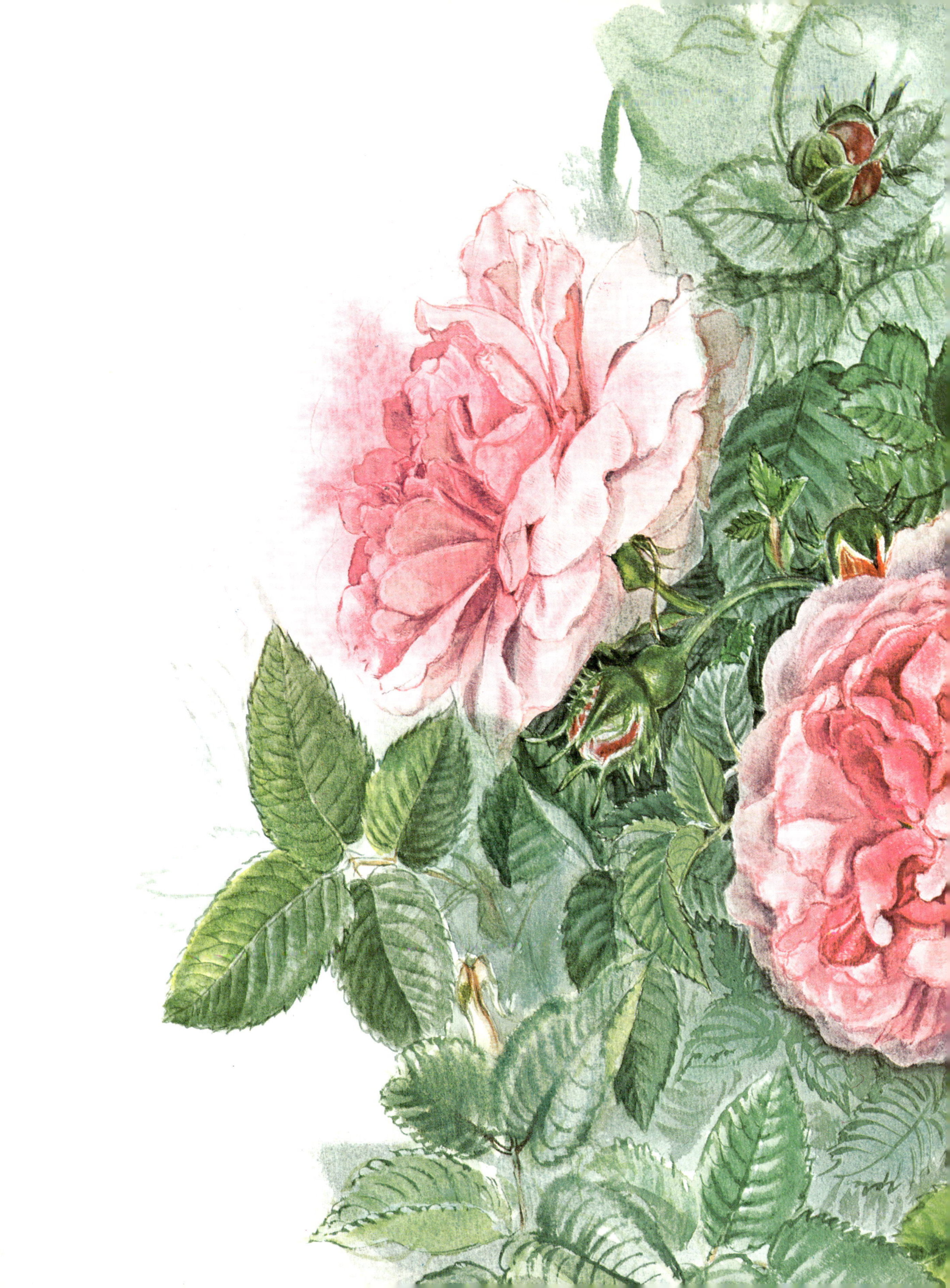

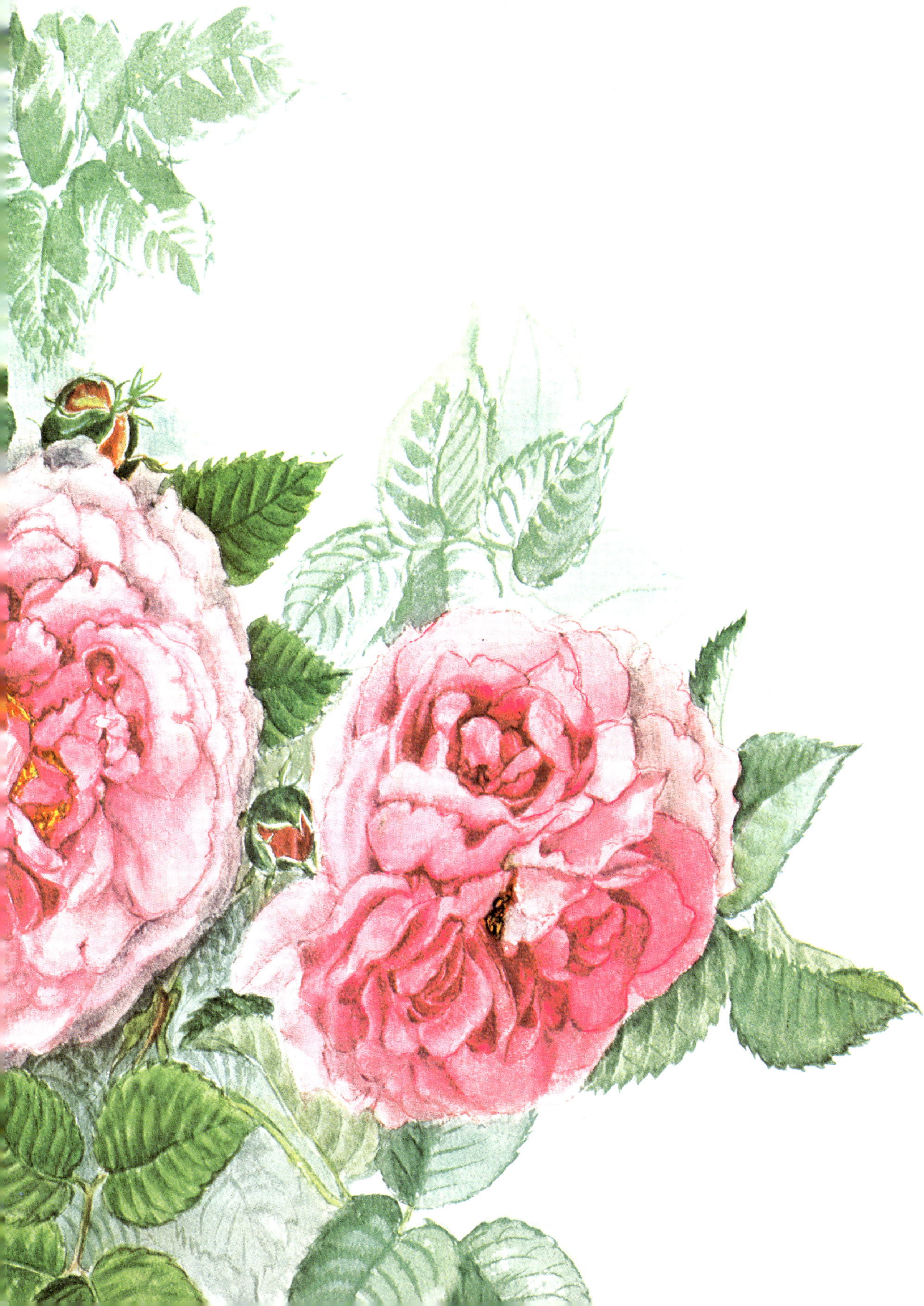

The advertising man for Armstrong Nurseries now came into action, and the advertising campaign began for the new rose. Already on disembarking from the "France", standing unobstrusively in the queue under the letter G at the quayside customs control, I was approached by a journalist who enquired about almost everything, and during this time the customs officer scrutinously examined our suitcases. He was also interested in the conversation, and as soon as he realised that I was a rose painter, we had to show him my rose book. "Beautiful, just beautiful" he said, enraptured, and at long last let us pass, after he had kindly helped us to repack our belongings. At the hotel, the telephone rang constantly, and many reporters, rallied together by the commercially minded advertising agent of the Armstrong Nurseries, visited and interviewed me. It was very amusing to observe how the different journalists posed their questions. Some questioned me most boringly, and chatted about so many insignificant things. A very charming young lady from the "United Press" was so refreshing in her manner, and asked such precise and adept questions, that it was quite a pleasure to answer her. We had a long and interesting conversation, with the result that a series of articles appeared in all the "United Press" newspapers with the title "Mrs Günthart does not think a rose is a rose is a rose – like Gertrude Stein". She had written her articles in a very humorous style, but very cleverly. During the interview I had told her, rather spontaneously, which I was later to regret, that those words from Gertrude Stein were actually nonsense, as in reality no rose is like the next, and each has its own individual characteristics.

The year 1964, when my rose was christened for the second time, was also a year rich with happenings. The events, and with them the excitement, began already at the beginning of the year. I had received an invitation to hold an exhibition in May at the Palazzo Serbillone in Milan. A Milanese friend of ours, who was the managing director of a large Italian company, wished to have five thousand of my rose books with an Italian text in order to use them as gifts for his business colleagues and friends. The president of the Italian Horticultural Society, and owner of the Palazzo Serbillone, as well as some of the most beautiful gardens and parks in Italy, Count C. Gola, had very kindly written the introduction to the Italian text. Our very generous friend had already commissioned an artist to copy eight of my rose pictures from a calendar on to finest Bemberg silk, a few years previously. In many hours of detailed hand work she had patiently created hundreds of roses; the pale pink "Souvenir de la Malmaison", the lilac blue "Sterling Silver", the yellow "Circus" and the deep red "Americana". These two thousand silk roses were presented to all the ladies at the

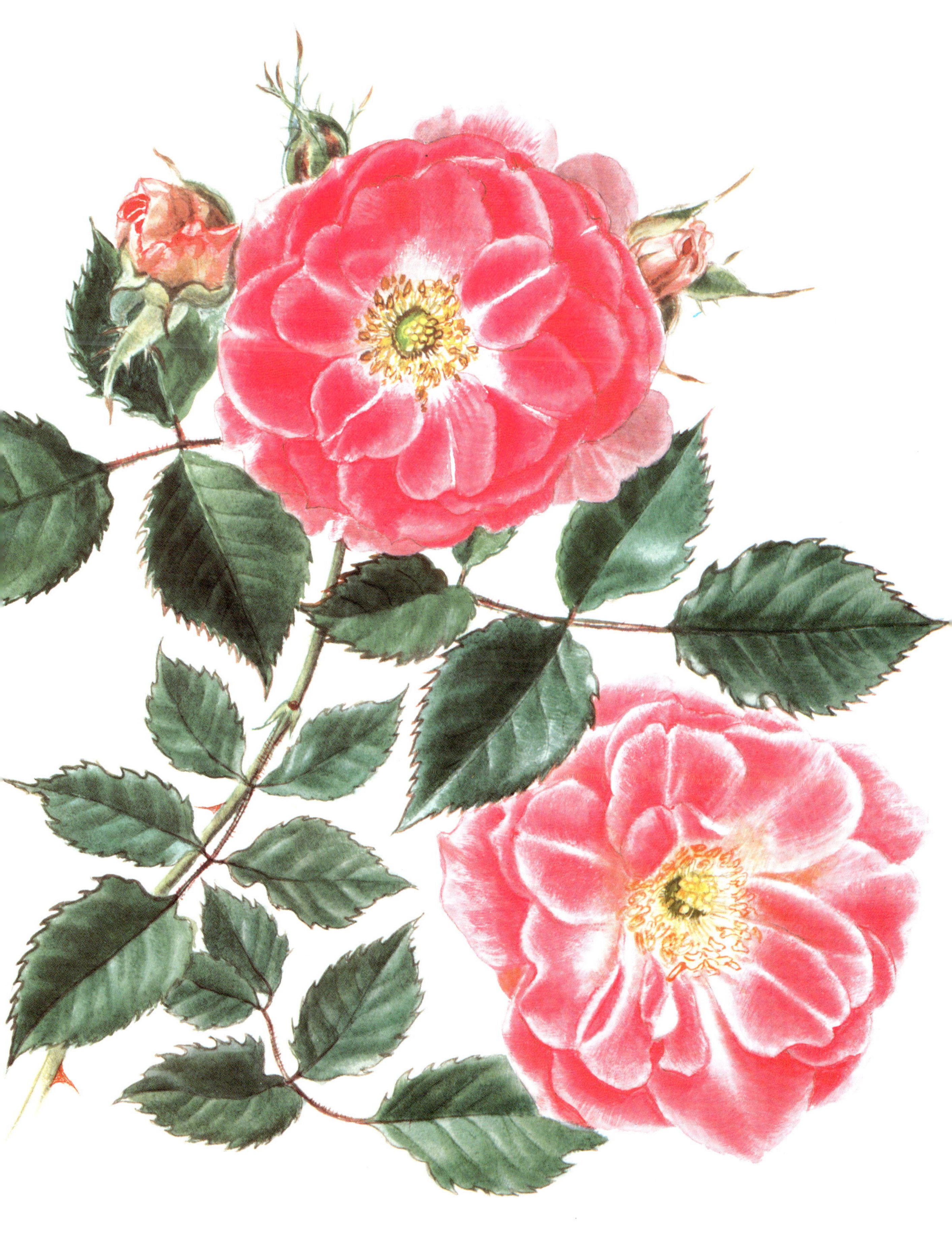

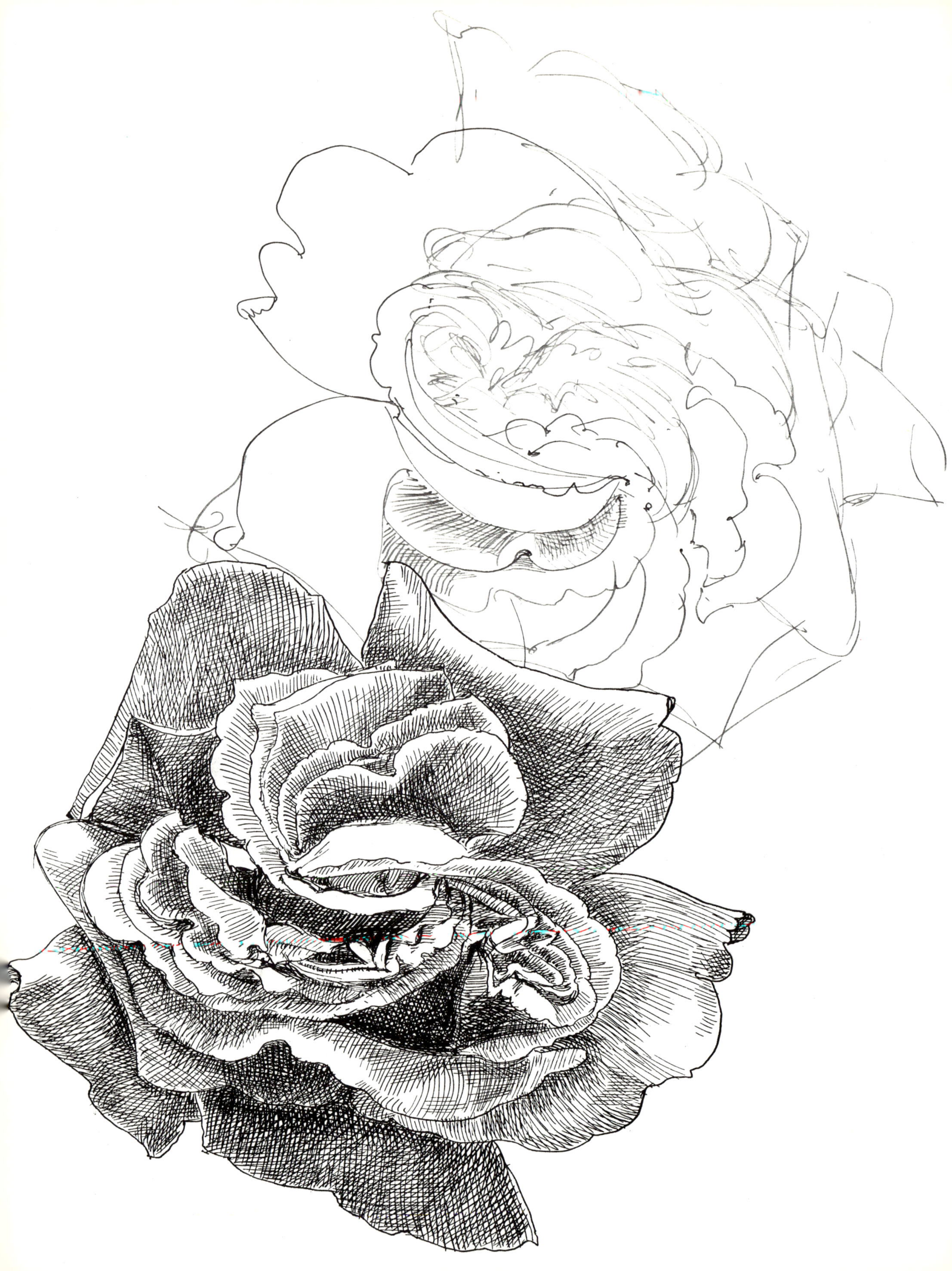

gala première of the "Scala". For the opening day of my exhibition these glorious silk roses were created again, and every lady visiting was able to choose either a pink, pale lilac or yellow rose to pin on her dress. It was a wonderful party; the high mantelpieces of the fireplaces were decorated with roses, and my books, bound in ruby red, shining silk were presented on the large round table cut from green malachite.

Before this day dawned, all manner of things happened. At one time the realisation of the exhibition was more than doubtful.

It was February, and Willi and the children set off for St. Moritz on their annual skiing holiday. I remained at home because mid-week I had arranged, some six months previously, to hold a concert with the well known Kroll Quartet from America, in our house. On Monday morning, the director of Lichtdruck Limited, where my book was being printed, telephoned to inform me that during the weekend there had been a serious leak in the plumbing, and that my books, all five thousand of them which were ready for dispatch to Italy the following day, had been damaged by water and were of no use. The prints were all spoiled; damage was estimated to be in the millions, and the five thousand copies of the forty rose prints had to be reprinted. The worst news was still to come.

The Dutch company which supplied this special paper suitable for the prints required many weeks notice for delivery. At this stage, I imagined the Milan exhibition and my five thousand books literally washed away. On that Monday morning my knees were truly shaky, and I was glad that Willi knew nothing of the matter, as he was very much in need of an untroubled vacation.

I retired early to bed after taking a sleeping tablet, knowing otherwise that I would be awake all night thinking about the problems. My sleep did not last long because that night, the main building of our factory, where the explosives are stored, caught fire.

Fire engines sped from near and far, even the fire brigade from the city of Zürich joined in the fight.

On the Tuesday morning, after the fire had successfully been extinguished, I telephoned our director and requested him not to inform my husband about the fire, hoping at the same time that the news had not reached St. Moritz through some unthinking gossip. That he heard nothing was mainly due to the fact that most guests in St. Moritz are foreign. In spite of these incidents, the problems relating to the exhibition were solved, in an amazingly short time. The insurance company reimbursed the damages, the paper arrived from Holland earlier than expected, and the exhibition was opened in Milan, even though a month late.

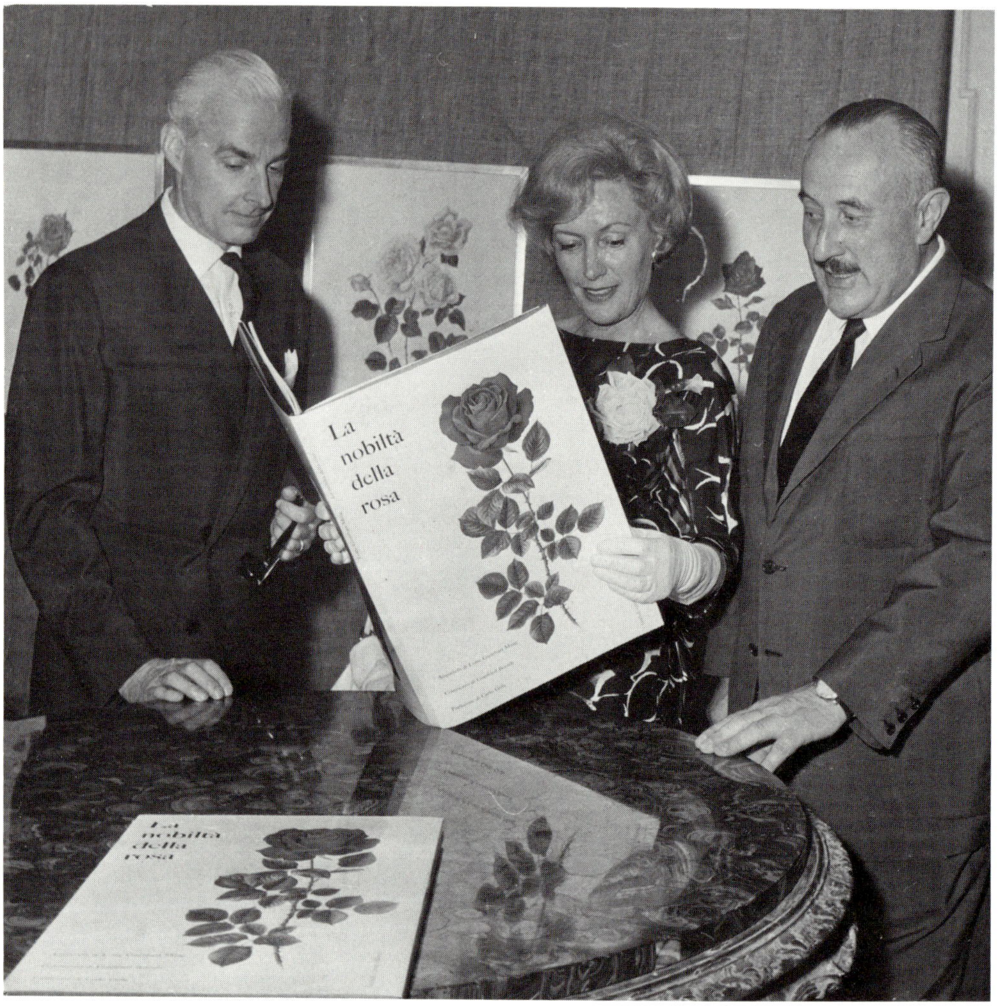

The Palazzo Serbillone, May 1964.
From left to right: The Consul-General, Swiss Embassy in Milan, Lotte Günthart, and Count C. Gola,
President of the Italian Horticultural Society.

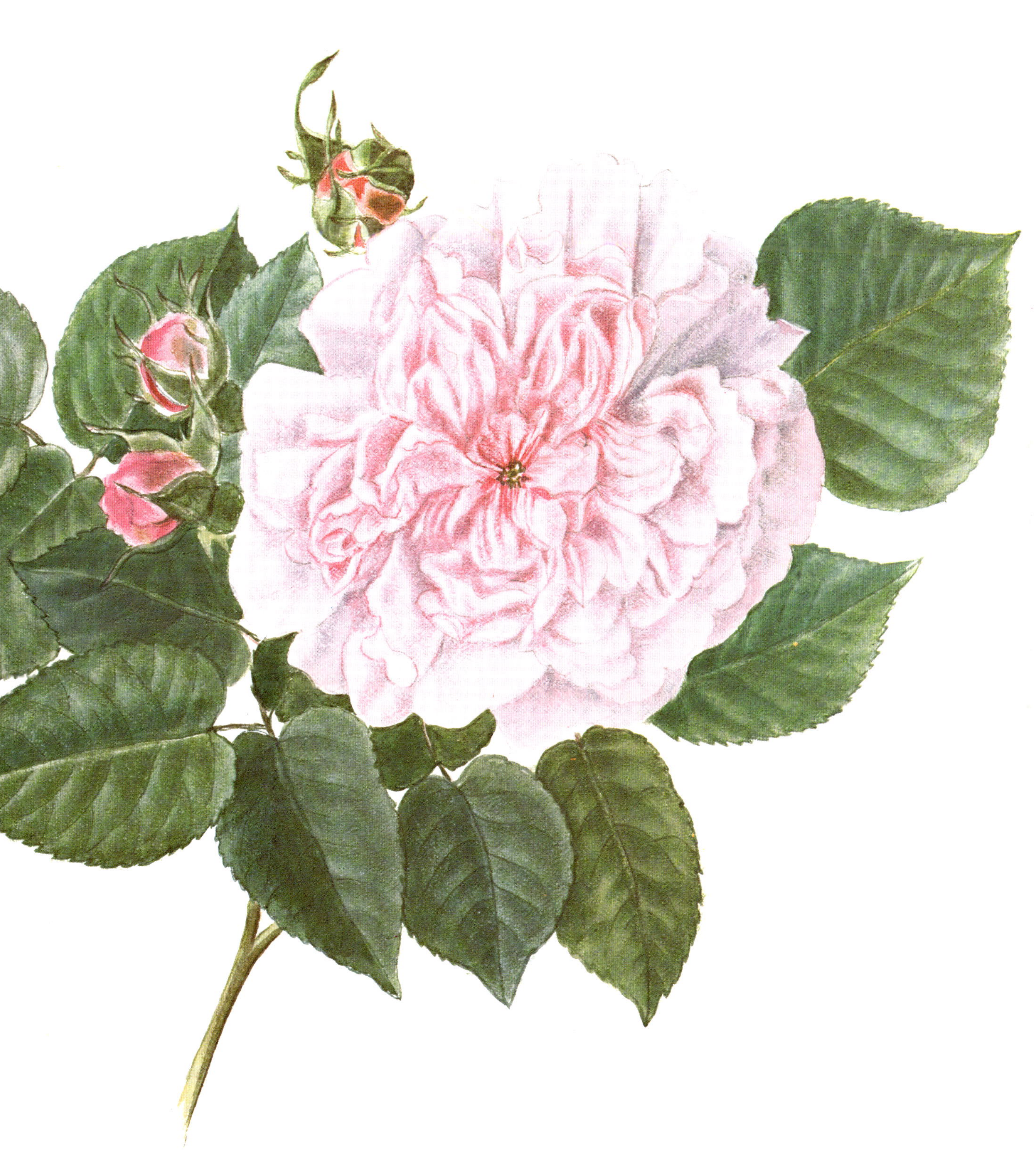

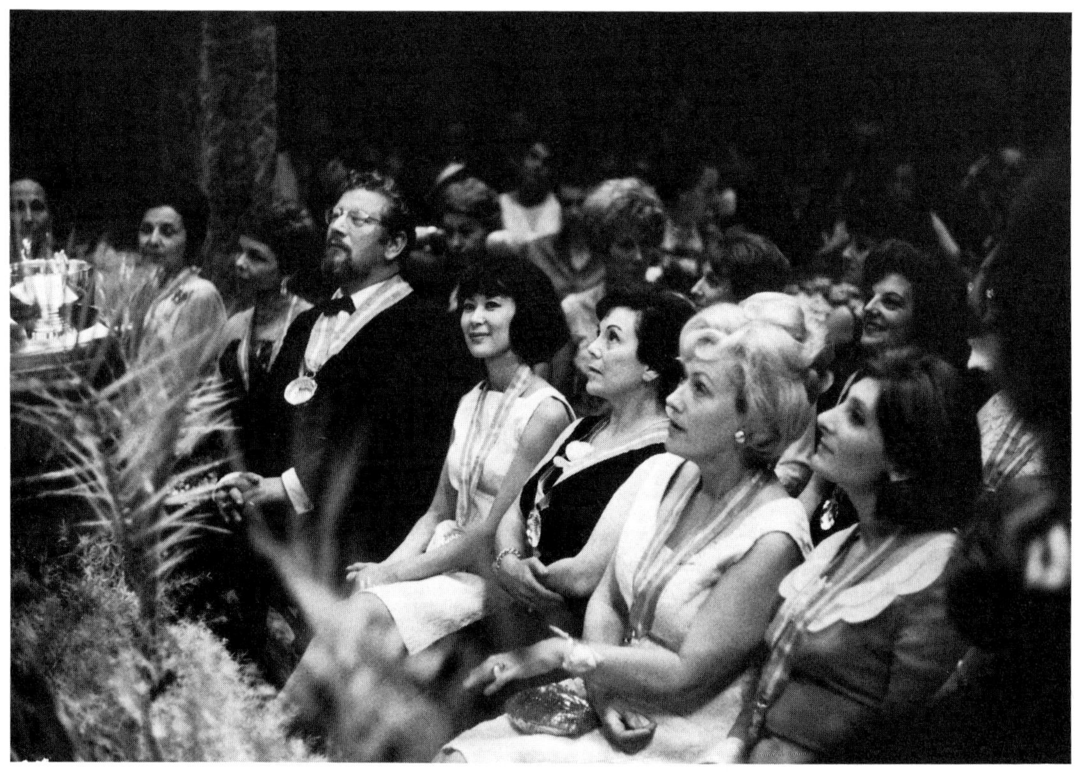

The festival of "Chevaliers de Tastevin", entitled "Chapitre de la Rose", held at the Château Clos-Vougeaut, France in June 1966. Peter Ustinov and some of the "Chevalières".

The concert was on Wednesday, and many more guests arrived than usual and filled the room and part of the hall. It was a wonderful concert and totally successful. Of course, most of the guests had read in the newspapers about the fire; the damage was tremendous. Many people were astounded because I managed to be so calm after this accident, and I told them that only the day before a similar accident had happened, only with water and not with fire. What I did not tell them was that my inner calmness had been found after walking for about four hours, accompanied by my dear French poodle, in the warm spring February sunshine.

In June 1966, I was invited to the festival of "Chevaliers de Tastevin", which was held in the Chateau Clos-Vougeaut, a famous castle built during the renaissance amongst magnificent vineyards in Burgundy, France. That year, the title given to the celebration was "Chapitre de la Rose". Six hundred guests were invited and the same number of "Lotte Günthart" roses were printed on the front cover of the extravagant menu.

Outside the tower, the trumpeters, who were dressed in mediaeval clothes, formed a guard of honour, and gave a superb performance, whilst we all admired the ancient presses and casks. The celebration lasted until two o'clock in the morning; it was held by candle-light in the cellar, which was over eight hundred years old, and with each new course of the meal, a different wine was tasted and served. After the feast, the nine new "Chevaliers", but this time we were "Chevalières", were ceremoniously inaugurated. Two actresses, Cecile Aubry and a lovely Japanese lady, a famous doctor, a renowned barrister, a distinguished journalist, three other ladies, and myself, all in turn had to step up on to the platform to receive the fraternal kiss, and to undergo the ritual set by the Great Master and the Chancellor, in the presence of the other high members of the brotherhood, who were all dressed in their ceremonial long costumes of satin and gold, after which we were ordained by the Great Master who solemnly placed the silver «Tastevin» which was on a silk band, around our necks.

In between the performances presented by various folk singers and sketches from Molière's "malade imaginaire", the honorary guest, the great Peter Ustinov entertained us with his wonderful and charming humour, sometimes in English, then in French, German or Russian, and all the time he managed to mix these languages together in a highly amusing manner.

In a small town such as Regensberg, every young man is expected to carry out an official duty. Since Willi's time was always too short, he decided to take over the office of an almoner, because this required only a few evening meetings annually.

The welfare officers numbered five, and after some years, only one case of hardship had to be dealt with, a somewhat grotesque proportion.

An elderly, friendly lady, Mrs Dünki, lived in a small house opposite to us. Every day, she had to fetch her water from the village well, and the house was totally lacking comfort or amenity.

There was no window in the kitchen, making it small, dark and smoky. The welfare committee decided that her house was untenable, worthless, and therefore should be demolished. The elderly lady could then either live with her son, or find a place in the old people's home in Regensberg. Previously, and independent of the welfare office, Willi had personally supplied the necessary finances to have the roof repaired, for it was full of holes and the rain dripped into the living room. He considered it deplorable that a house, whose charm was temporarily lost through neglect, should be destroyed. He proposed to the council that they acquire the house from Mrs Dünki, but this was met with laughter, even more so because the county's property officer estimated the value of the house at a maximum of Sfr. 12,000.-. When the poor lady was told that the council did not wish to purchase her house, she came to Willi, dissolved in tears.

In her imagination, she had already received the Sfr. 12,000.-, and her son had even purchased a car in anticipation. The poor soul had taken every word spoken by Willi at face value, and was now bitterly disappointed. Therefore, Willi decided to purchase the house himself, in order to retrieve the charm and beauty which had been foolishly lost through many years of negligence. He bought the house from her at a much higher price than the estimate, and also undertook to pay her a monthly pension, for the rest of her life.

The locals mocked at the man who had bought this ruin of a house, and at such a high price. Mrs Dünki remained in the house until all the renovation plans were complete, and when the building commenced, she moved to live with her son and his wife.

During the building phase, the house was nicknamed "the unfinished symphony". Five long years passed before the house emerged, surprisingly beautiful, like a Phoenix arising from the ashes, and the "Dünki House", as it was named by one and all, became the Red Rose House. It was a masterpiece, affectionately planned and painstakingly achieved by

my husband. The house itself held many unexpected rooms. When viewed from the outside, the small and charming timbered building, sited between two other higher houses,
appeared small, and it was difficult to imagine the spaciousness within. There is a huge
cellar, which, later furnished in a rustic style, became the favourite place of many business
functions. Also our many guests, often numbering over a hundred, prefer to sit in the
cellar in the late evening, and many amusing hours are spent there. The great barn at
ground level is now an exhibition hall. My paintings cover the walls, and various "rose
items" are displayed for sale on a large oak table. Table-cloths and handkerchiefs with rose
motives, prints of my rose water colours, and collotypes of my garden scenes and
sketches. Naturally, my rose books are also on sale. Following the German editions, they
had in the meantime been translated into the English, French, Italian and Polish language.
These items, in addition to other books and prints also offered, were sold by Christa, our
youngest daughter, every day between two and six in the afternoon. On fine days, the constant stream of visitors completeley occupied her. Christa would have loved to manage
everything herself, but with time, their numbers increased so much, that this proved to be
impossible. It involved conducted tours of the house for people from India, Japan,
Sweden, Finland, Australia, America, France, England and Germany, during which she
talked to them about my paintings, the founding of the Red Rose House, and finally,
about the history of Regensberg. The outcome of all this was that her circle of friends was
very large, and international. Christa received invitations to Japan, New Zealand, America
and South Africa, from visitors charmed by her natural friendliness. Each Christmas, her
list is longer, and over a thousand calendars and cards are sent all over the world.
She replies to the many letters personally, and also handles the despatch of pictures and
books ordered, as well as taking care of the reservations for the Red Rose House, which is
in great, and still growing, demand for business functions, weddings and balls. For, on the
first floor, facing south, is the large, long room, at which many a wedding party has been
assembled. Beyond this is a balcony, of the same length as the room, which is bordered by
pretty window-boxes in summer. Here outside, sitting at small folding tables, and perched
as though on a tree top, one can admire the breathtaking view. Enjoying tea, or coffee and
home made cakes; even this is now possible since we have two additional assistants, who
serve our guests in the afternoons. If a woman's social club wish to meet in an agreeable
and homely place, then we lead them to the room in which the antique, green tiled stove
gives a pleasing warmth; this is comfortably furnished, with a sofa and matching chairs,

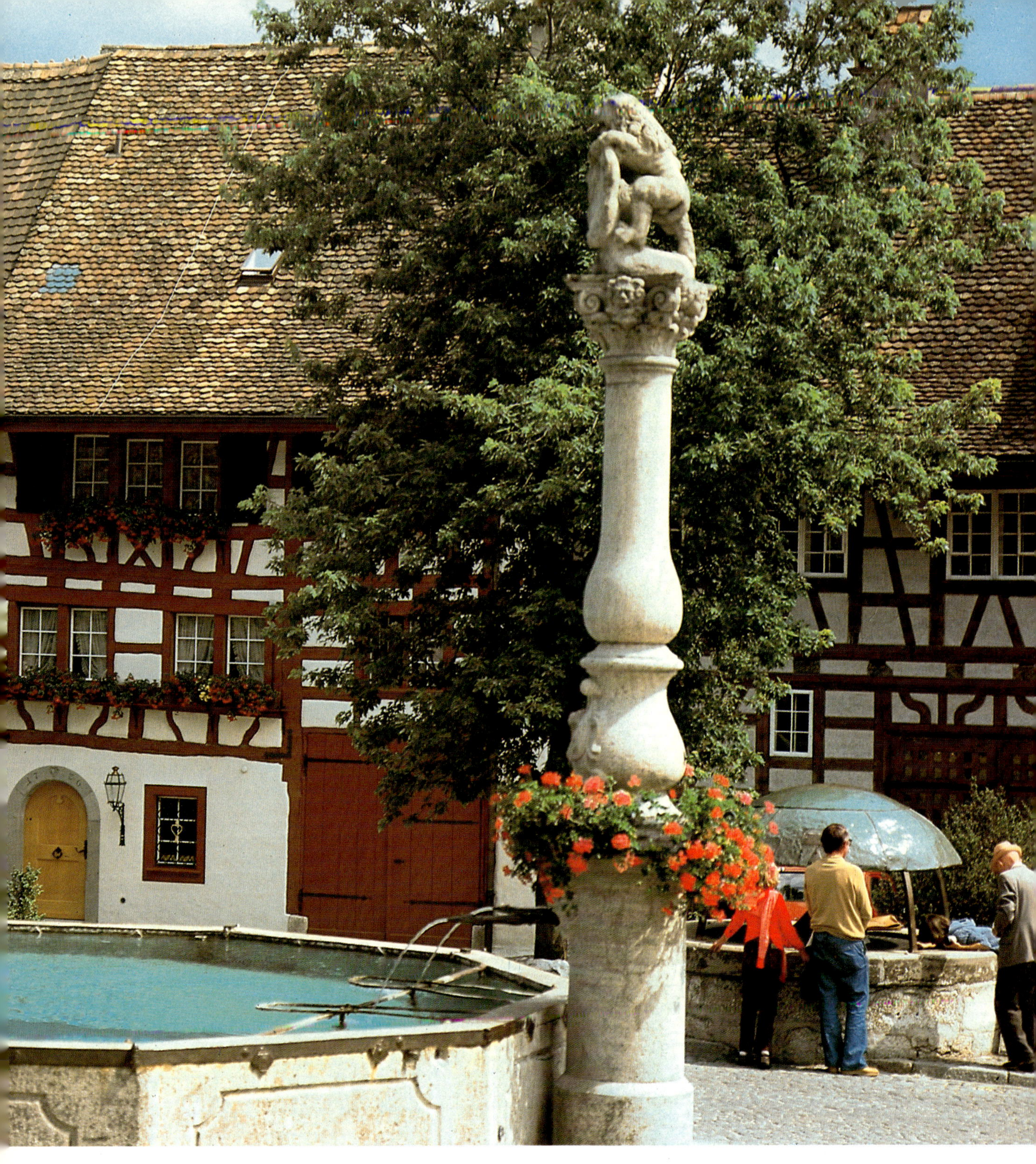

The Red Rose House, Regensberg.
A permanent exhibition of the works by Lotte Günthart, open to the public every afternoon.

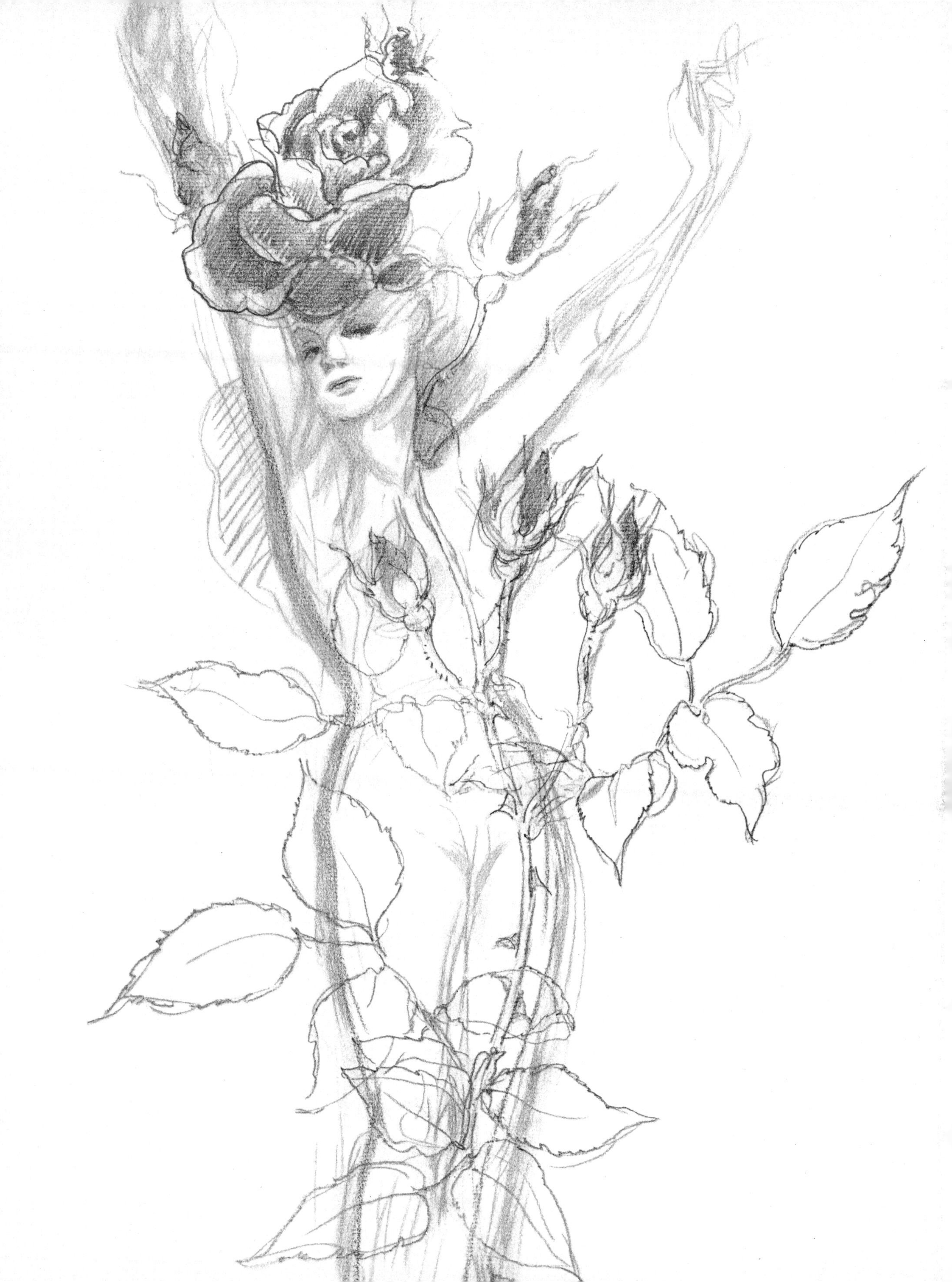

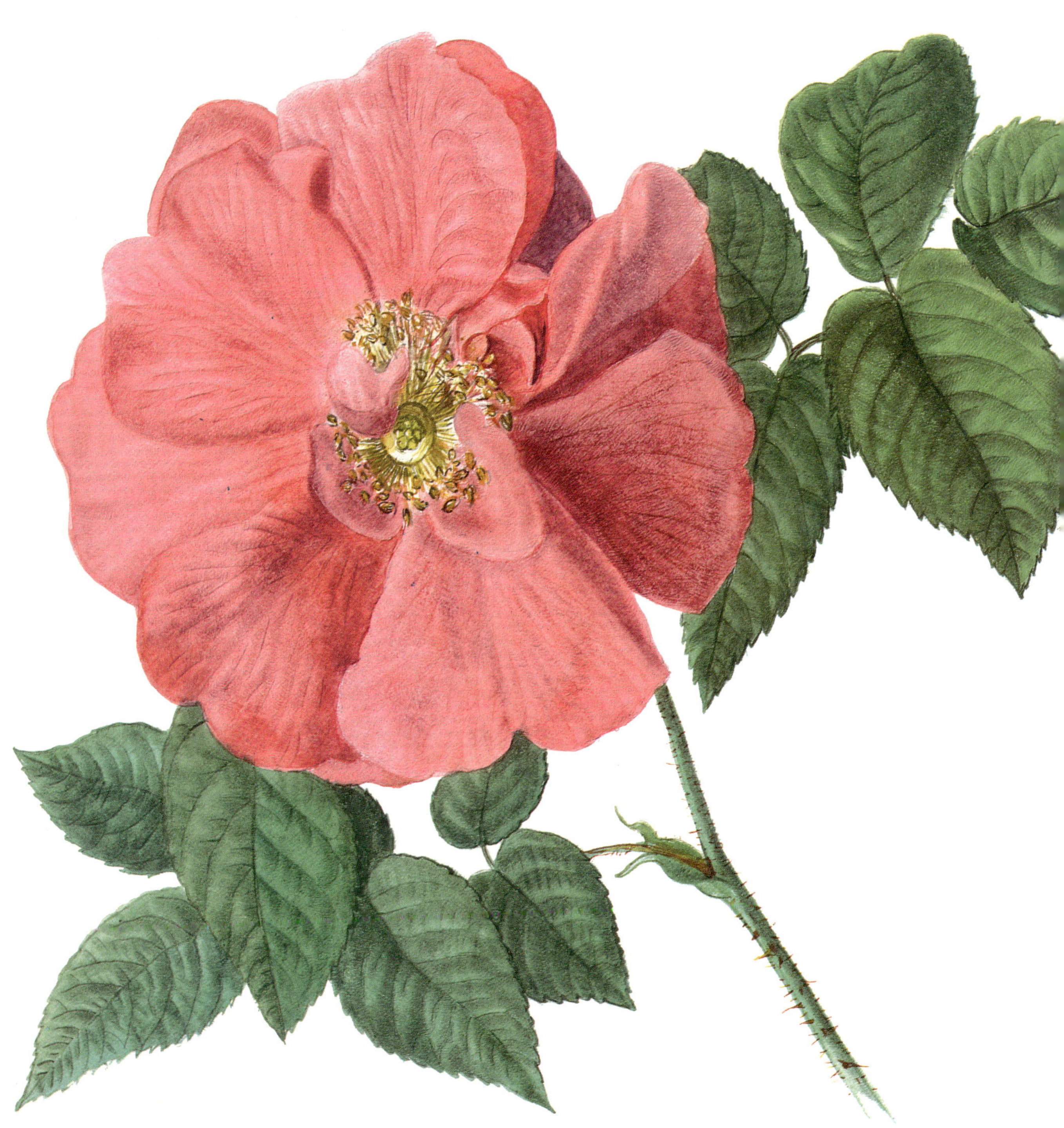

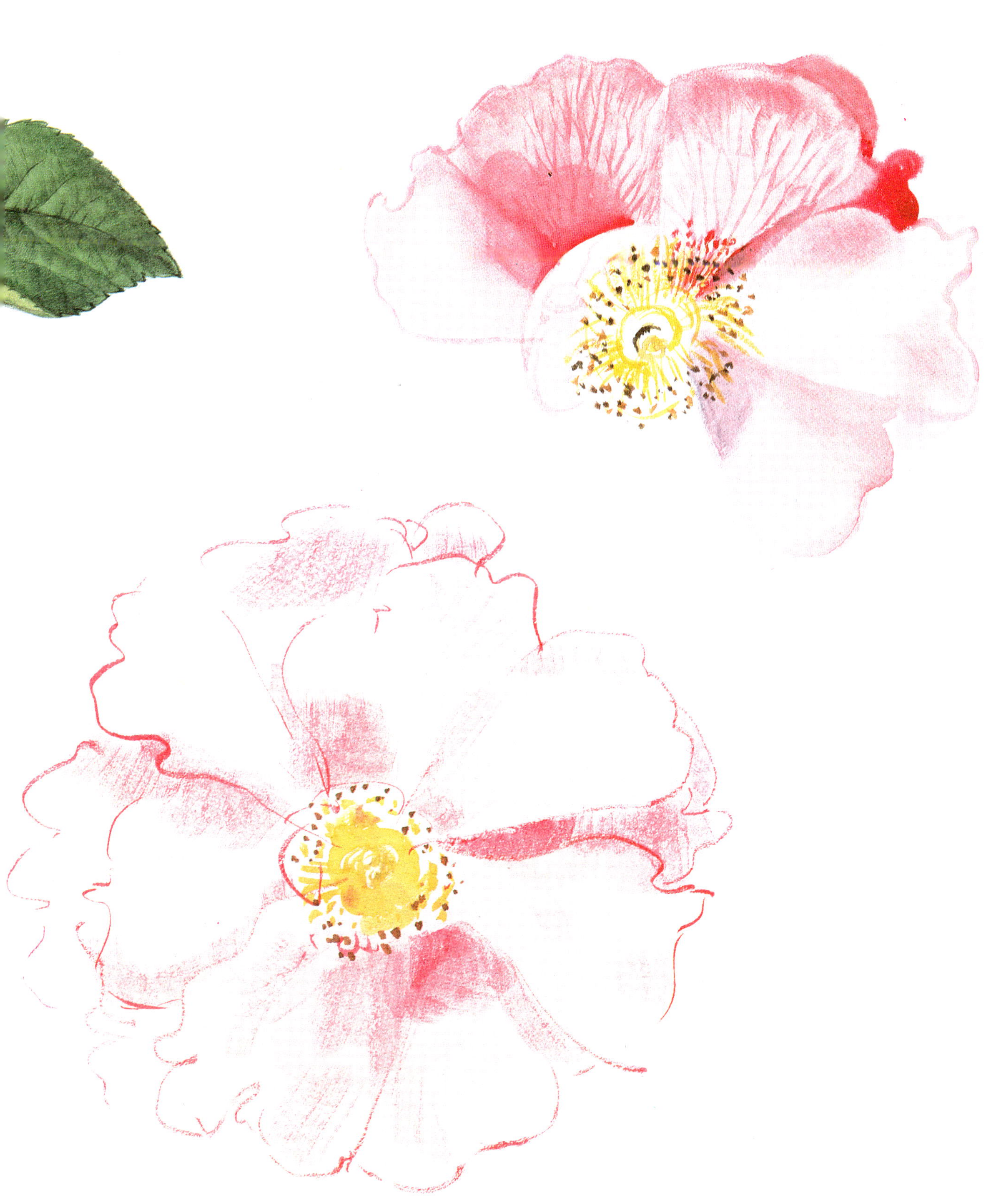

also antique. Two glass show cases hold miniature dolls dressed in finely embroidered Swiss national costumes. The exquisite creations were kindly donated to us by an artistically gifted friend, who had produced them in many hours of patient and exact work. A modern and functional kitchen is also well equipped to handle catering, either from other hotels, or from our restaurant "zur Krone", which regularly prepare large wedding and business banquets.

The very top of the house is most delightful. Here, in glass cabinets, father's drawing pads are exhibited, and a few sketches, amongst which is to be found a rose sketch quickly drawn; amidst the rose buds is his small daughter, aged one and a half years.

Almost an omen!

The dark room is also here, where the company can present films and slides showing our company, the factory, and the plants in the surrounding gardens, to their business guests, who are often entertained in the Red Rose House. The library too, is situated on this floor, and here we have our most valuable books on plants, particularly roses. This collection is becoming more extensive, and the shelves are well stocked.

The two small two-room apartments, complete with individual kitchen and bathroom, are furnished with specially chosen antiques, lovely carpets and curtains. The walls are decorated with old prints of Regensberg.

The apartments face south, and on a clear day the view into the far distance and the snow covered alps can be admired.

In spring and summer, they are reserved usually by guests from America, and many of them have become our friends. Many charming guests come from Germany, France and England, and of course, also from Switzerland, who wish to celebrate their first, tenth or fiftieth "honeymoon" with us.

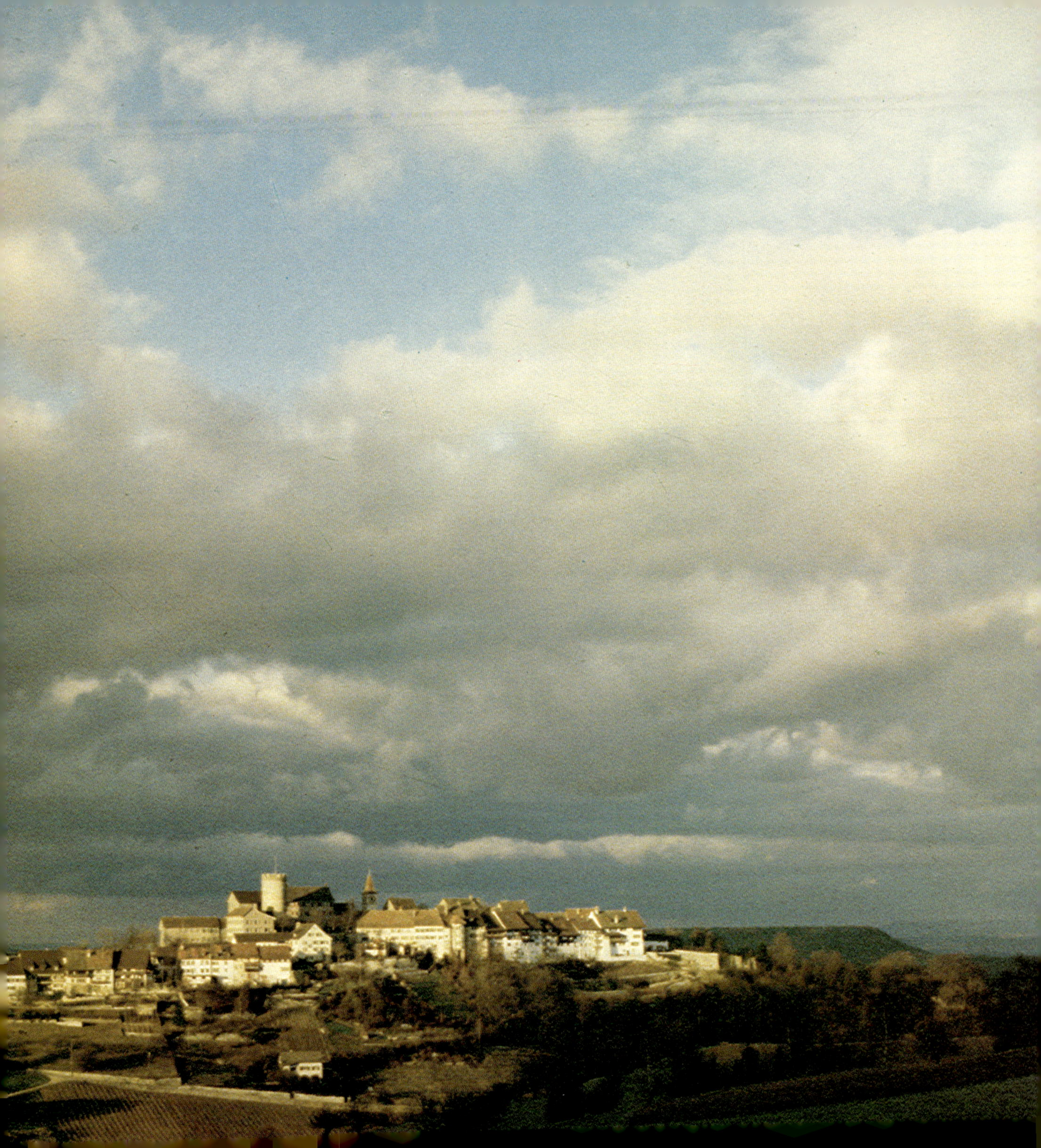

"Regensberg A Swiss Surprise".
An article from the New York Gourmet Magazine, March 1979, written by Joseph Wechsberg.

"Regensberg had been founded in 1245 by a knight, Lüthold the Fifth, who ruled over a large part of what is now the canton of Zürich.
Regensberg, perched on a hilltop of the Swiss Jura, five hundred feet above the surrounding Unterland, was a natural fortress. There Lüthold had a small, sturdy castle built with bailey, moat, drawbridge, a round tower with nine foot thick walls, and an entrance twenty feet above the ground, accessible only by means of a removable ladder.
And from there, he terrorized the people below.

But even the smart men make mistakes, and Lüthold made his in 1267 when he became involved in a feud with Rudolf I of Habsburg, an impoverished Swiss nobleman from nearby Aargau. Lüthold foolishly led the Regensbergers in a battle against Rudolf, supported by some mercenaries from Zürich. Lüthold was beaten; and that was the beginning of the end of Regensberg.

Six years later, Rudolf was elected King of the Holy Roman Empire of Germany, and became the founder of the Habsburg line, which ruled an empire for 645 years where "the sun never set". In 1302 the Regensberg knights sold out to the Habsburgs, and the small fortress town passed into the hands of Zurich".

Three times during twenty-eight years, we have had to overcome hefty opposition to save our beloved Regensberg from disfiguration.

In 1946, the authorities planned to erect a high and ugly prison building in the midst of the vineyards. At the last moment, when everything appeared lost, because even the Society for Conservation of Ancient Monuments and Countryside voted against us, Willi decided to ask Gottlieb Duttweiler, one of the most highly individual and courageous personalities in Switzerland, for assistance. As Willi was explaining the background story, this very enterprising man spontaneously said, "I like you, you're my man", and faithfully promised to help us. Thereafter, a pamphlet was circulated amongst the electorates of the Canton Zürich, with the slogan "We have it, and we'll pay", which was a synonym for "we're sufficiently affluent to squander our money", for the building project was tremendously expensive. This striking sentence achieved a miracle amongst the population, and opened their eyes. The general opinion completely swung about face, and the building was rejected with an overwhelming majority.

The second episode was in 1960.

A private venture was unveiled to build a row of houses at the foot of Regensberg, which is the smallest town in Switzerland. This would have totally obliterated the sensational view to the mediaeval city, which is like a crown on top of the hill. This new housing estate would have been a lucrative business for many. Willi, and the Pro Regensberg Society, newly formed with congenial people, and whose dedicated president was Hans Arnold, the art restorer, then had to destroy the hopes of those who had planned to attain a grand profit. Amazingly, their efforts were rewarded, due also to the perseverance and patience of my husband, who never resigned.

By this time Willi Günthart had become a hero to many people in Switzerland, but a Don Quixote to others. This victory was the result of never ending and untold arguments, negotiations, conferences, meetings with politicians, as well as many intrigues. It was a victory achieved over the seemingly impossible. Even the village mayor of the time had ordered the "pack of artists" as he called us, to leave the village within three days. Nevertheless, we stayed. Finally, the land owners were well compensated by the Canton for their expensive sites, that no longer would be built on, and the scaffolding on the future plots disappeared. The passions and anger declined, slowly subsiding, and those citizens who were so hostile towards us, mellowed.

Peace returned again to our small community.

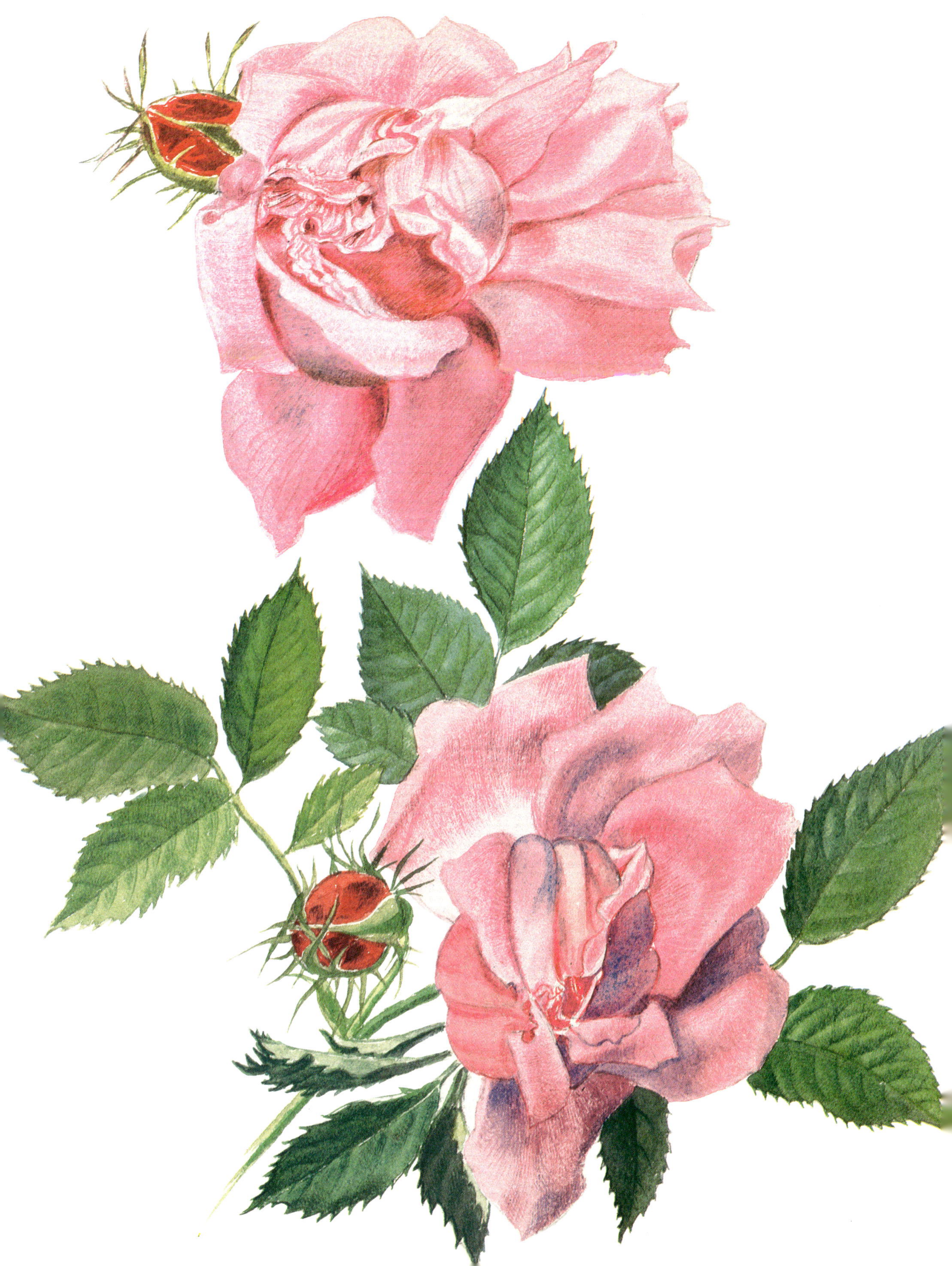

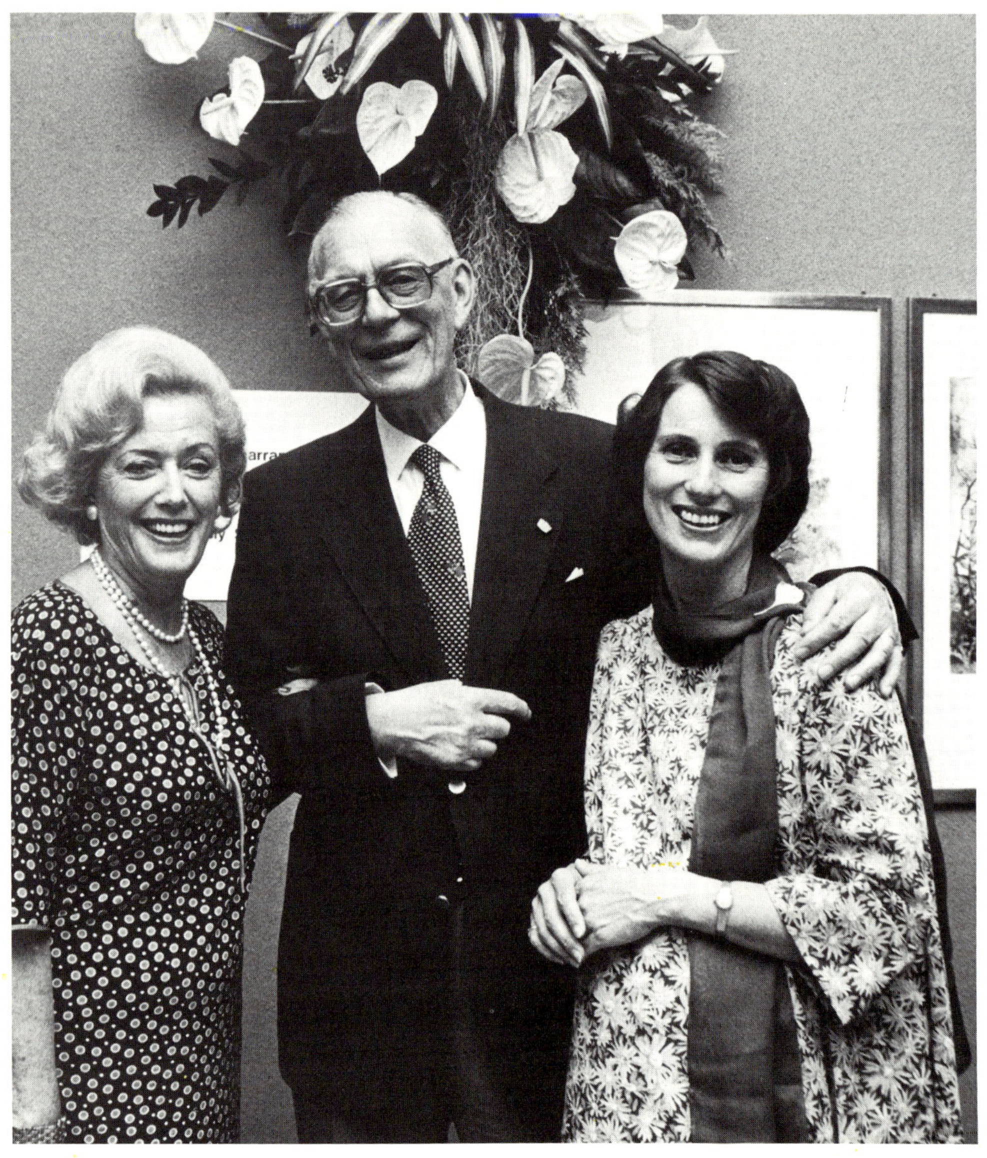

Mainau Castle 1980.
From left to right: Lotte Günthart, Count Lennart Bernadotte, and his wife Countess Sonja on
the occasion of my exhibition in the castle.

A "flower Island" in the heart of Europe, the Isle of Mainau is a huge park surrounded by
the Lake of Constance, and a paradise of the most beautiful flowers and trees. It is the result
of 50 years of dedication by Count Lennart Bernadotte, who turned the wilderness which he
inherited from his grandmother, the Queen of Sweden, into a jewel of nature. Millions of
flower enthusiasts visit this unique spot every year.

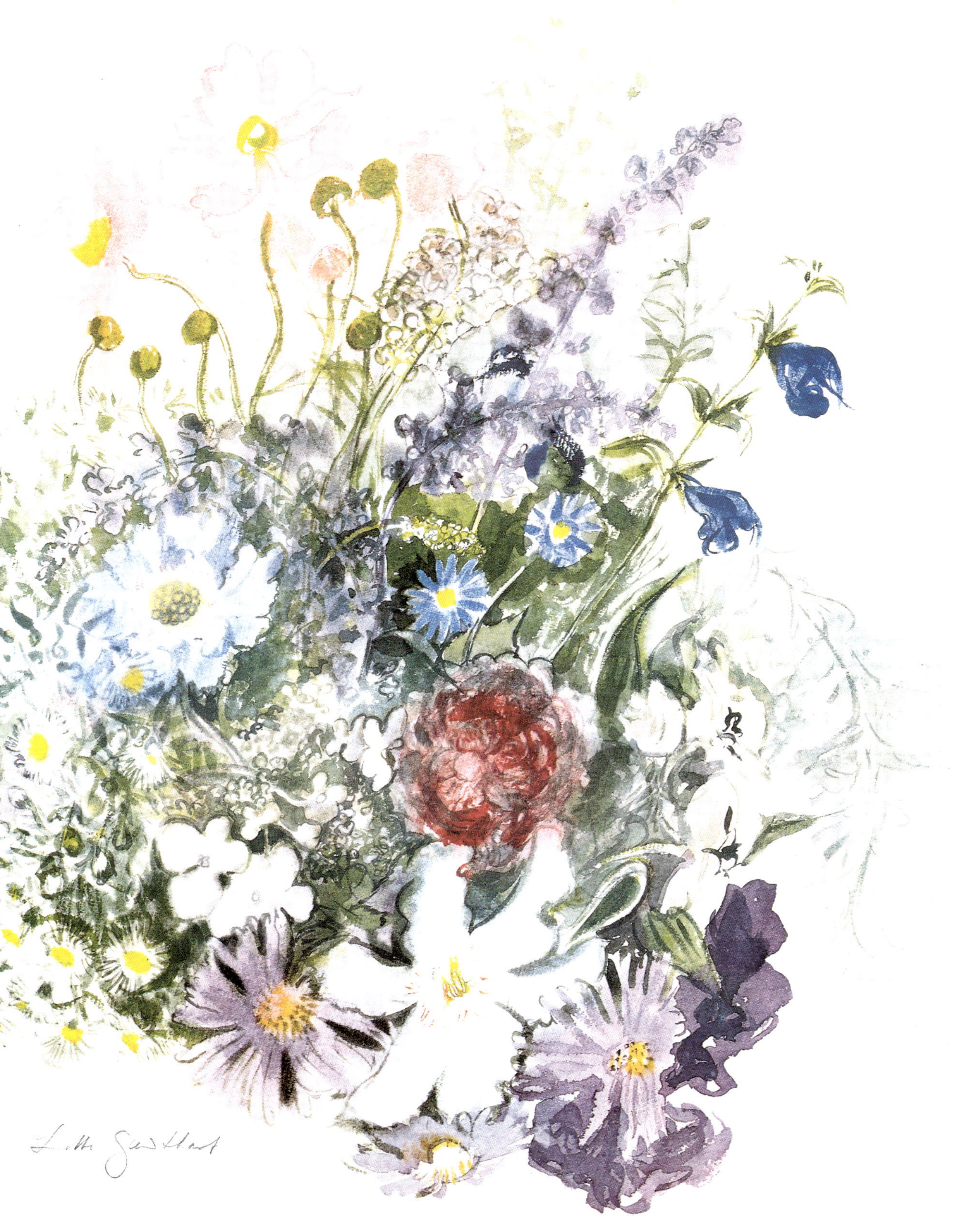

Our last struggle, from the beginning of 1973 till the end of 1974, was to defend Regensberg against circumstances which would have irretrievably ruined the beauty inherited from the middle ages. This lengthy process personally cost us much courage and nervous energy.
In spite of the Society for Conservation of Ancient Monuments and Countryside, who supported us least of all, it was planned to build a terrace of town houses.
This massive structure would have entirely stifled the charm of Regensberg. Rows of existing houses were also to be demolished to make room in the lower part of the town for new and modern styled buildings. The plans looked disastrous. An underground garage was constructed under the tower, and for this reason, the lovely old lime trees were felled. This, even though the garage could have been built further down, involving far less detonation. There, it would have been easier to build, less expensive, and without the loss of the attractive lime trees.

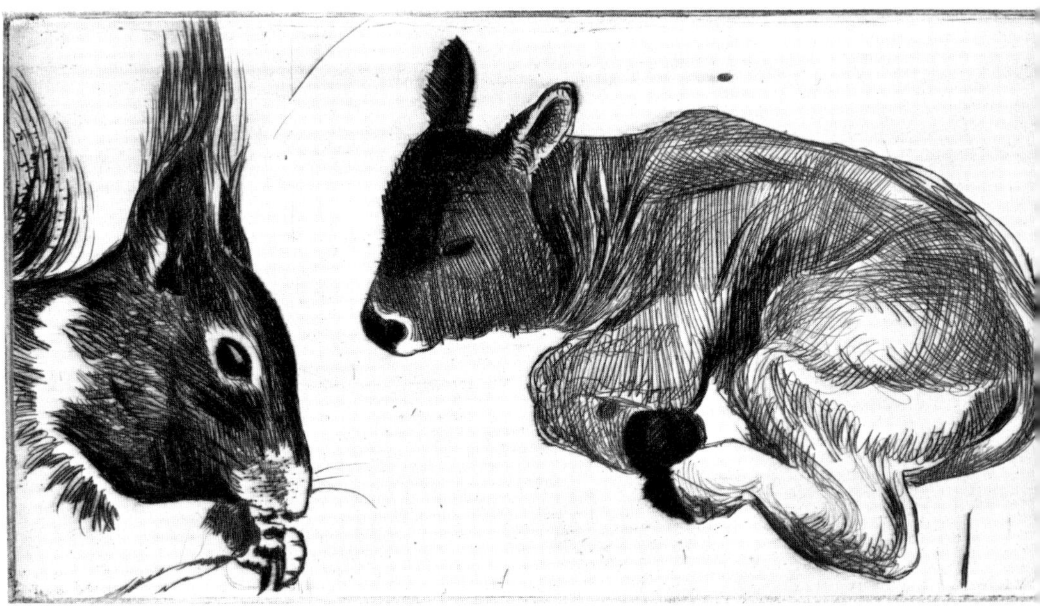

This process was extremely unpleasant, and we were under pressure from all sides.
Until success neared, we were literally bombarded with many insults and adversities.
Our opponents totally lacked civic courage, and all measures of mendacity, even from the authorities, were apparent.
It was almost a miracle that we were able to save our village from ruin. After this dispute, lasting over two years, the high authorities appropriately reimbursed the council of Regensberg for the land which was no longer to be urbanized.
Now, "our castle", as it is fondly called, is still proud and beautiful as it was hundreds of years ago, rising above the vineyards. And, instead of rows of houses, the delectable local wines are cultivated; "Pinot noir", the amber coloured "Pinot gris", and the pale "Riesling-Sylvaner" (Müller-Thurgau).

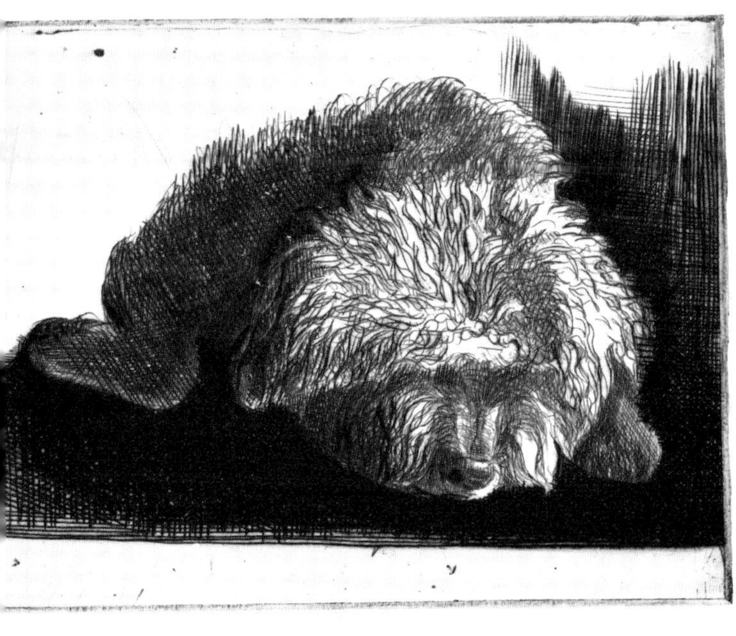

It was the first week of January 1961, and about midnight, when I was awakened by the telephone. The call was from New York; it was Mr Harrity, my manager at that time. He was probably enjoying his first whiskey of the day because there it was only six o'clock in the evening. "I have just arranged a fabulous deal for you" were his first words. He went on to say "Our friend Mrs Y. had the most marvellous idea that we could do something with your rose paintings, and so I immediately went to the Manager of McCall's Magazine, with a print of one of your roses". The very strict and critical Mr Myes was apparently enthralled with the idea of publishing ten new varieties of American roses, in full size, in his magazine. Mr Harrity was so enthusiastic on the telephone that he almost became hoarse, and then explained how lucky we were that McCall's was financially well situated. With a voice full of excitement, he said "We'll split the sum they're paying between three, Sfr 16 000.– for you, the same for Mrs Y., and the same also for me, because I settled the whole business with the very influential Mr Myes". At that time, Sfr 16,000.– seemed a lot of money, and I was extremely pleased. On recollection however, it now appears rather little in reward for the excessive amount of work involved, especially because none of my original paintings were returned to me. And, to think that Mrs Y. also received the same amount for her casual idea, was rather vexing. A hectic time followed; none of the varieties were obtainable from any European florist, and no roses bloom outdoors in January. I then telephoned Mr Harrity for assistance, and he immediately had a solution to the problem. He enquired at all the large rose cultivators in America, if these varieties were available. At Armstrongs, in California, all ten varieties required were in full bloom, and at their best. Armstrong then telephoned me to clarify when, and how often, I would require the roses to be sent. I told him that for a true to nature portrait of a rose, I required at least fifty hours work, and that early every Monday morning I would commence painting a new rose, and so therefore dispatch every Saturday would be most suitable.

Every Friday I received a telegram indicating the arrival time and flight number of the "rose aircraft", which was mostly routed over the North Pole. On each Saturday for five consecutive weeks, my husband drove to the airport to take prompt receipt of the rose consignment, to ensure their freshness. Each parcel contained a hundred roses, and the stem of each individual rose was immersed in a small container of water. On arrival of the third delivery, the customs officer could no longer contain his curiosity, and asked my husband if "this Mrs Lotte Günthart" had a birthday every week, to which my husband replied that Lotte Günthart was painting these roses for an American womens' magazine.

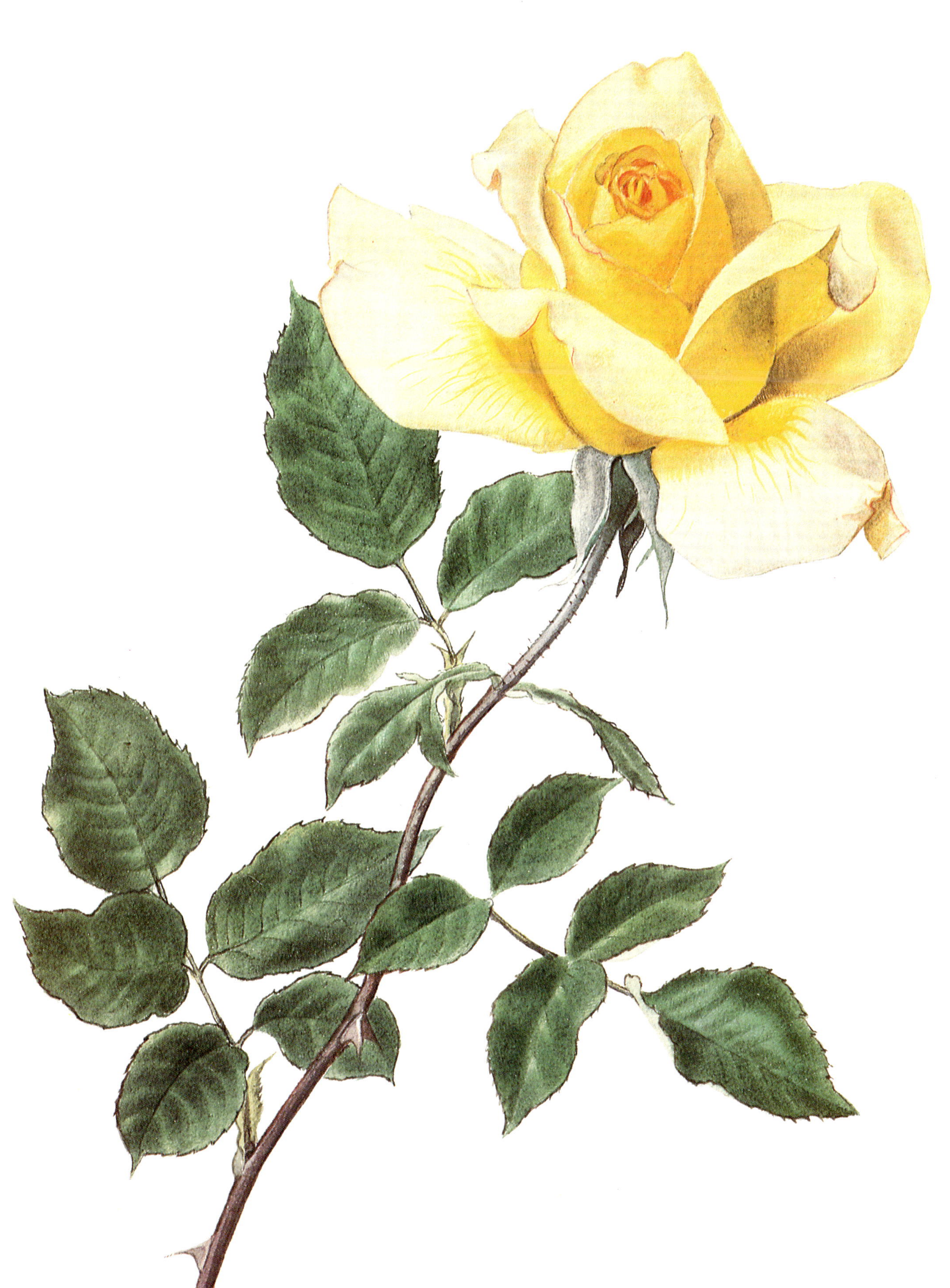

This took him completely by surprise, and rather puzzled him, and he remarked "Don't they have an artist in such an enormous country as America who can paint roses? That would be far less complicated". In actual fact, of course, he was right. The definite date for the paintings to be in America, the so called dead-line, was Monday, the 20 February. The paintings had to be at the editors office in New York by ten o'clock in the morning, failing this the contract would be cancelled. There was no clause allowing a delay.

I had six weeks in which to finish the paintings; from Monday morning till Saturday evening, I was able to complete one painting. Very fortunately, during the previous summer, I had unknowingly painted four of the required varieties in great detail, with their long stems, as they were now requested. These four paintings proved to be my saving grace, because ten paintings, each requiring fifty hours work, could otherwise never have been accomplished in the short time of six weeks.

Having to paint the six remaining roses presented me with a problem great enough, and on Saturday, the 18 February, I made the final strokes with my brush at six o'clock in the evening. Then I noticed my legs; the ankles were swollen and felt numb.

Well, I thought, this ailment will pass, the main thing is that I have finished on schedule. I telephoned Mr Harrity in New York, telling him that the paintings were finished, and that we would dispatch them in a specially constructed wooden package. Departure was with the Swissair afternoon flight from Zürich to New York on Sunday, 19 February, and he was to take receipt of the paintings that same evening.

Sunday dawned, and we drove to the airport with our precious freight. Oddly enough, at the last minute, I had put my husband's passport and some money, all that I could find in the house, in my handbag. On arriving at the airport, the Swissair personnel laconically informed us, that due to snow storms in New York, the next flight would not be until Monday. We were in despair.

My husband immediately rearranged the plan, and went to the counter of Air France, who also had a flight scheduled for New York, via Paris. This proved to be fruitless, because several celebrities, returning from their winter vacation in Klosters, had completely filled the aircraft, and, to our annoyance, their excess baggage required all the available freight allowance.

By now rather agitated, my husband hurried to the KLM counter, where they told him that an aircraft was shortly leaving for Amsterdam with a connection for New York. However, it would not be possible for KLM to guarantee expedite handling of the package, as

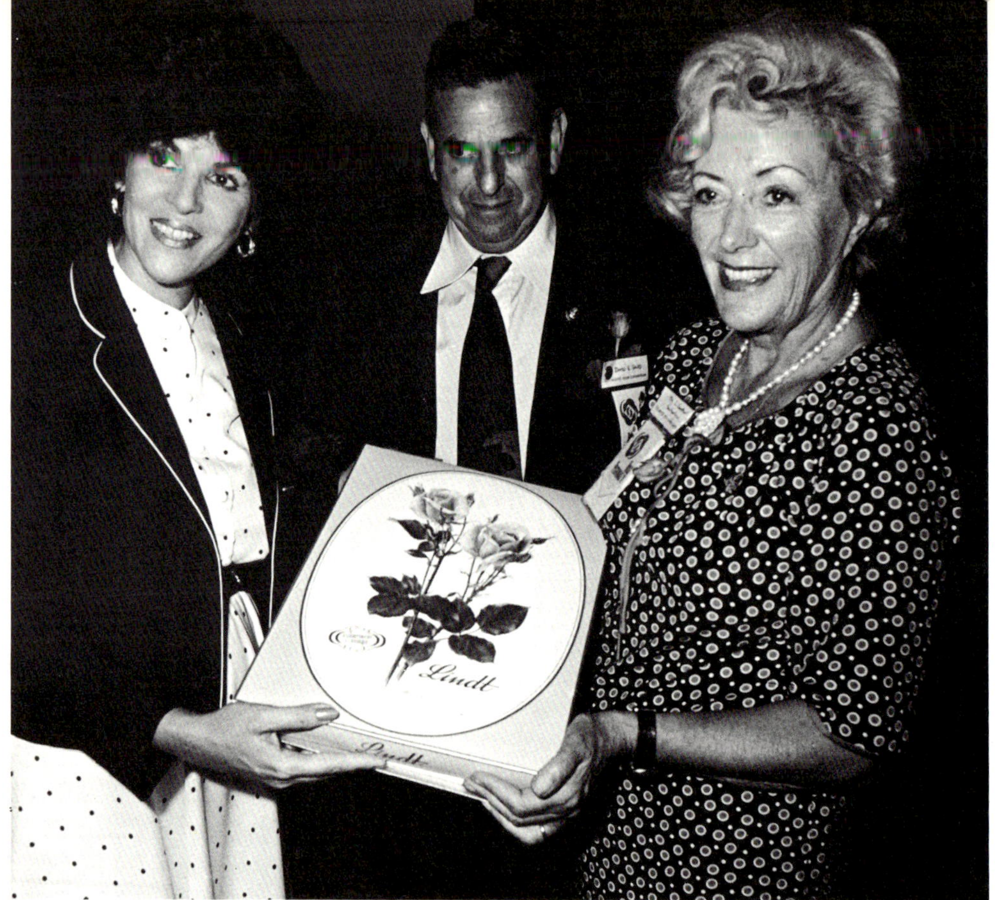

The 5th International Congress of the World Federation of the Rose Society, held in October 1980 in Jerusalem.
From left to right: Ophina Navon, First Lady of Israel, receiving a box of Swiss chocolates, David Gilad, President of the World Federation of the Rose Society during 1980, and Lotte Günthart.

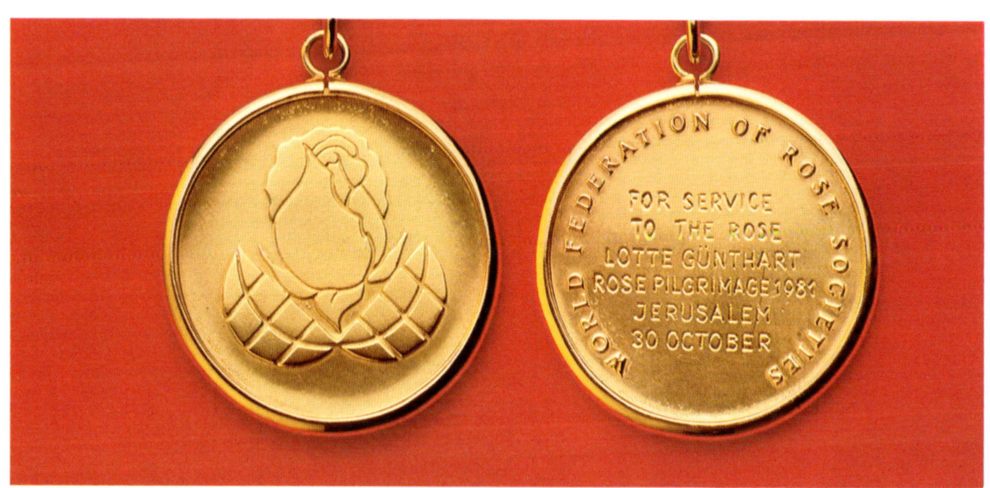

Gold medal presented to Lotte Günthart by David Gilad at the 5th International Congress of the World Federation of the Rose Society in Jerusalem, October 1980.

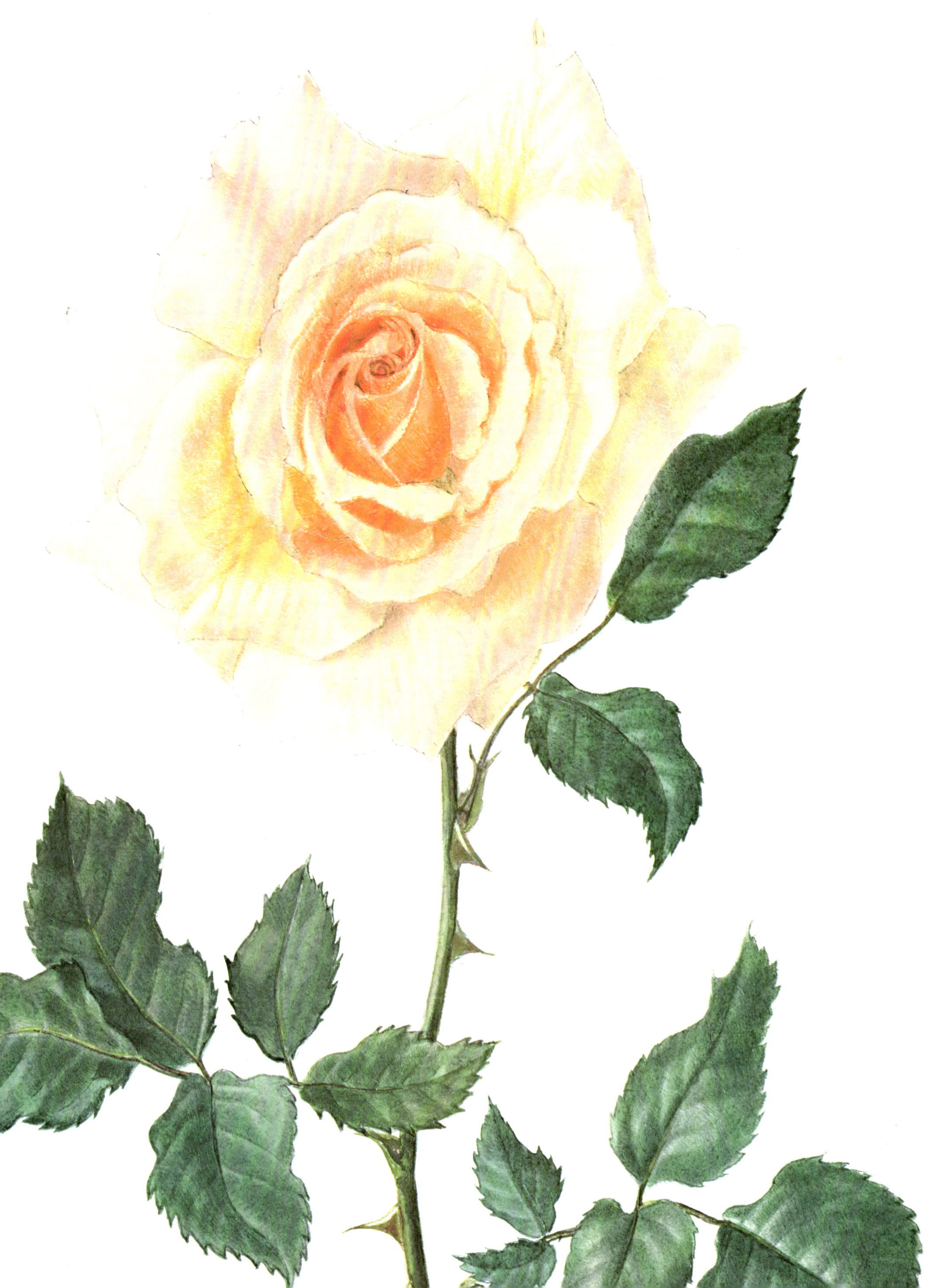

on Sundays there was always a staff shortage.

Therefore, they suggested, it would be best if he travelled to Amsterdam himself with the package.

Looking very dejected and pale, Willi returned to me and said that if only he had his passport and some money, he would go to Amsterdam to load the package himself on the flight bound for New York. "You have your passport and some money", I said, and took these so essential items from my handbag. He gave me a great smile, and rushed off with the package to the KLM counter where they had a seat for him. As the aircraft landed in Amsterdam, he noticed that swirls of fog were approaching. He hurried to the departure gate of the aircraft bound for New York, which was almost due to take off; the main steps were already pulled back, and only the rear door was still open.

A charming hostess, walking daintily on her high stiletto heels, came to assist him and said "You're just in time, in a few minutes it's taking off, and the airport is closing down due to the fog, this is the last flight leaving today". She took the package from him, and ran out to the aircraft, handing it through the rear door. Whilst running, she had twisted her ankle, and my husband hugged her with happiness and gratitude. She was our saviour.

A few minutes later, thick fog encircled the airport, and all flights were cancelled.

My husband telephoned me from the hotel in Amsterdam with the good news.

Awaiting his telephone call, I had spent many hours of uncertainty, and had become rather doubtful as to the success of the venture.

I had taken a taxi home from the airport; it was a dull and grey winters day, and I was rather depressed, and very tired from the events. Then, quite unexpectedly, I noticed a large placard, which read "KEEP SMILING" in bold white letters. I could hardly believe my eyes, after all, this was not America. I smiled secretly to myself, and suddenly all my worries were swept away. I was determined, that whatever the outcome of the whole affair might be, to keep smiling.

In the meantime, our Mr Harrity had found out that the flight from Zürich to New York had been cancelled, and spent a terrible night waiting at the airport for any information. He telephoned me every half hour, and when at last I told him the good news, he gave a great sigh of relief. The poor man was not relieved for long though, because the snow storm in New York seemed to be never ending, and the KLM flight was diverted to Montreal. At long last, and with a delay of many hours, the flight landed in New York, at eight o'clock in the morning of the 20 February. Time was now precious, and Mr Harrity

DR. F. T. WAHLEN
BUNDESRAT

Bern, den 29. Mai 1965.

Sehr geehrte Frau Günthart,

Meine Frau und ich danken Ihnen bestens für Ihre Zeilen vom 25. Mai mit den beigelegten Unterlagen über die Ausstellung Ihrer Werke in London. Es freut mich ausserordentlich, diesen Beilagen den grossen Erfolg entnehmen zu können, den Ihre Ausstellung davongetragen hat. Auch ist es mir besonders angenehm, dass Sie dabei auf die Mitwirkung unserer Botschaft zählen konnten.

Mit freundlichen Grüssen, auch an Ihren Gatten, und der Versicherung meiner vorzüglichen Hochachtung.

Letter received from Dr F. T. Wahlen, President of the Swiss Democracy during 1965 congratulating upon the success of the London Exhibition, and that he was pleased about the official support from the Swiss Embassy in London.

hurried to collect the package and then rushed by taxi to the McCall's offices which were located in the skyscraper of the Grand Central Station. He arrived at a quarter to ten, just fifteen minutes before the dead-line, feeling completely exhausted and very hot, but tremendously happy; his Sfr. 16,000.– was safe!

The ten rose paintings were published in the May edition of McCall's Magazine, together with a charming story about the painter, who had called herself Carlotta Hart because of the difficult English pronunciation of the name Günthart. It was a marvellous success, and I was particularly pleased because the paintings, in spite of the fact that circulation was over seventeen million, were excellently reproduced.

Christina Foyle, of the family who own the world's largest bookshop, arranged a special launch for me in June 1965 when the English edition of my rose book was published. Later, I was also invited to attend one of her literary luncheons at the Dorchester Hotel in London.

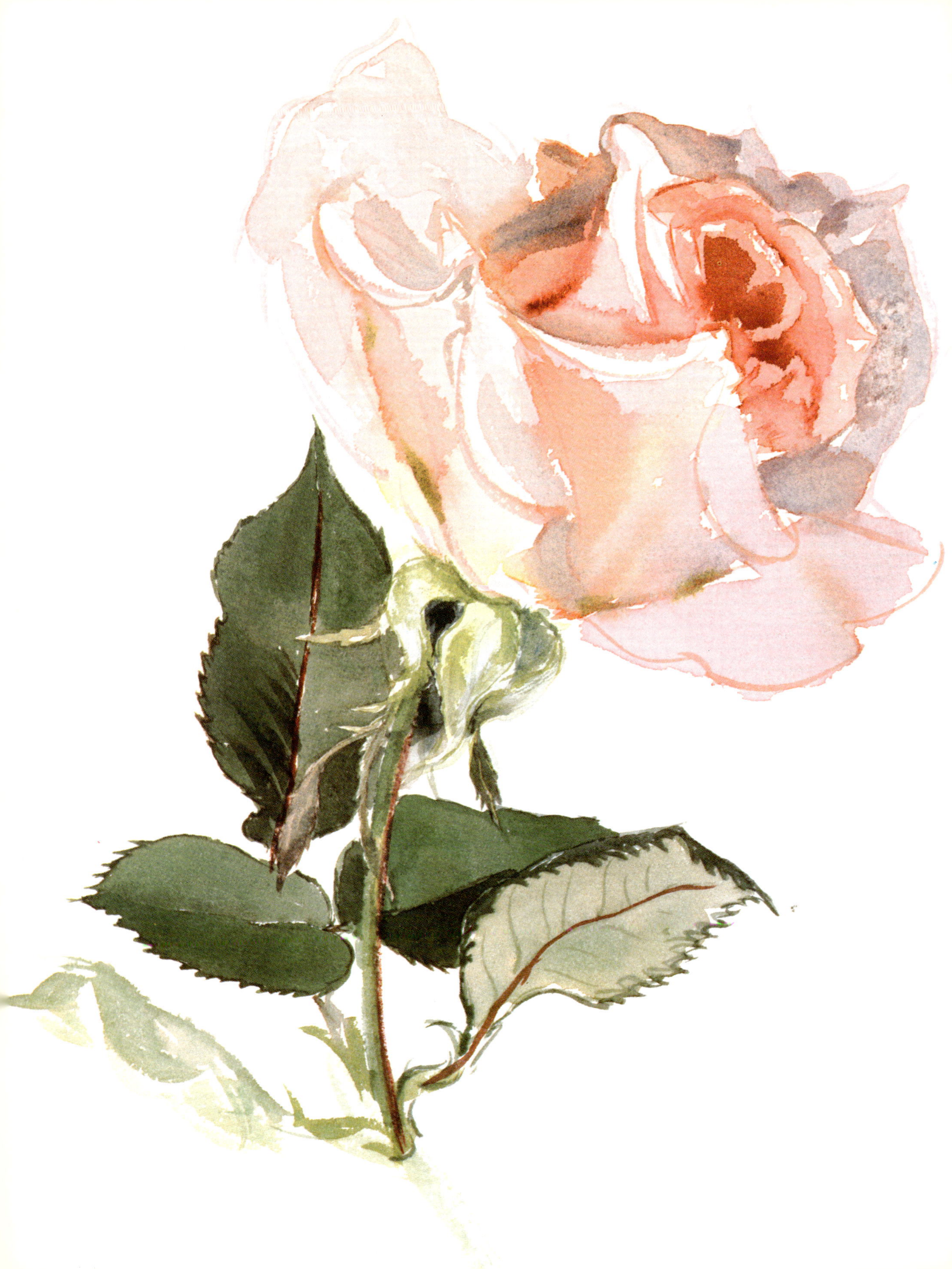

Thanks to her efforts, I was invited in 1968, by Professor George H. Lawrence to participate in an exhibition, together with thirty-five artists from all over the world, which was to be held in the Hunt Botanical Library of the Carnegie-Mellon University, in Pittsburgh, America.

This exhibition in Autumn 1968 gave us the opportunity to visit our business partner in Philadelphia.

Mr H. kindly invited us to lunch with him in his new house, and during the dessert, Willi politely asked if we could possibly hold a short business discussion.

The Director of Mr H.'s company, who was also present at the lunch, appeared extremely surprised at this request, almost shocked, but Mr H. remained calm. He said that it would be the first time that he used his study for business purposes, but … this was an exception. Willi immediately came to the point, and explained his reason for the talk. He asked Mr H. to return the "right of first refusal", which had been granted by my father in 1958. At this time, he was already unwell, and most likely did not fully realise the seriousness of his acceptance to this clause.

Willi continued; his sole objective was that Maag should remain Swiss and not become American. If the contract could not be retracted, it would be our downfall, and with it, our company's, and neither would benefit Mr H. We convinced Mr H. that the best possible solution, for one and all, was to invalidate the contract, and he agreed to do so.

It was a miracle. We were so relieved; it seemed as though a huge burden was removed from our shoulders. Alas, too soon was our joy.

The difficulties which we encountered, lasted for two years, and took a great toll on our health. We were strongly opposed by the most ingenious attorneys, for which we could thank the doggedness and persistence of Mr H.'s Director. We were called, several times, to exacting negotiations, sometimes in New York, then in Paris, Milan and London, with hardly a pause in between. From Mr H. himself, I sadly bade good-bye, for he was the most human and amiable person of all in his company. A few years previously, I was introduced to his mother, who had many interests, and a friendship grew between us. We corresponded until her death, and in my desperation, I even used these letters, to attempt to change Mr H.'s opinion.

Mr H. became ill, and in the end there was no further communication from him.

During these so very difficult years, I felt like the mouse that had fallen into a bowl of milk. It was so determined to survive, that it ran round and round the bowl, until there

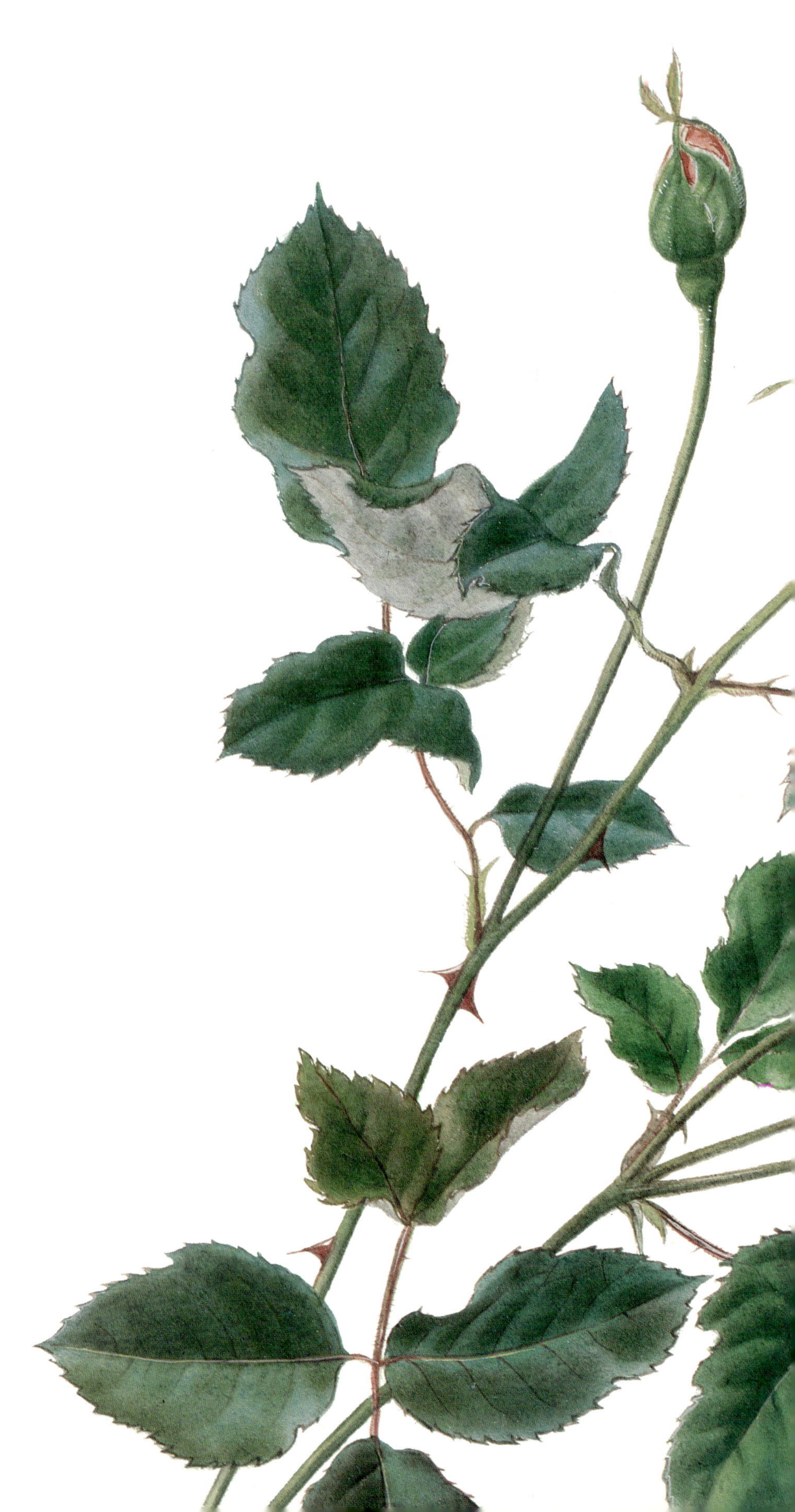

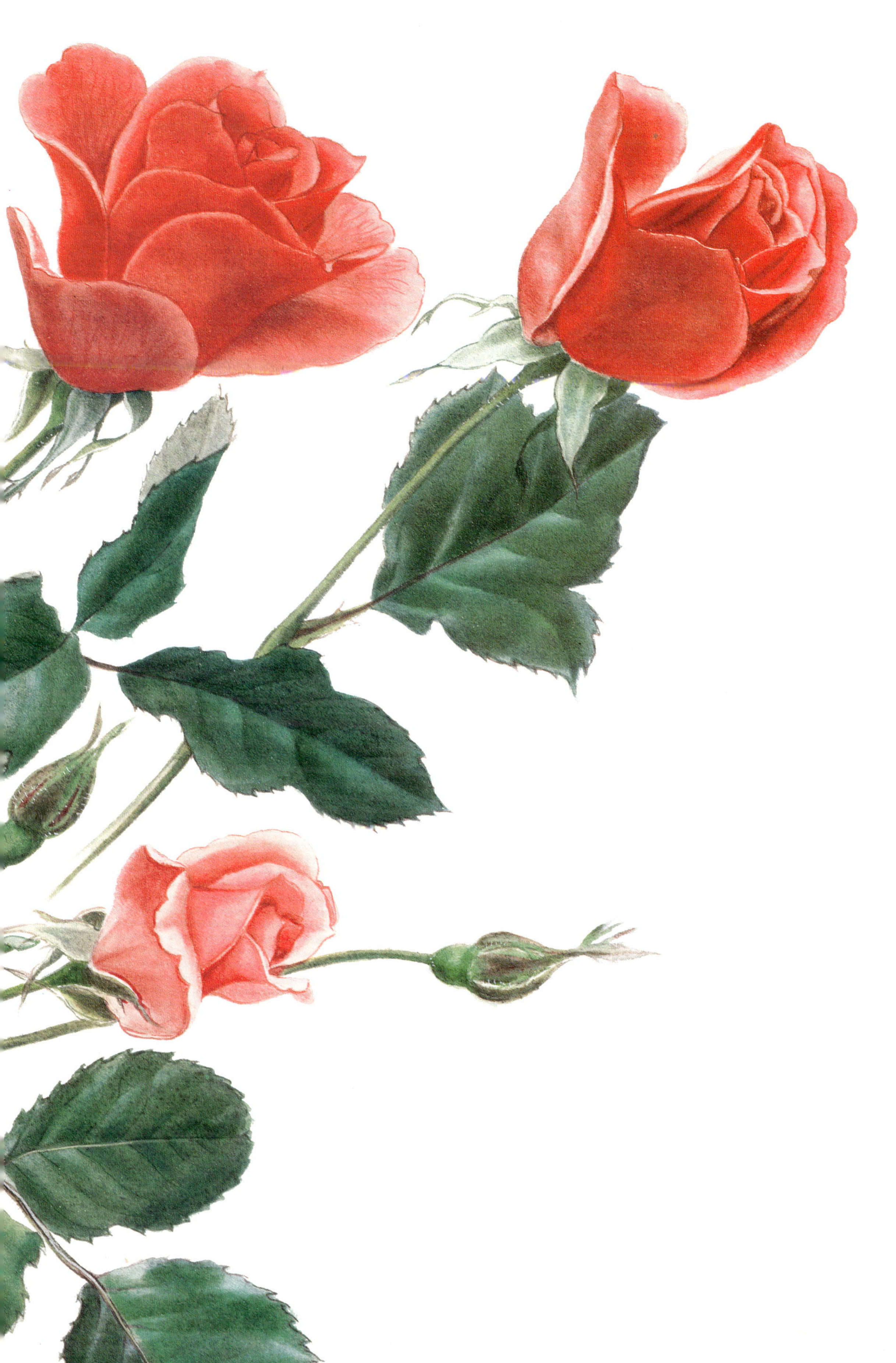

was a ball of butter on which it could jump out.

My constant thought was that if I did not struggle for success, I would not survive, and as long as there was a slight chance, I was game to fight. I then wrote several hundred pages on the topic, and showed the document to one of the top attorneys in New York's Downtown, Mr Graubard. After reading it with interest, he then asked me if I was a lawyer. "You're far off the mark, I'm a painter", I replied!

He appeared to be impressed with my effort and said, "In the long run, you'll win. Americans have far less staying power than you Europeans". The two other attorneys had paid no attention to us whatsoever, probably because they thought we stood no chance. During this negotiation, Mr Rosenwald tried to reach Willi by telephone, and when Mr Moskovitch heard this, it had the same effect as an electric shock. "Do you mean the Mr Bill Rosenwald? Do you know him?", and Willi was suddenly lifted in his esteem from rock bottom to the highest pinnacle.

In the end, we did win, as Mr Graubard had prophesized.

The exhibition in the Hunt Botanical Library was wonderful.

During the delightful celebrations, I became personally acquainted with Alfred Hunt and George Lawrence. Professor Lawrence, at that time the Director of the Hunt Botanical Library, suggested that I hold a "one-man show", in their exquisite exhibition rooms, from April to October 1970. Quite naturally, I was absolutely thrilled, and spontaneously accepted the invitation. Without delay, I commenced with the preparations for the catalogue, which for this occasion had to be suitably splendid, and interesting.

Prior to the exhibition, we met George Lawrence again in New York, to discuss the final edition of the catalogue. It was a pleasure to collaborate with him; he was an expert specialist on books and bibliophile rarities, and took great pride to produce excellent publications. We were of the same opinion, and the work progressed well.

We travelled to America in March 1970 on the "Michelangelo", taking with us a huge wooden crate packed to the brim with my water colours and sketches. When the ship arrived in New York Harbour with a considerable delay, a friendly customs officer boarded, and came up to the deck where close on two thousand passengers were patiently waiting to disembark. My husband and myself, as well as the wife of a senator from Washington, were shown into a side room. When the lady noticed my apprehensive face, she comforted me with the words "They are doing us a special favour". The trustworthy looking customs officer added "I'll take care of you, don't be afraid". We had every reason

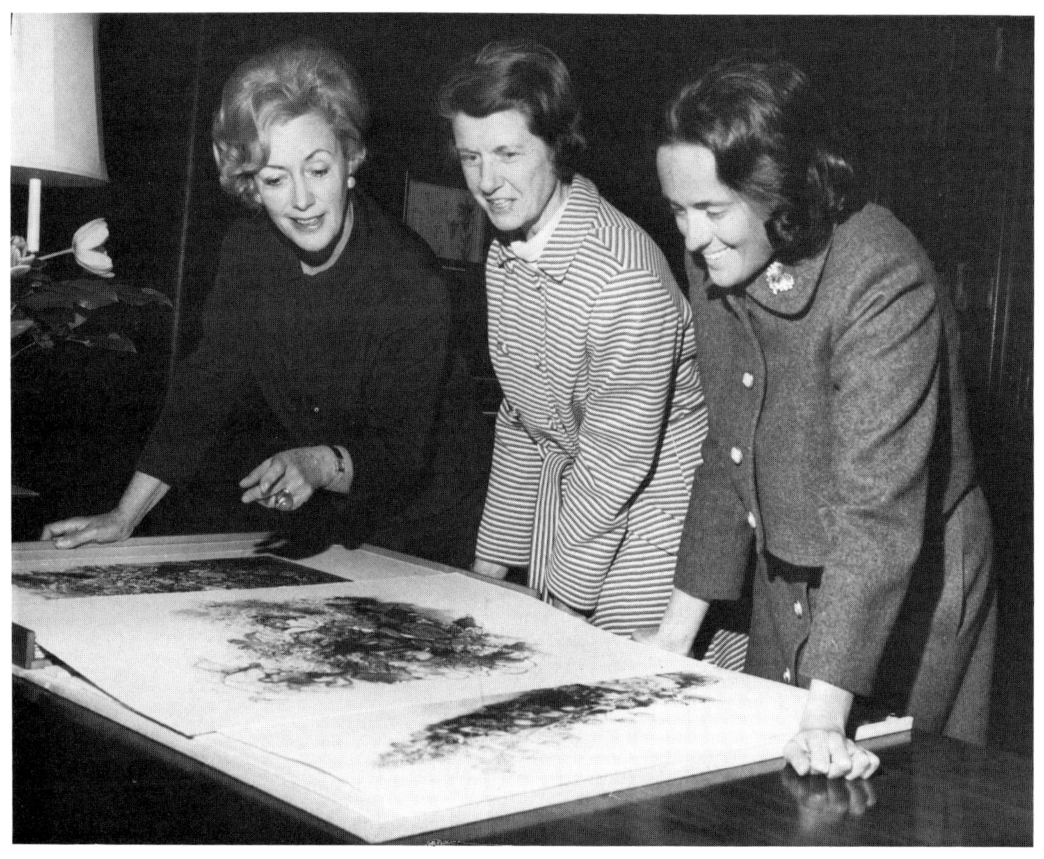

From left to right: Lotte Günthart shows some reproductions of her work to Mrs H. Guyford Stever,
wife of the President of the Carnegie-Mellon University, and Mrs James M. Walton,
wife of the President of the Carnegie Institute and Carnegie Library.

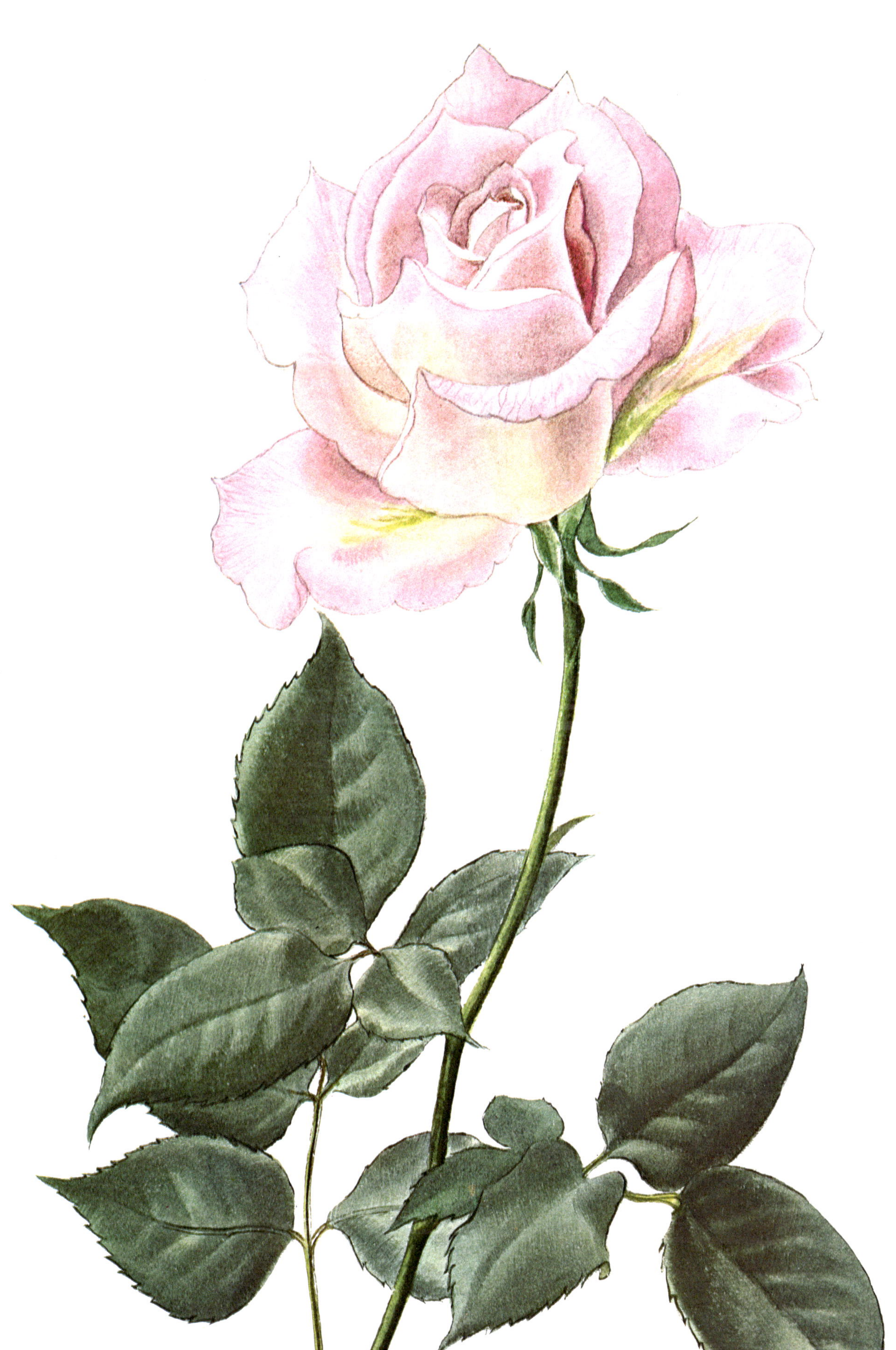

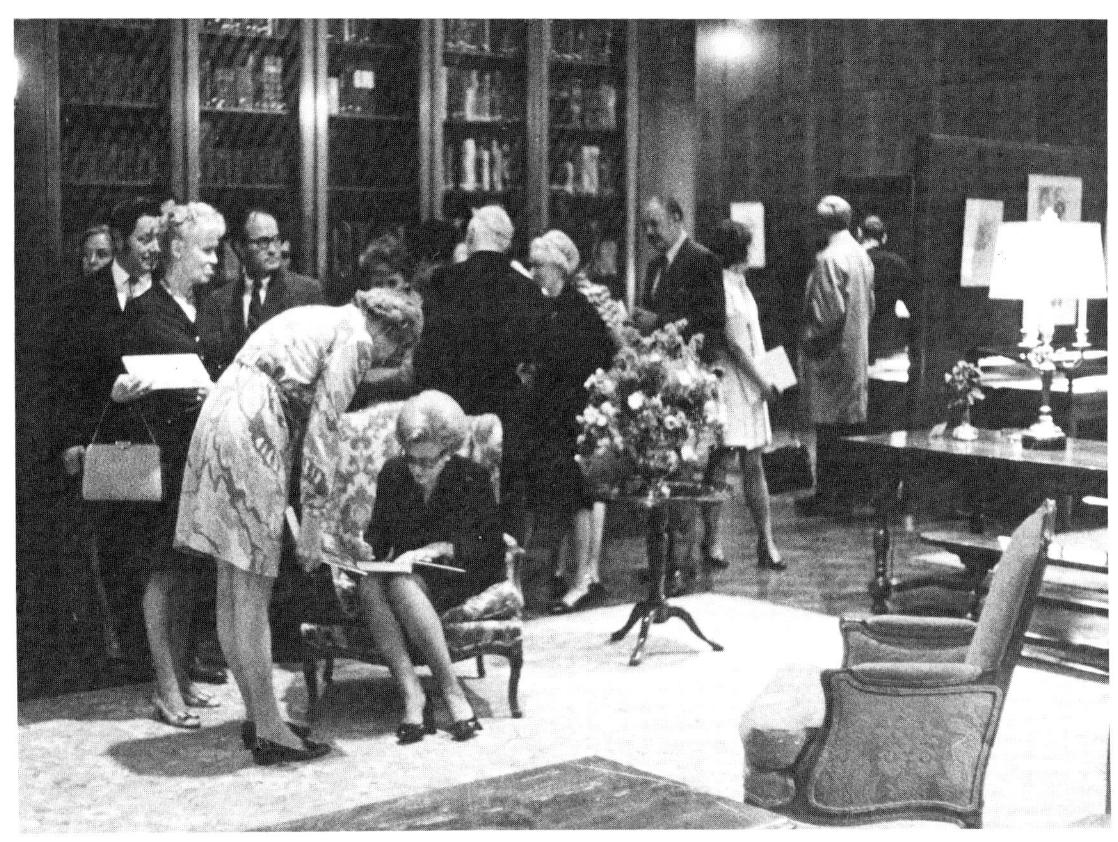

The glass cabinets house the books chosen by the plant enthusiast Mrs Rachel Hunt, which she has collect-
ed since her early youth. These exquisite editions, leather bound in many different colours, with gilt
edges, titles, and subtle ornamentation, are proof of her aptitude and excellent taste, herself a bookbinder.

to be nervous because we disembarked almost three hours before the other passengers, and many viewed us with contempt and jealousy, probably wondering who we were. At the small customs office on the pier, we were kindly offered hot tea, whilst waiting for our luggage. We passed through without further control, and were amazed at the hospitable reception which was given to us in America. We were certainly given the VIP treatment.
My exhibition at the Hunt Botanical Library at the Carnegie-Mellon University was opened in April 1970, and continued till October. For me, it was the most rewarding and beautiful exhibition of my life, an absolute jewel. The rooms were unbelievably lovely, and my paintings were effectively displayed. Grand flower arrangements had been strategically placed, and seemed to have been created by an artist to compliment my paintings.
I was so happy at the celebration on the opening day, that I remarked to my husband, that even if I lived to be a hundred years old, never again would I relive such an experience.
So many interesting and pleasant people were in attendance, that I was immediately surrounded by a sense of well being. Alfred Hunt gave a speech in my honour during the gala dinner, indeed the finishing touch to an unforgettable day.
During the exhibition, I had time to befittingly admire the large rooms comprising the Rare Book Gallery and the Botanical Library. These libraries are housed on the entire top storey of the building, and were furnished and decorated with great taste by Mrs Rachel McMasters Miller Hunt. As a plant enthusiast, she has collected books and paintings on plants and gardens since her early youth. She generously donated the funds to found the new Institute of Botany, and has bequeathed it to the Carnegie-Mellon University. As a crowning glory to the new Institute of Science, the two top storeys of the building are devoted to the artistic and botanical presentation of plants.
This inspired us to follow suit, and initiate our own Foundation of Plants. The first award was presented in 1973, and since then, on an annual basis. The handsome prize is endowed in the Engelfried House to a person who has made a notable contribution to plant life.
In honour of my father, who was a connoisseur of plants in the very widest context, it is called the "Dr Rudolf Maag Prize".
The Foundation of Plants is subject to the Swiss Ministry of Internal Affairs.
On the occasion of my exhibition in Pittsburgh, I was requested to give a thirty minute television interview on the educational Channel 13.
The lady who was holding the interview was unknown to me, and I was therefore understandably somewhat nervous. To speak fluently in a foreign language under the heat of the

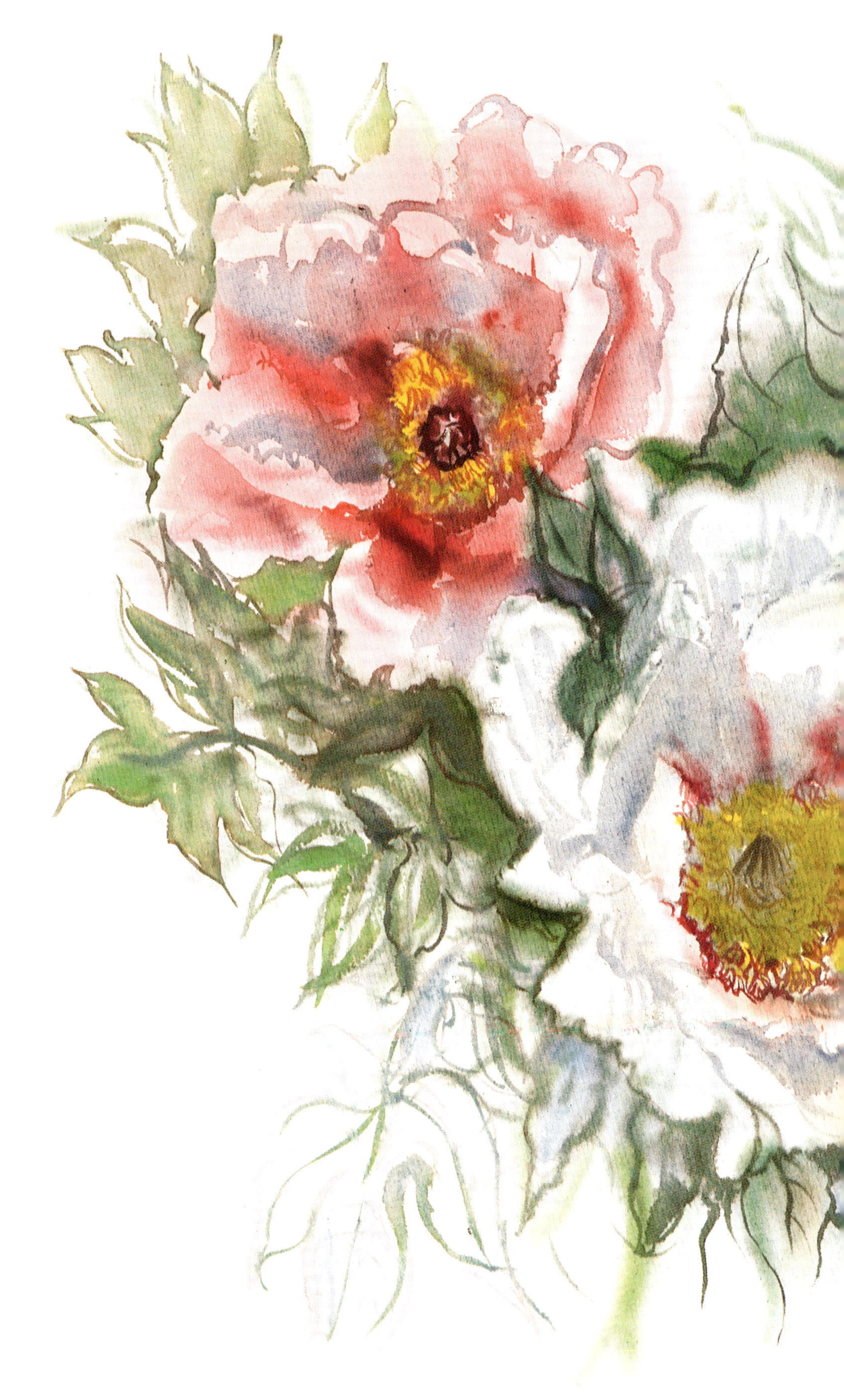

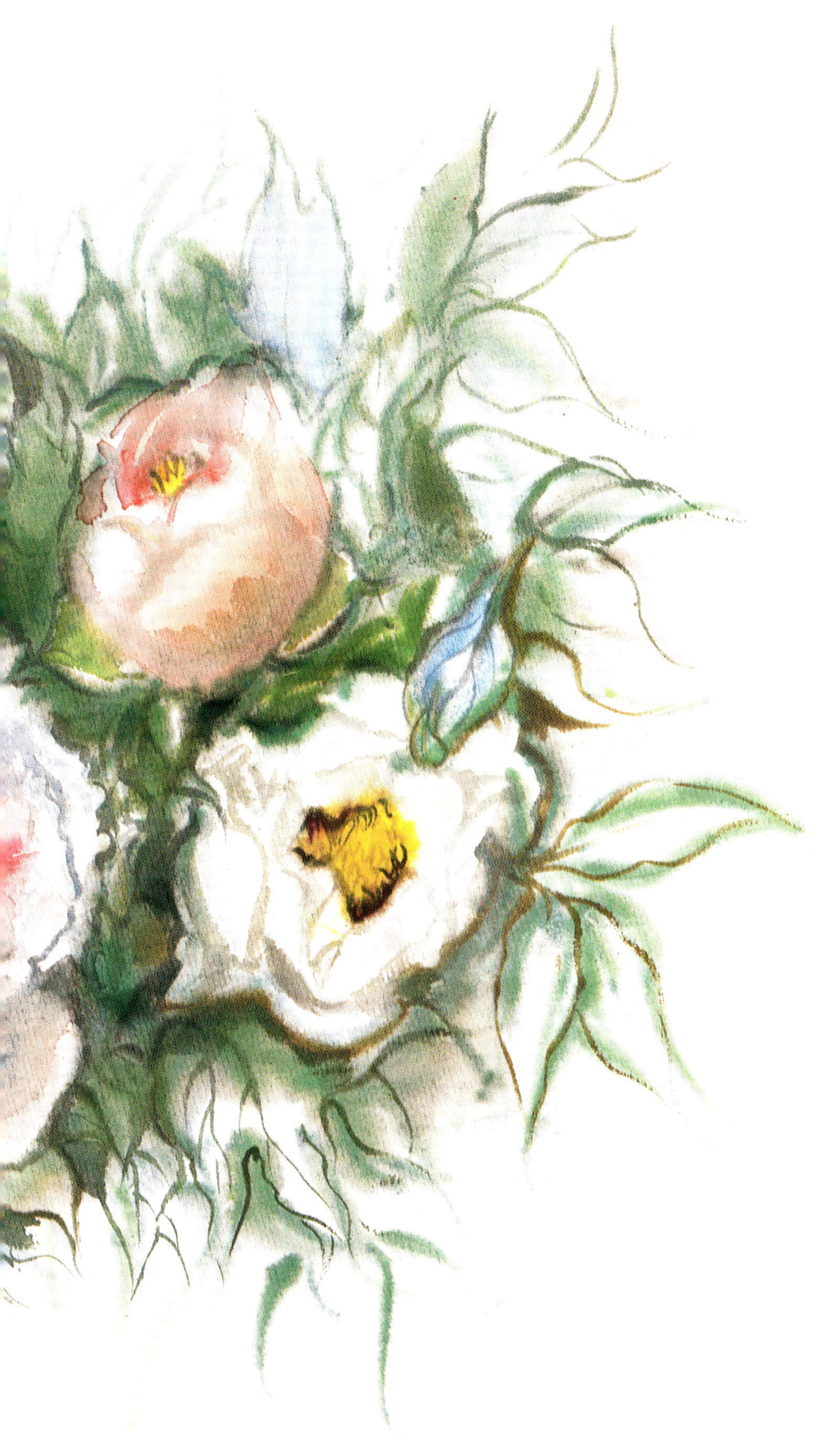

television studio lamps, was certainly a new situation.

The date was set for 13 April, and my interview was scheduled for five o'clock in the afternoon in the studio, which in my imagination would be a "torture-chamber".

On this very same day, Apollo 13 was in space, and at 13.13 hours, as the whole world knew, was undergoing an extremely hazardous phase, and the astronauts safe return to earth was in doubt. Everything hung on a fine thread, on the luck of the astronauts, and on their Swiss precision timepieces.

Leaving New York, we arrived in Pittsburgh in the early afternoon. At the hotel, we were allocated room number 1013. I was born on the thirteenth, and now here was the seventh occurrence of the number thirteen. It was all too much for me, and in a state of slight panic, I kindly asked them to find us another room with no connection to the number thirteen. It was a poor exchange; room number 1013 was spacious and well furnished with every possible comfort, and our new room was rather bare in comparison.

My anxiousness was unfounded, for the lady interviewing was intelligent and we were compatible from the start. To this day we have remained friends. The questions were exactly right, and quite naturally I was able to give the right answers. After twenty-five minutes, the technicians called out that it was perfect, and we both congratulated each other. But, then the thirteens entered the game, and we were informed that due to a fault, the sound had not been switched on. Since we were not producing a silent film, the whole procedure was repeated. Leonore Elkus' face became damp with nervous perspiration, and her make-up had to be renewed. To my surprise, I was very calm; not even the heat from the studio lamps bothered me. Deep inside, I knew that I had overcome the barriers set by the number thirteen, and that there would be no other mishap, and the film was successfully accomplished. Later that evening at the hotel, an elderly lady in the lift told me the news that the astronauts had overcome all their difficulties and were now safe. We both had emotional tears of relief and happiness.

During my Pittsburgh exhibition, I also became acquainted with Vivian Lehman, who was to become my dear friend. Several years later, she asked me to contribute a painting for the bicentennial of America which was in 1976. All the eleven other artists contributing were American citizens, and I was naturally rather perturbed being the only foreigner amongst them.

But who could resist such a request from Vivian?

I painted an American eagle with a rose in it's beak.

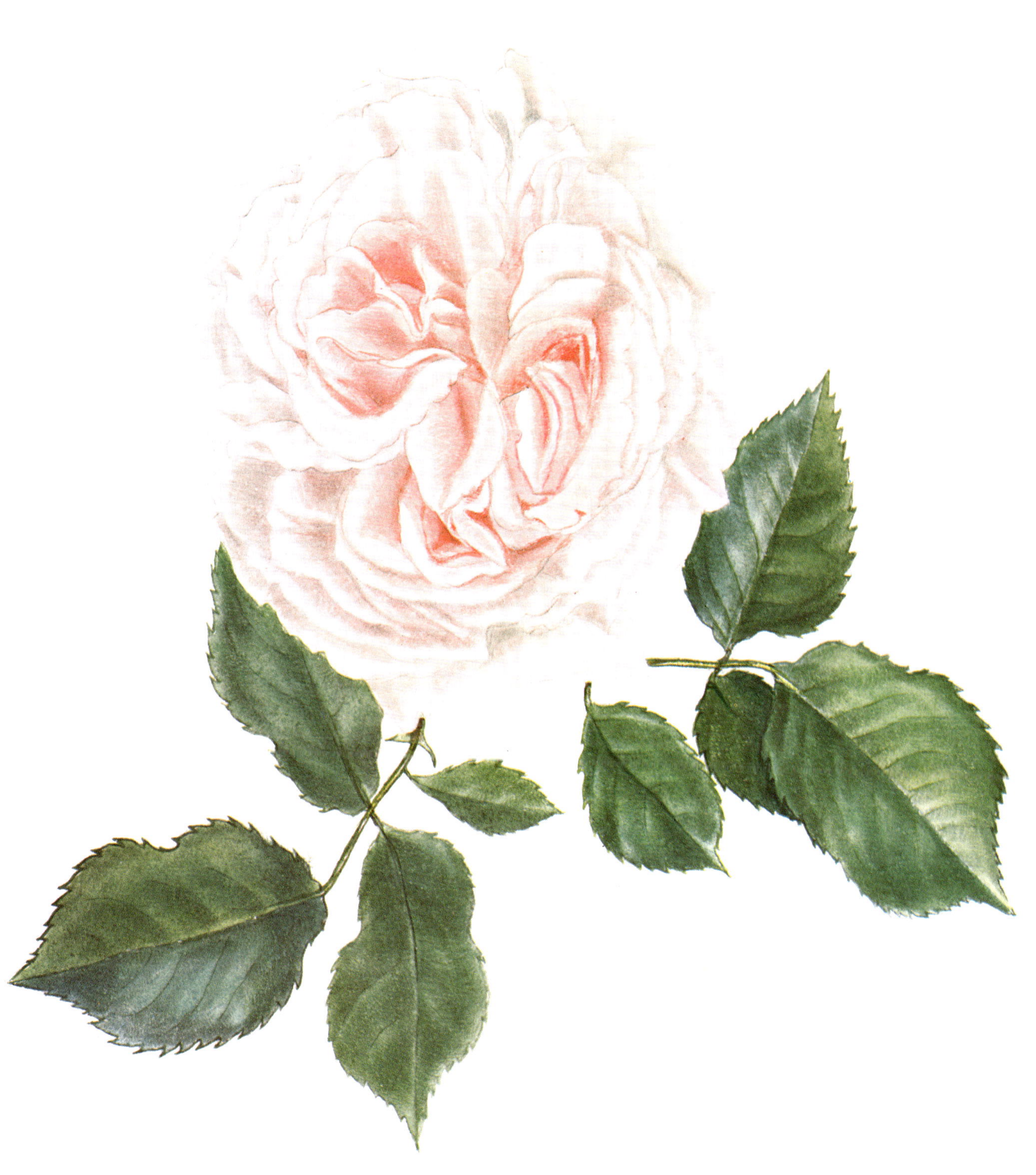

„Sieh jene weisse, die sich selig aufschlug
und da steht in den grossen, offnen Blättern
wie eine Venus aufrecht in der Muschel; "
Aus: „Die Rosenschale" von R. M. Rilke

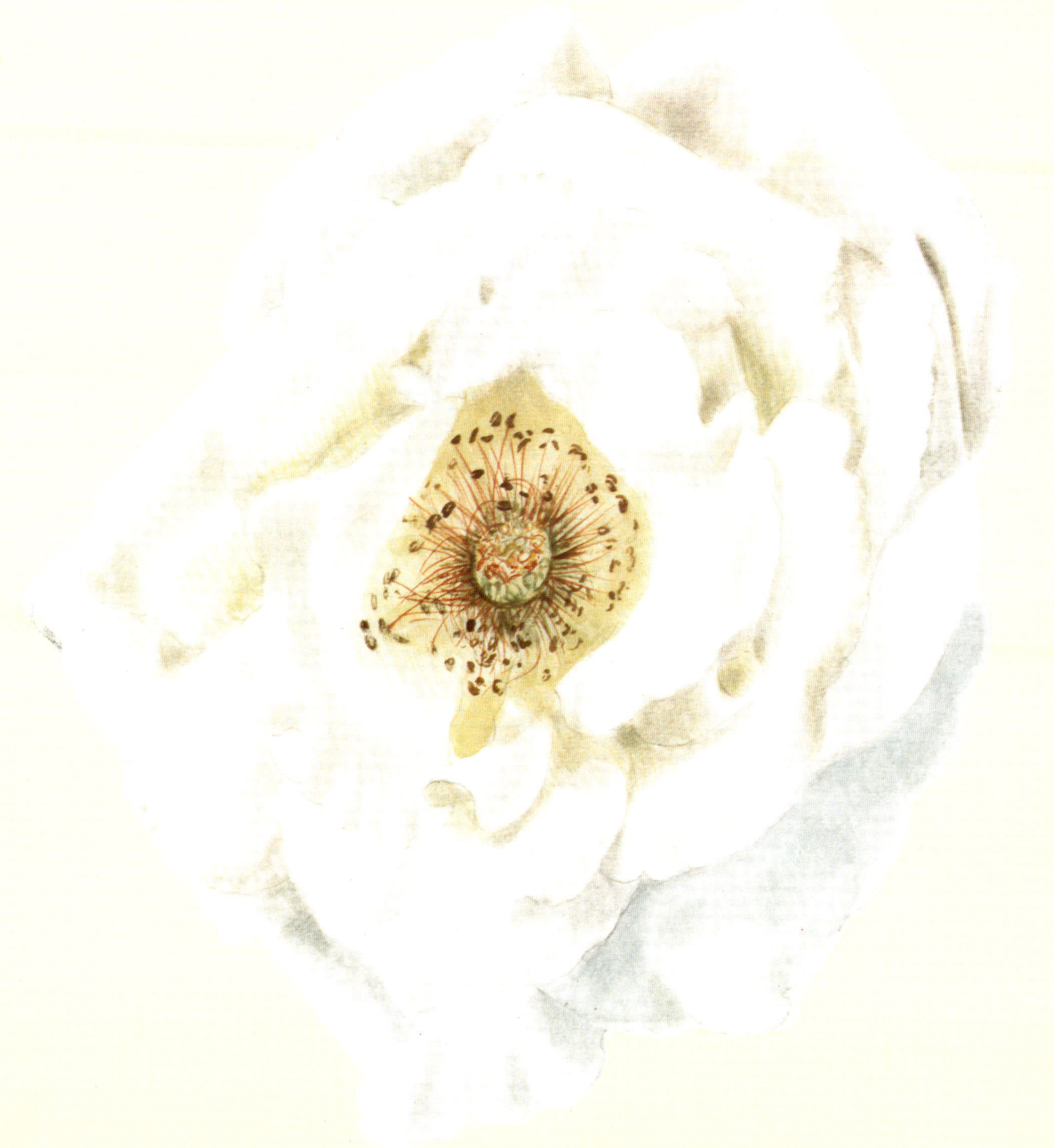

Underneath, I wrote the words "America's 200th Birthday 1776–1976".

At the immense celebration in the Carnegie-Hall in Pittsburgh, eight hundred people were invited. The main event of the evening was when Vivian Lehman was presented with the "Molly Pitcher Award", to the accompaniment of thunderous applause. I was placed at her table, where the Mayor of Pittsburgh sat next to her. Alfred Hunt was on my left, and on my right was General Wright. After mustering me somewhat, he asked full of scepticism, how it was, and why I, as the only foreigner, had donated a painting for the bicentennial. I confessed to him about my early inhibitions, and about the request from Vivian, and then added that maybe it was not quite so inappropriate as first thought. After all, I suggested, the largest democracy had perhaps certain connections with the smallest and oldest. Whereupon his first distrust was completely banished and he commenced to show me photographs of his children and grandchildren.

Vivian Lehman contributed greatly to the National Flag Foundation in Pittsburgh, and bequeathed her total fortune to this institution. A large number of my paintings decorate the walls of the Flag Plaza.

Through Vivian Lehman, I became acquainted with her best friend, Berta Gerney, a great Russian lady like Karinska. She lives in an enchanting house in Lausanne, surrounded by a wonderful park, and overlooking the Lake of Geneva. To stay in her house is like something out of a fairy tale.

One of the most splendid and interesting personalities we have met, is surely Salman Schocken. He often visited us in Regensberg during the fifties; sometimes with one of his sons because, in his words, he wanted the friendship to extend beyond his lifetime. With his son Theodore, we were later to enjoy a sincere friendship.

Once Salman Schocken noticed a poster which I had designed for our company, and approvingly remarked that this kind of advertising would have international recognition.

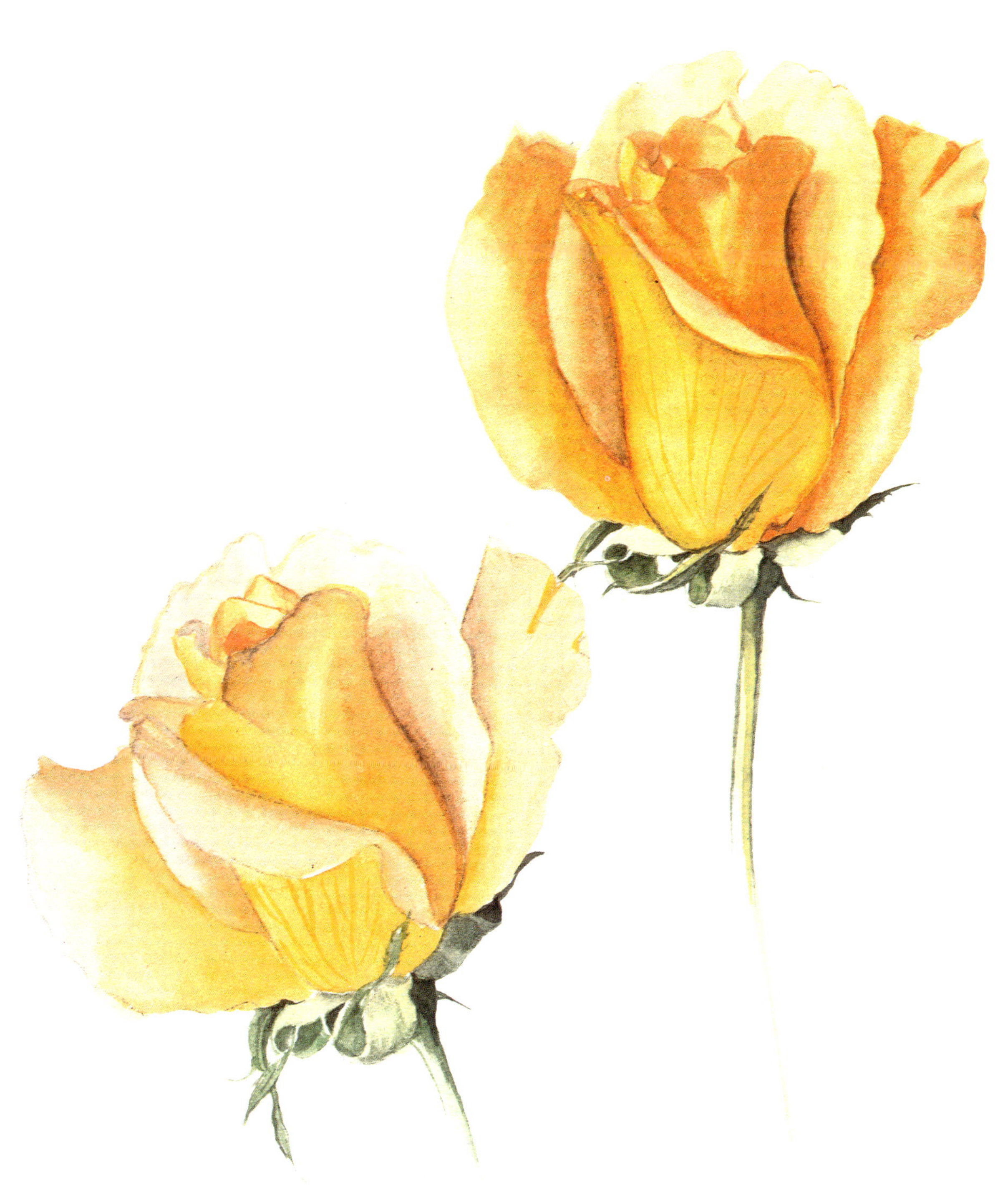

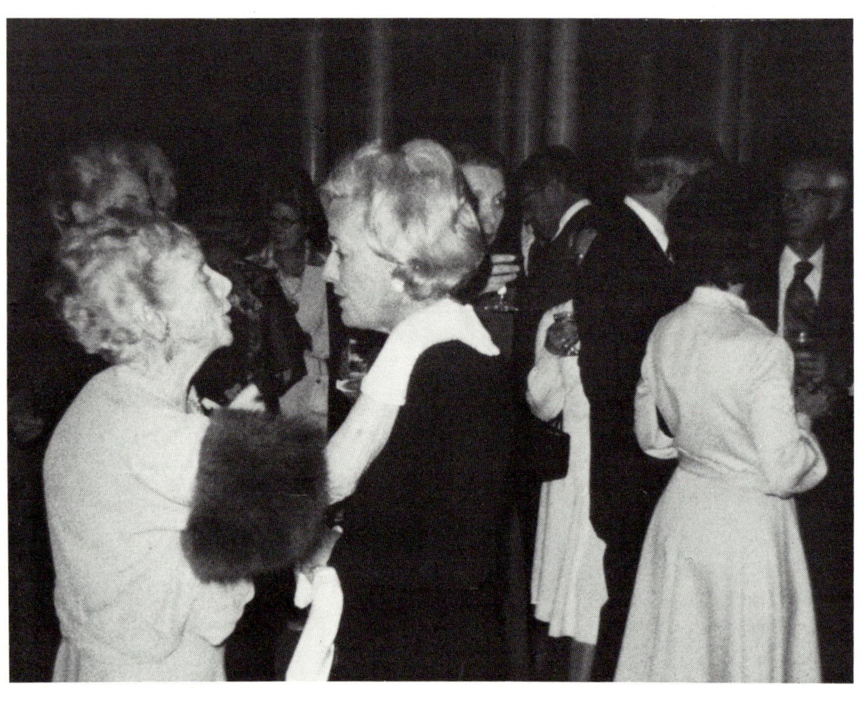

Mrs Chester Lehman, who tendered her final salute in May 1977, innovated and funded America's most extensive memorial to the Flag of the United States. She is the first and only Honorary and permanent Director of the National Flag Foundation.

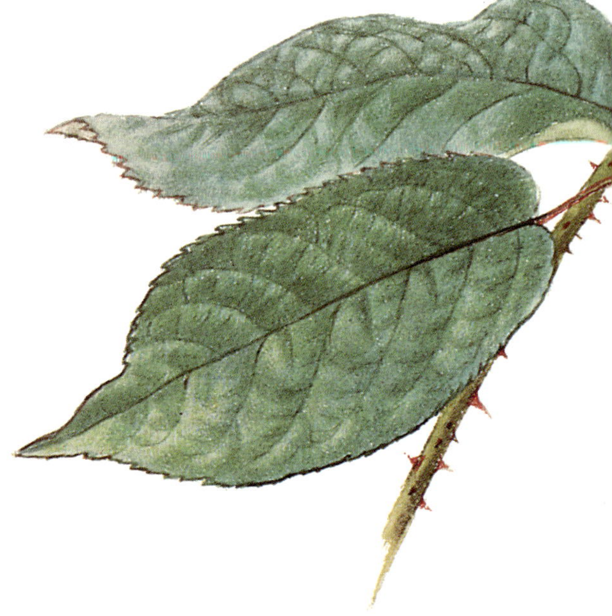

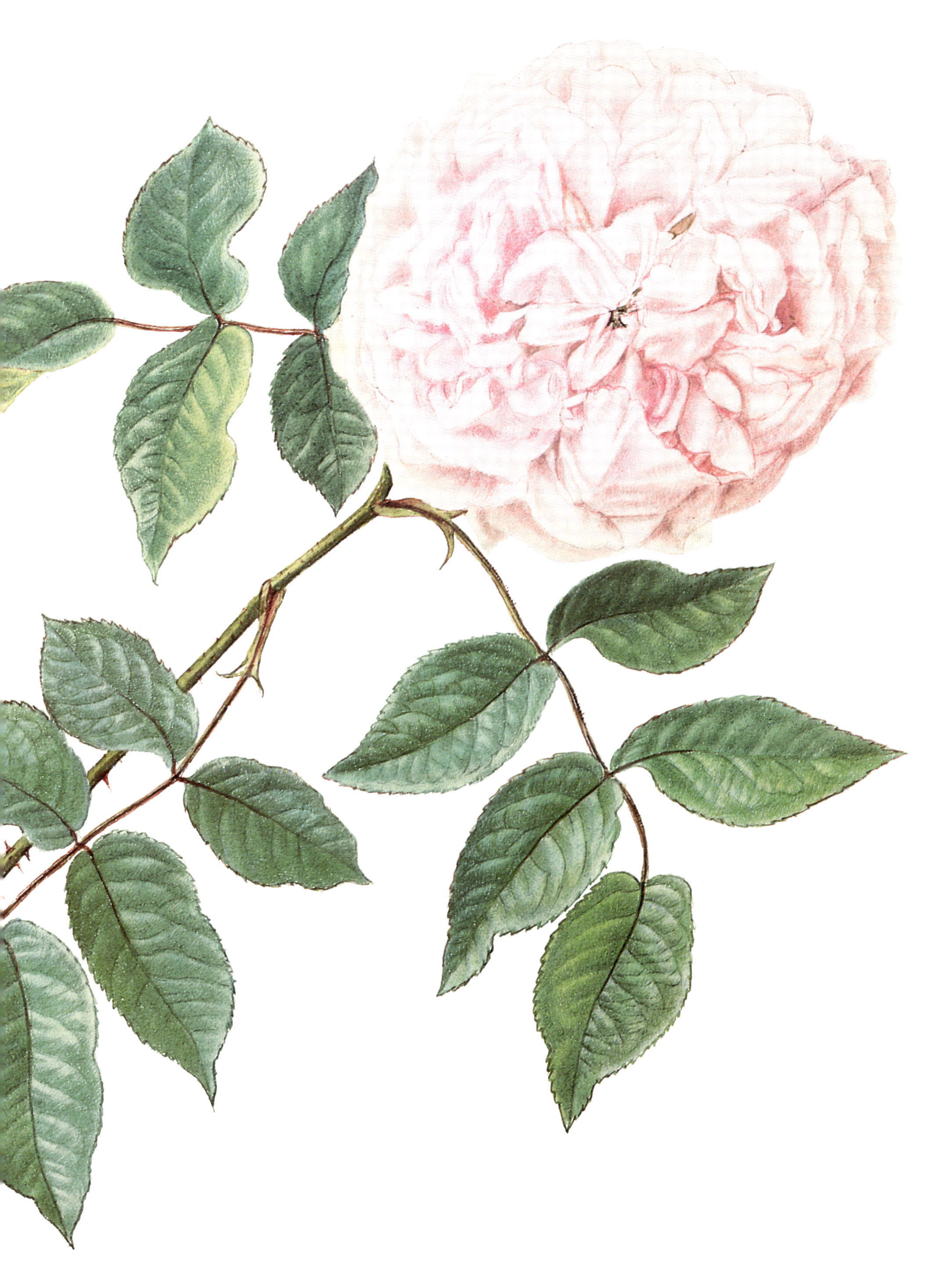

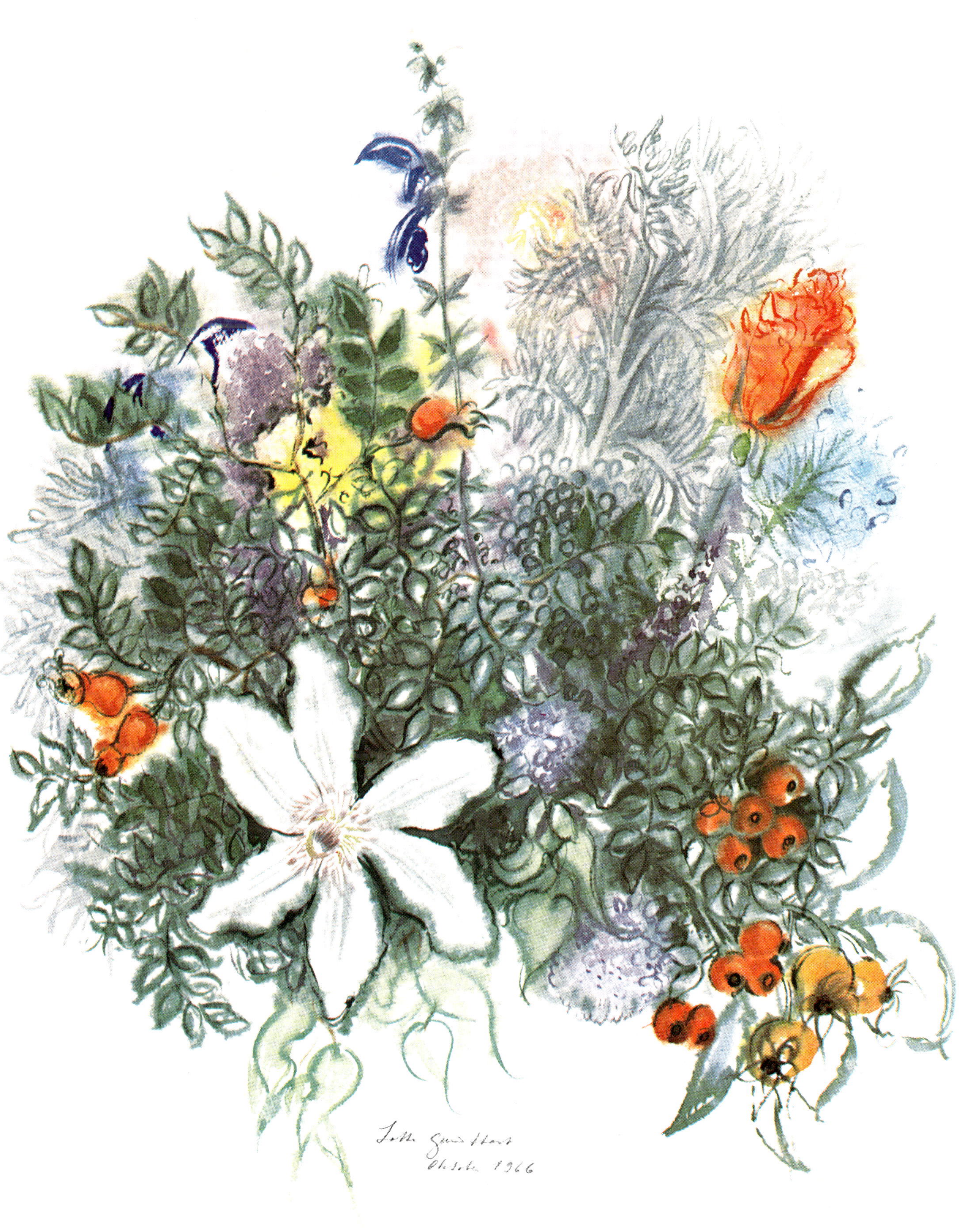

Lotte Günthart
Oktober 1966

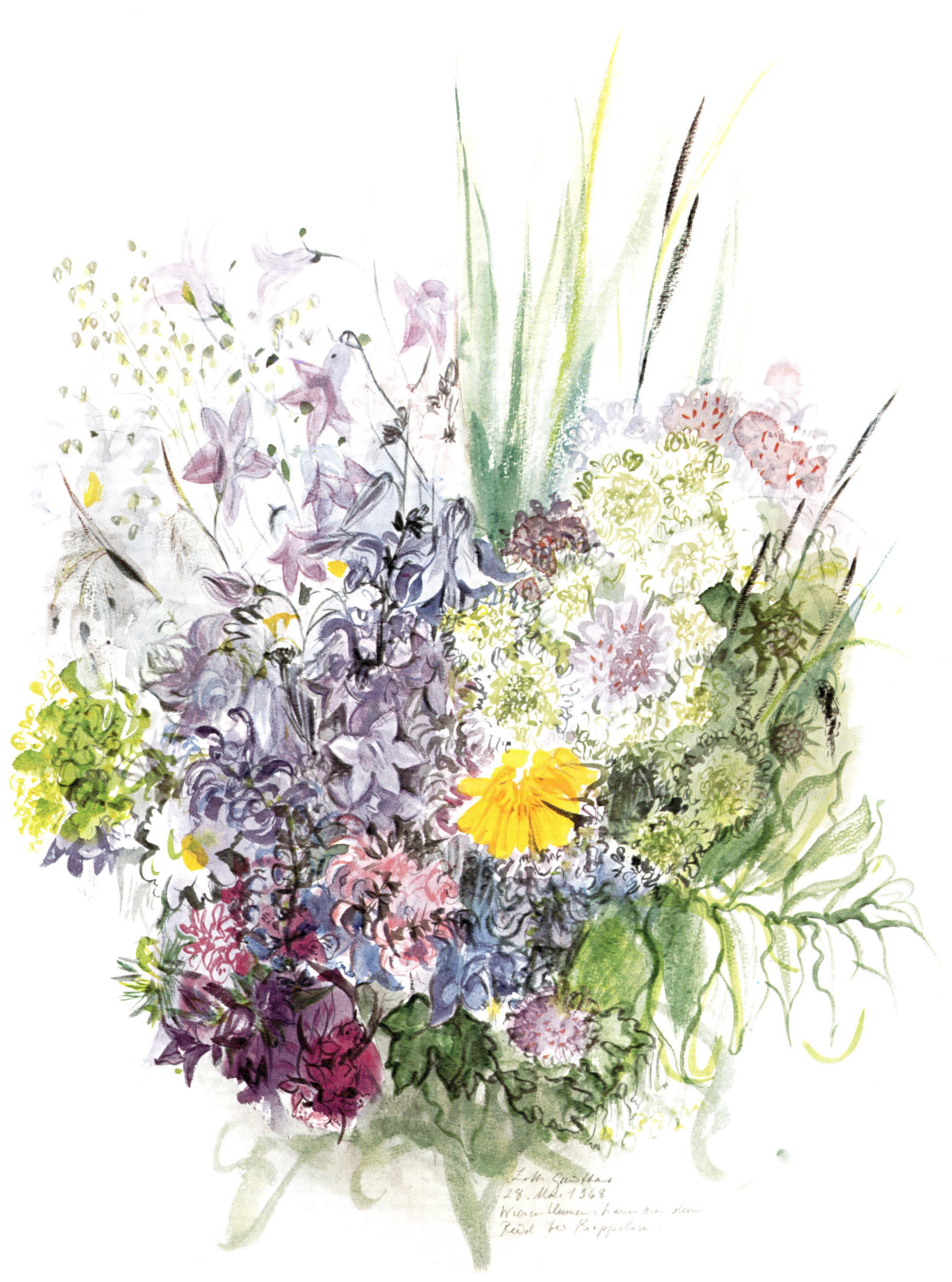
Lotte Günther
28. Mai 1968

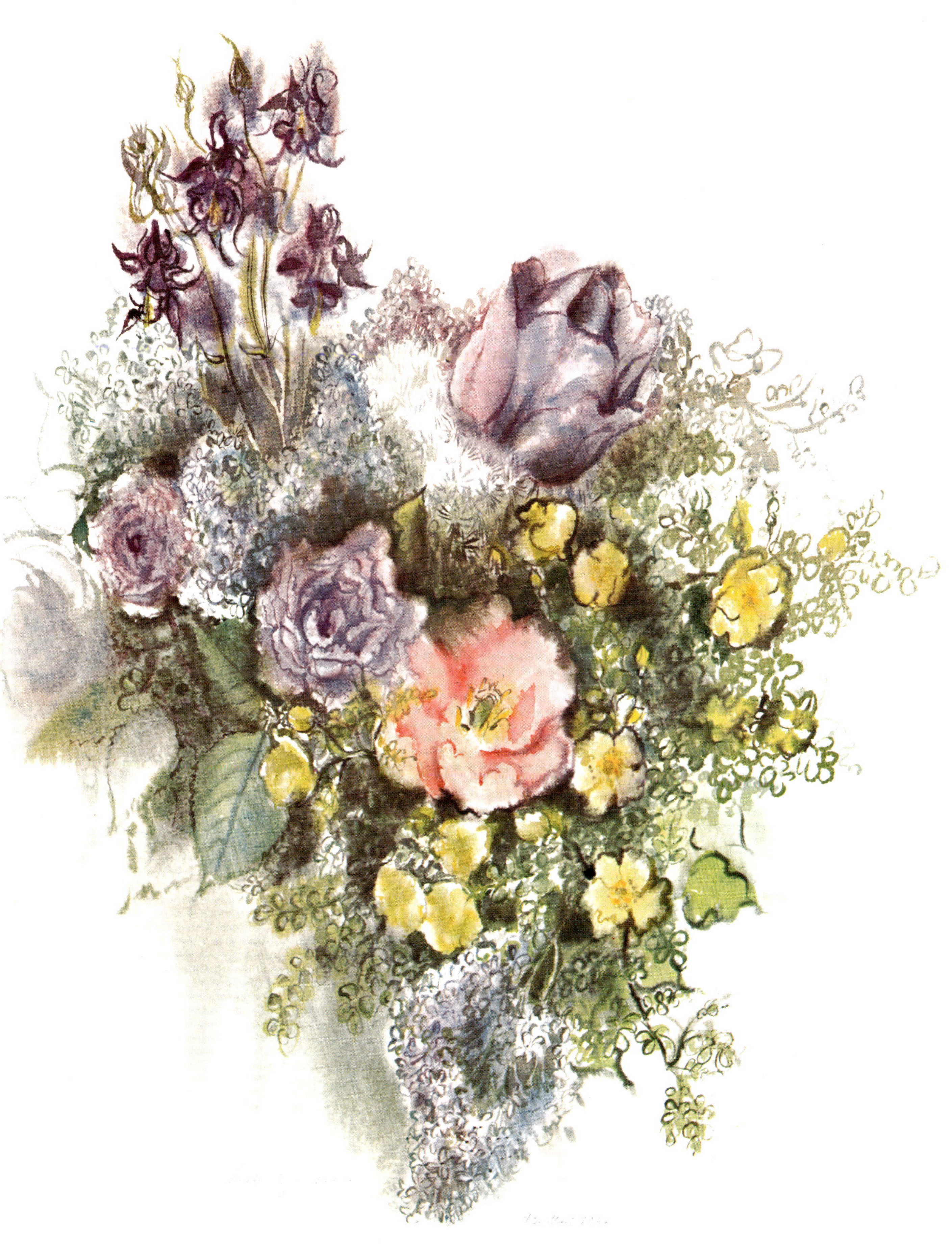

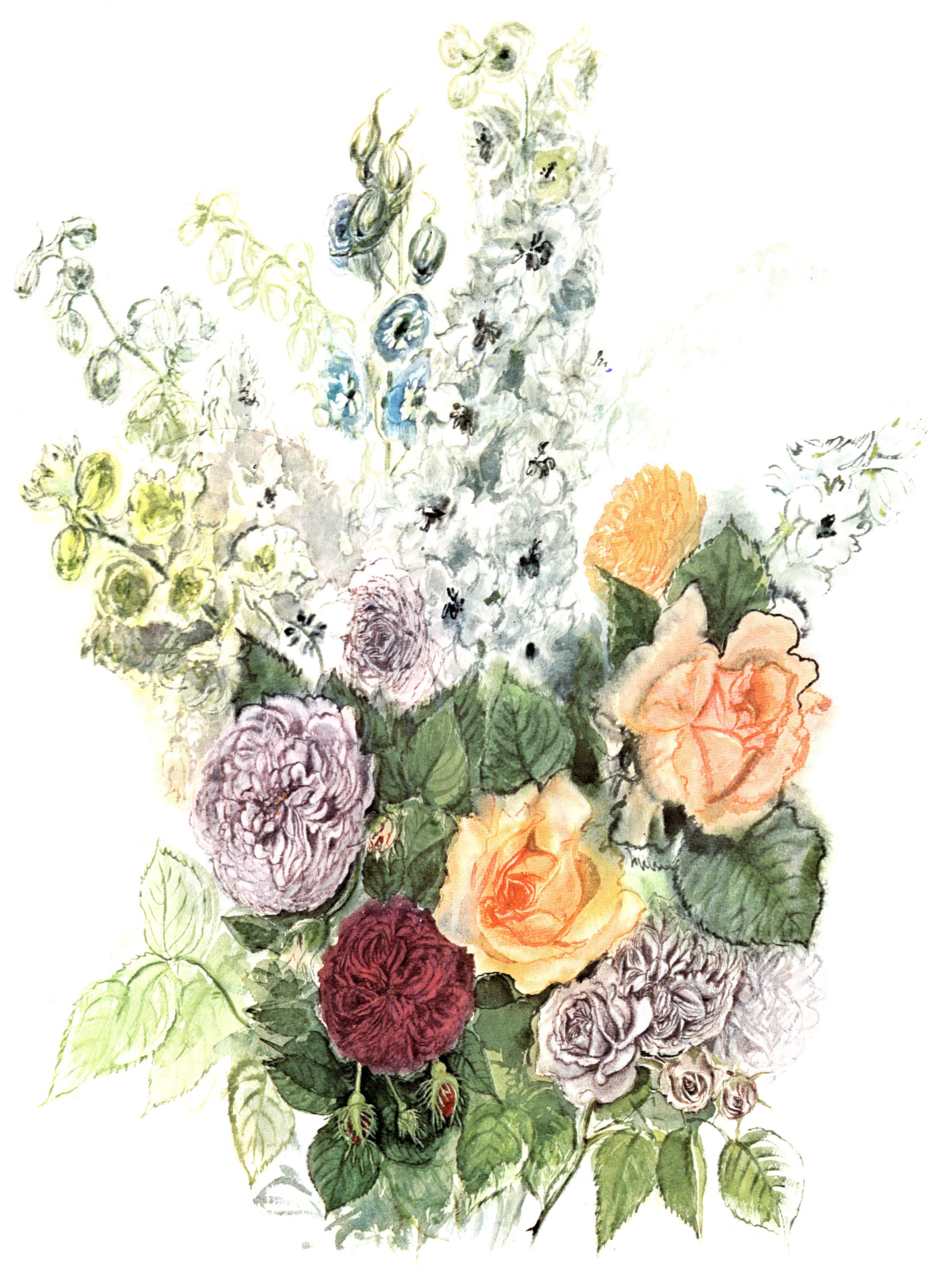

Our first "abode" in New York was for many years the Wentworth Hotel on the 46th street. It was rather small and simple, definitely not a three star hotel, and since demolished. But, in no other hotel have I ever felt so much at home. Returning after an absence of two years, all three porters greeted us like old friends, "Back home again", they chorused, and we felt truly welcome.

New York's taxi chauffeurs are an interesting mixture of nationalities. Unforgettable for me, was Henderson. We conversed in the purest French, and I asked him where he had learned to speak so well, with no trace of an accent. He explained that he had studied at the University of Tours, where they speak the purest French in France. Then we noticed, on the front seat next to him, piles of French books, Baudelaire, Mallarmé, Proust, A. Gide, and others. "When do you find time to read all these books when you have to drive all day long?" we inquisitively asked him. He replied that he read at night, because he only required four hours sleep. He did not look very healthy, and we thought that a brisk walk in the fresh air would have been more beneficial than sitting reading books. Somehow he seemed fanatical, full of ambition and energy. I promised to send him a copy of my French book, "La femme, le poète et la rose".

Unbelievingly, he gave me his address. I sent him the book, and received a six sided letter of thanks, written in perfect French. He had not believed that I would actually send him the book, because so many people gave him empty promises. I had given him great pleasure, and he wrote that he would now start to study German, so that he could enjoy my other books. Not much later, I received another letter, this time informing me that he was now a Professor for French at the University of Columbia, New York. Euphorically, he wrote "Such a tremendous honour for me, a taxi driver and also black. What did I think of that?" He had already attended German lessons, and soon hoped to read my other books. We corresponded regularly for two years, then nothing was heard from Henderson, and my letters remained unanswered. He had probably taken on too much.

"La femme, le poète et la rose" also brought about an acquaintance with a veritable "clochard" from the Seine, Paris; however only by letter. He wrote a long, enthusiastic poem, and also sent me an amusing sketch in which he had depicted himself as the "Cavalier from Côte d'Azur".

In every life, there are people who one never forgets. Often because they have a special significance, or because they have in some way enriched oneself. The great artist Barbara Karinska was one such person. I first met her quite late in life; she was eighty-three, and I was fifty-three. Born in Khartow, Russia, as one of the ten children of a wealthy industrialist, the family lost their possessions when the Bolsheviks came to power, and were forced to flee to Belgium. Later, Karinska went to Paris, and from there to America. A few years before we personally met in her New York house, she had written to me a fond and original letter, being herself a great rose lover, because she had been given my rose book by a friend, and spontaneously wanted to tell me how much she admired my paintings. Invited for the first time, after many years of correspondence, I was amazed to find out that the eight storey brown stone house which was in the most sought after area of New York, belonged to her. At the top was her roof garden, beautifully planted, and here she once served countless vodkas to my husband, who had visited her with a large bouquet, and unflinchingly held her own in true Russian style.

She used the old and spacious lift, which had a green velvet seat, to go up and down in her large house. She showed me her water colours by Chagall, and other works by Matisse, Miró, Modigliani and Picasso, all of whom she was on friendly terms with, and some of the works were framed and hung on the walls. The costumes for "Firebird" were by Karinska, based on sketches by Chagall, and this she was then working on. Karinska explained to me that she had to translate the paintings from Chagall for her over thirty employees, to correctly understand the meaning which was to be transferred by embroidery on to the costumes. One tailoress concentrated on cutting only, another tacked the pieces together, and yet another expertly embroidered the dazzling colours on to the bodices, sleeves, skirts and the head-dresses, which were to be worn by the ballerinas of the New York City Ballet. Karinska continued to work solely for the New York City Ballet and its famous choreographer, George Balanchine.

Exhibited at the Lincoln Center in 1970, it was an extravagant display lasting for six months, entitled "Firebird, Chagall – Karinska". Whoever failed to enjoy a performance of Firebird by the New York City Ballet, was fortunately able to visit the Lincoln Center to admire the well matched fantasies of Karinska and Chagall. At this exhibition, models were dressed as replicas of all the performing dancers, in their richly embroidered original clothes, complete with head-dresses, bouquets and jewellery. This exhibition turned out to be Karinska's swan-song; shortly afterwards, an increasingly serious eye ailment hindered her more and more with her beloved work. Every morning, she walked for thirty minutes to her studio, where she worked from nine till five. She often said that was what kept her young and mobile, implying that it was the fresh air and hard work. For an eighty-three

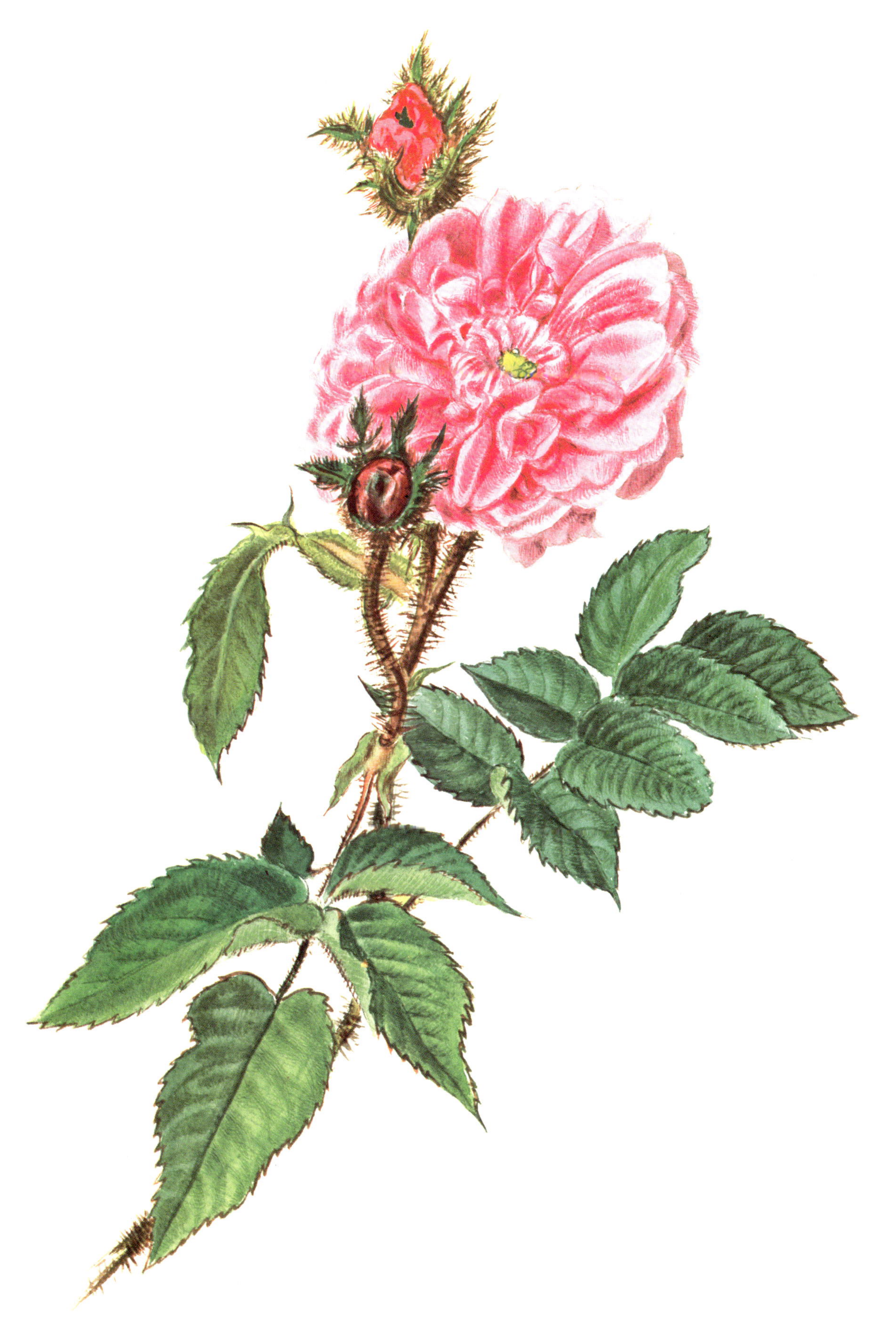

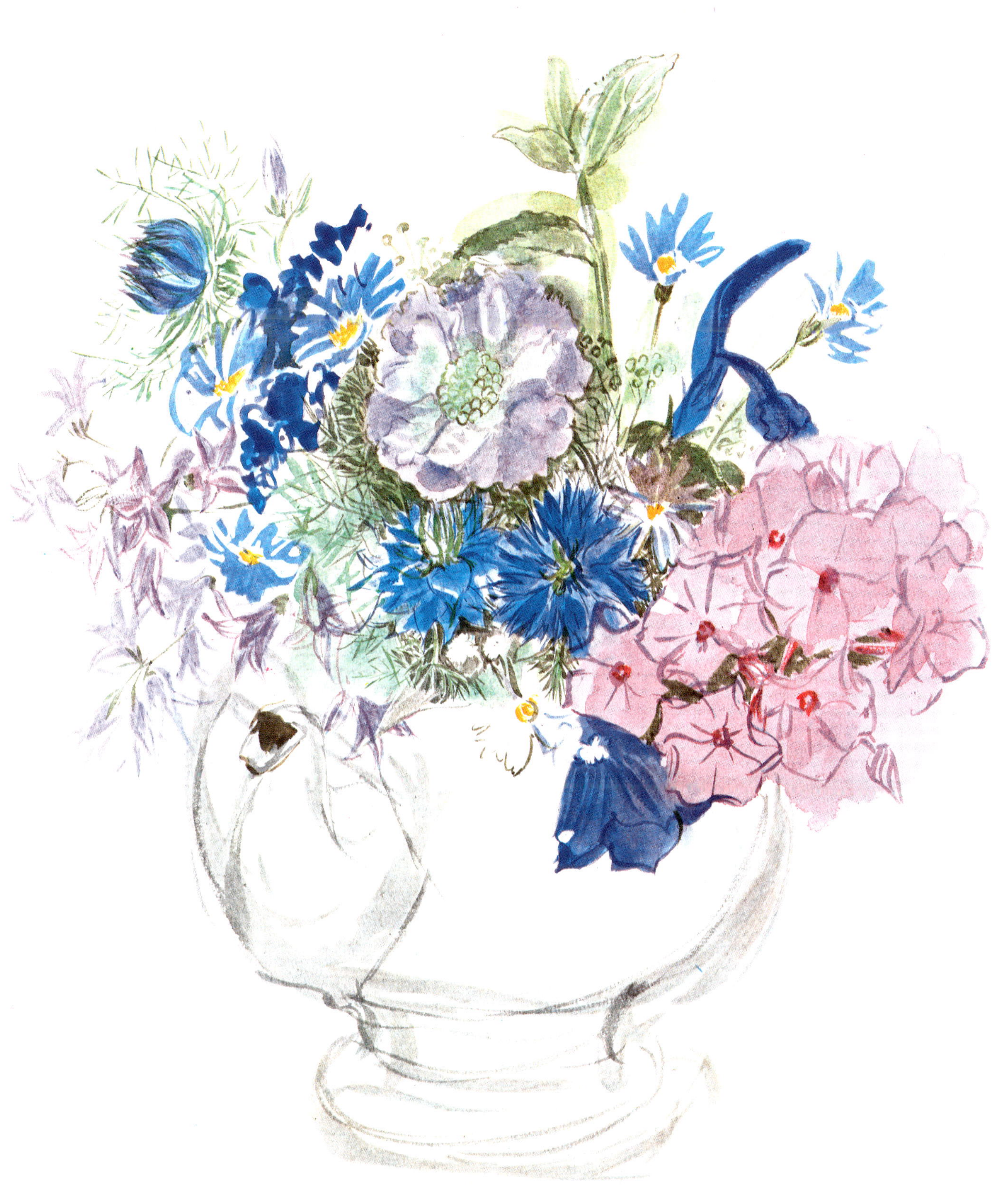

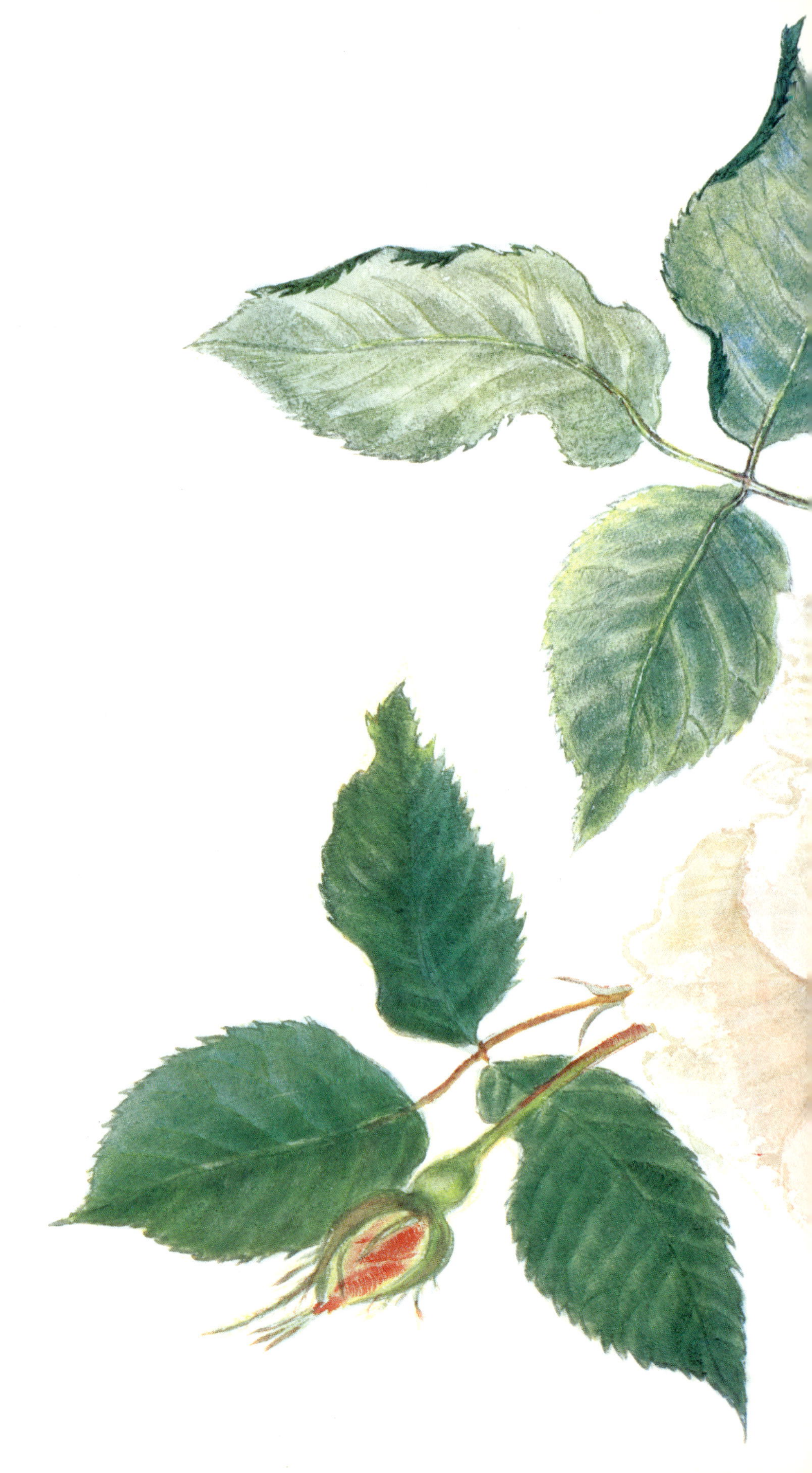

year old, she was amazingly fit. Most likely very beautiful in her younger days, she was still very attractive, tall and with a good posture. Her only daughter and grandchild live in Paris, and there she visited them every year. Karinska expressed herself with equal brilliance in either French, Russian, English or German.

Whoever loved art and beautiful objects was loved by Karinska.

During a visit, we sat drinking vodka from blue crystal glasses, and then took our places at the dining table. The other diners were her young and charming designer, and an elderly Russian dancer, who had now become her house-keeper. The rather overweight and asthmatic Chinese cook served an exquisite meal, and we drank red burgundy; wine from her cherished country, where she owns an estate which resembles one large rose garden. Her second home is in Sandisfield, Massachusetts, where she regularly retires to relax, it being only a few hours drive from New York. Here she has planted all her favourite roses; the roses from times past, which are sweetly perfumed and so delicate, but sadly wilt too soon. Her absolute favourite, the white "Mme Hardy", with its green eye and full bloom, is also here. These old species, partially forgotten, were all obtained from Dorothy Stemler in California. From Stemler's, who specialise in old species, my own almost two hundred different old rose shrubs were ordered in 1964. Due to this "mutual rose supplier", Karinska was introduced to my rose paintings, and later to my person, and so in reality, we must thank the roses for our friendship.

"My dear Rosalotte, that is your name for me", she once began a letter, and since then in every letter, I am her "Dear Rosalotte". She is exuberantly and rapturously Russian, "My biggest kisses" were sent to myself and Willi, ensuring me that there was no one else she loved more, and ending with "Love, forever love". She made abundant use of the word beautiful, and if something pleased her, it was written with a double letter l. For her, it was always full, opulent, rich, in short "beautifull". It was not possible to admire the objects in her house, for she would spontaneously say "Take it" and would insist that it was immediately taken. "Take it all, it is yours", spoken with slightly guttural, and rolling Russian r's. Unknowingly, I once admired a round handsome glass bottle, which had a graceful dolphin poised on the stopper. Pressing it on me, she said it was filled with genuine Russian vodka. I flew over the North Atlantic holding this precious object in my hands, to be sure that it would not be damaged. It is now in my glass case, still half full. At Christmas time, we received a parcel from Karinska. Lovingly packed, as only she knew how. First a layer of golden paper, then pink velvet bound with paler pink ribbons, and in the centre of the bow, a bouquet of tiny, pale pink roses. This enchanting package held a red velvet purse, which was embroidered with pearls like a girland of roses. On the small note, Karinska wrote that it had been made from part of a jacket belonging to the Empress Catherine the Great, and that she had acquired it at an auction. It was her most beloved possession, and therefore I should have it.

Her home in Sandisfield, St. Joan's Hill, was named after the film in 1950 "Joan of Arc", for which Karinska had won the Oscar for costume design, starring Ingrid Bergman and José Ferrer. In the house, almost every room contains reminders of the Saint; statues, paintings, and a bed cover relating the entire legend.

One such tapestry, showing the Maid of Orleans with flames leaping at her feet, was hanging over her bed, and it was partly charred and blackened. Karinska gave me an amazing explanation.

One night whilst asleep, the tapestry had caught fire, and she was almost burned.

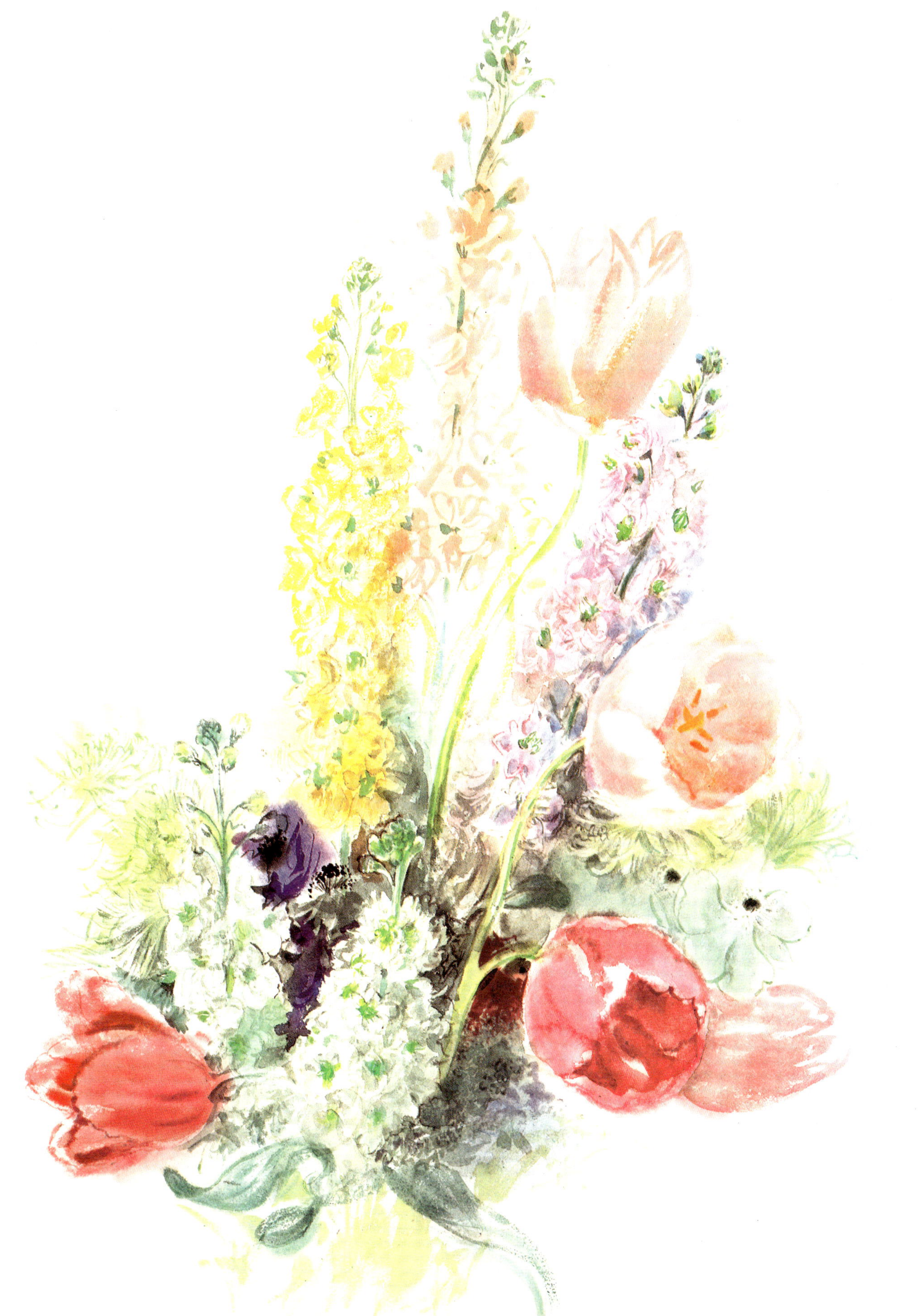

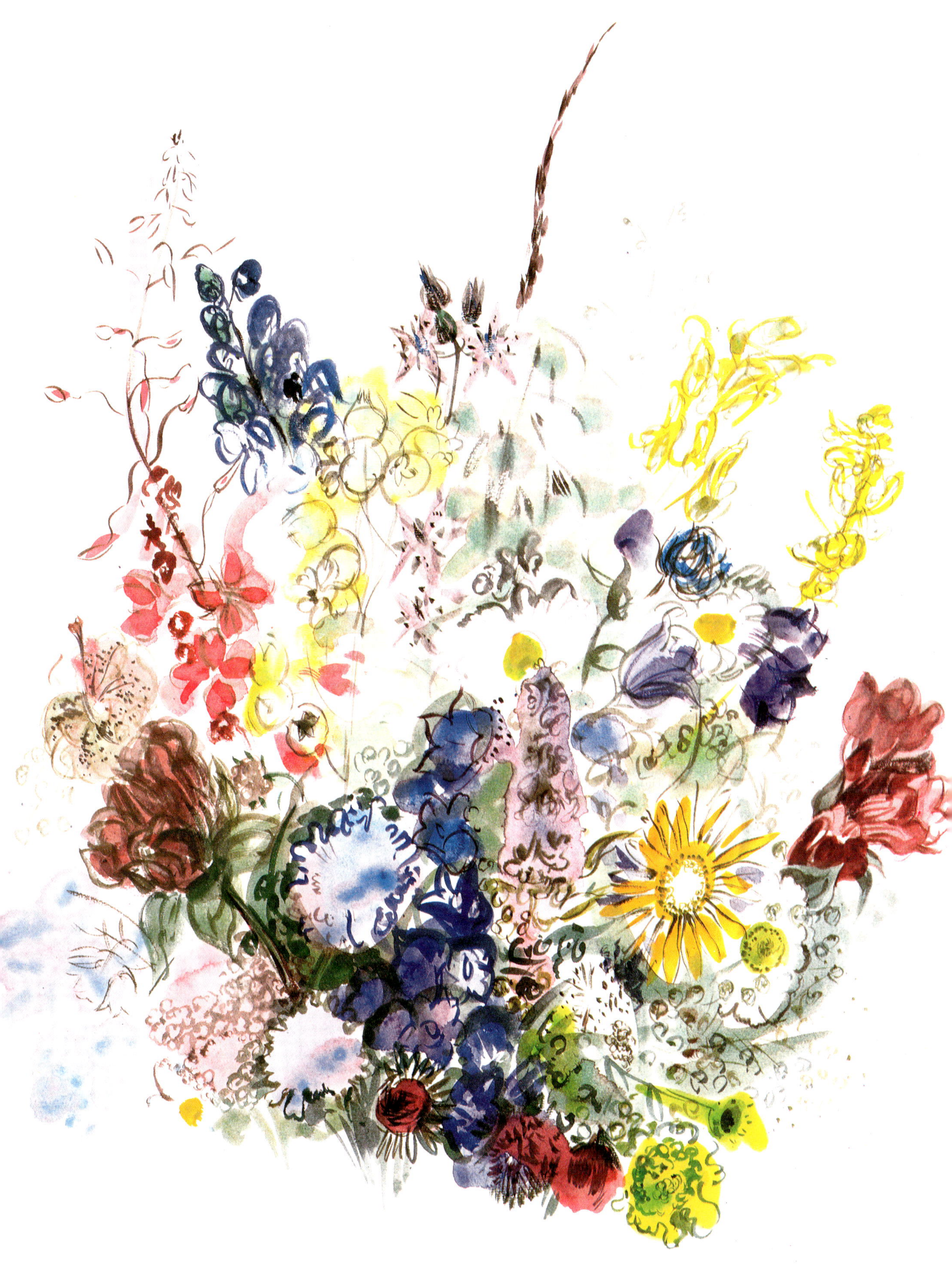

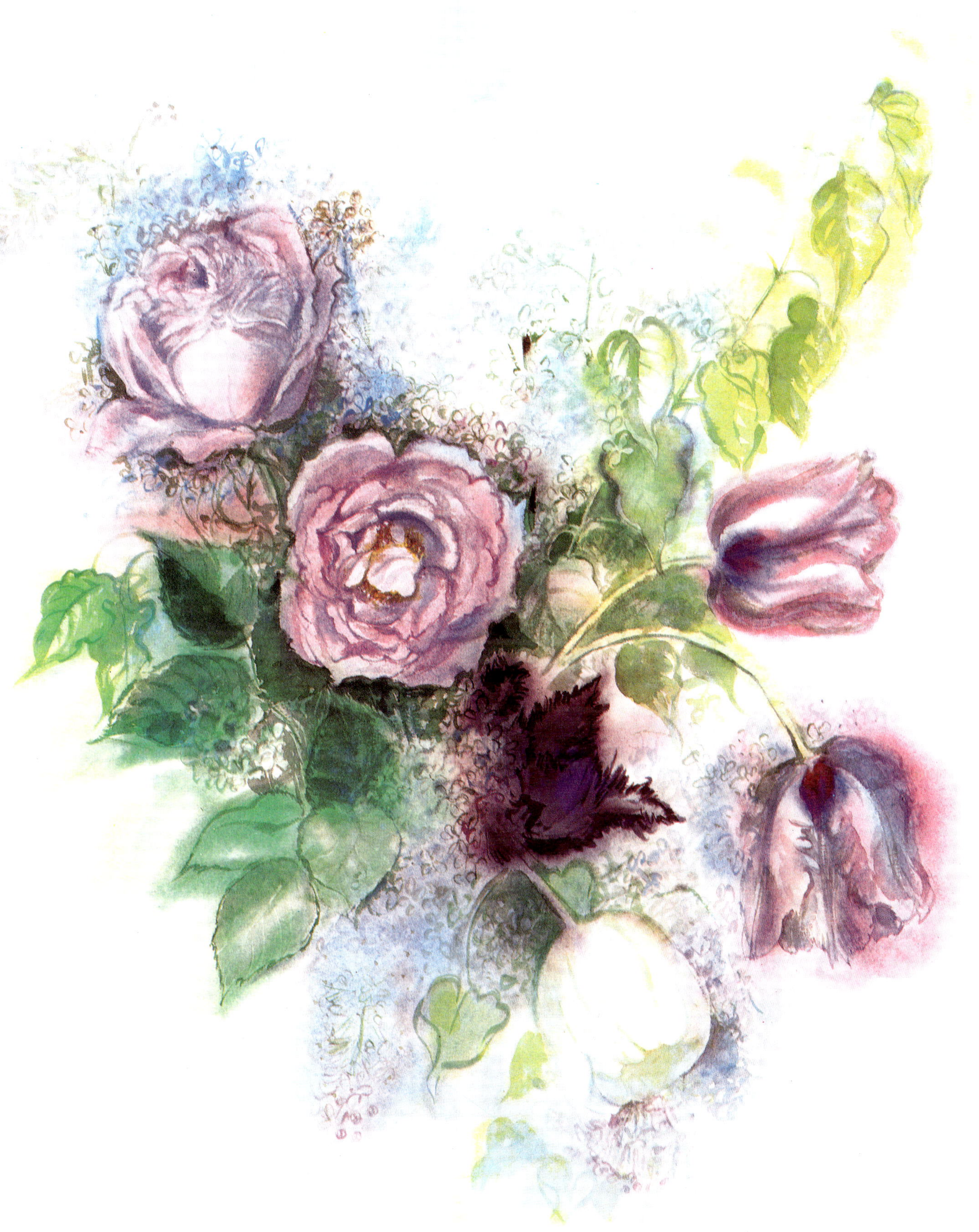

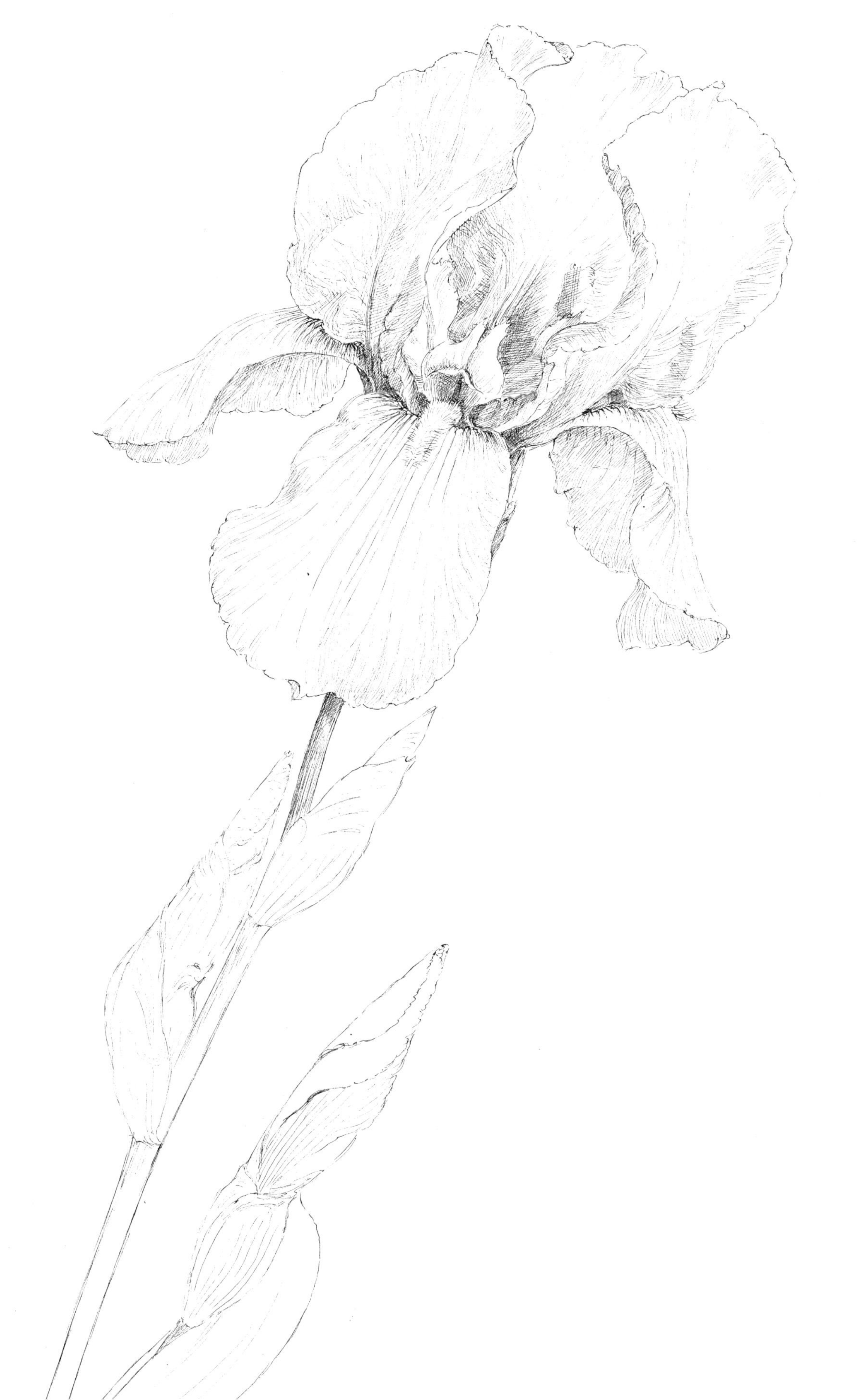

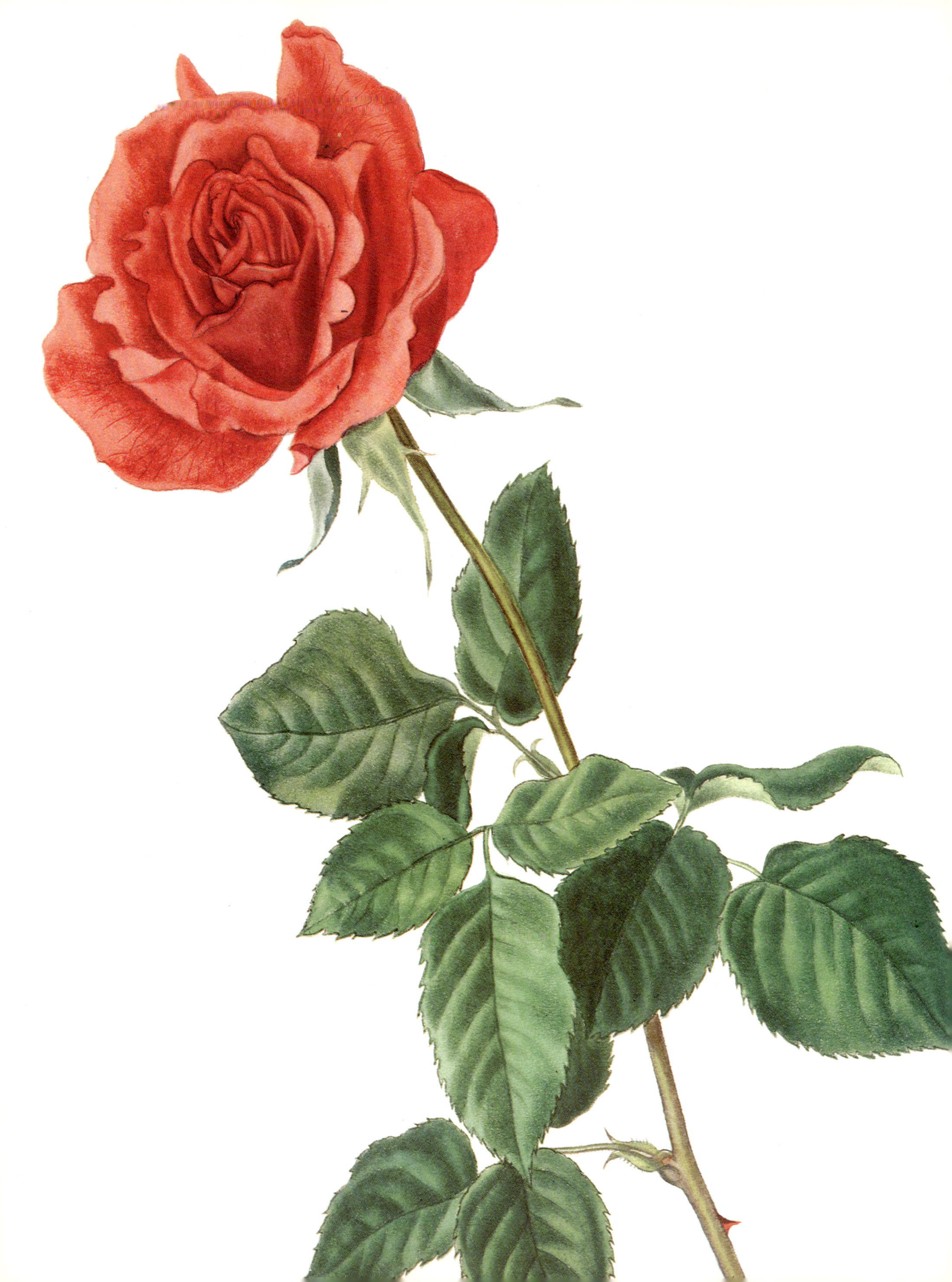

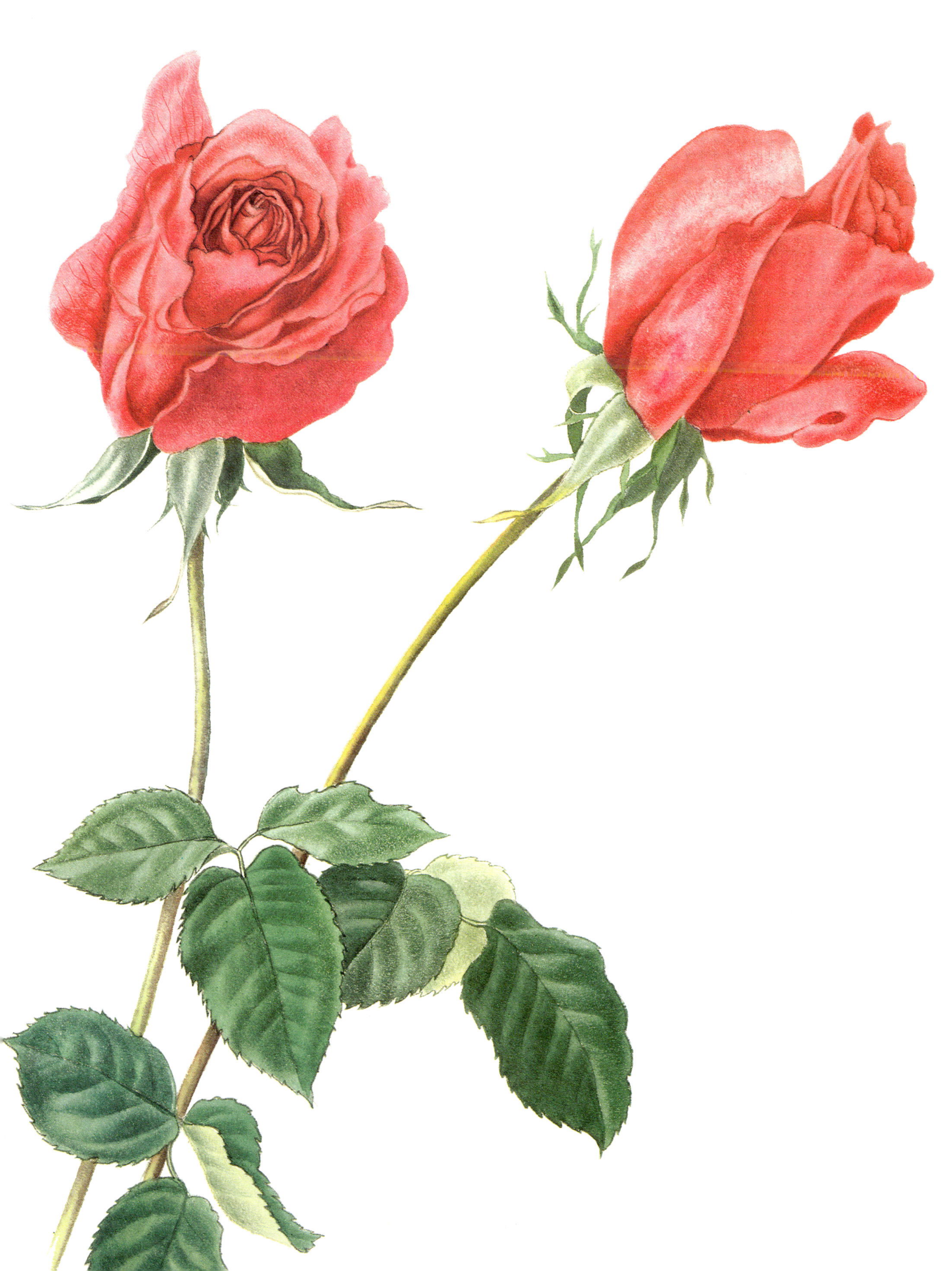

I return to my painting, …

I remember having been in love with colours since a very early age. For my second birthday, my father gave me a box of coloured pencils that made me very happy. Later, when I was about five years old, I remember that my greatest delight in midsummer was to sit among the many flowers in my parents' garden. I took a small stool and put it carefully into the middle of the pale yellow achileas, the high grown altheas, the large white marguerites, the heavy scented pink and red phlox, the campanulae and the tall bushes of delphiniums, shining in different shades of blue. Thus I was quite hidden in my "flower-house", with the exquisite perfume intoxicating me, and the sun's warmth was a gentle caress. It was perfect bliss. In rare fortunate moments, I am able to capture in my garden and flower paintings a glimpse of those delights.

These "hours of grace", as Professor Carl J. Burckhardt, President of the International Red Cross Geneva during the second world war and Ambassador of Switzerland in Paris, once called it, when looking at one of my favourite paintings, are unfortunately very rare, but they are the highlights of my life.

I feel happy if I succeed in finishing a water colour painting with firm and light strokes of the brush without superfluous colouring and daubing with white, as it makes the colours dull and heavy looking.

When painting, I prefer the clear and transparent water colours, which lend themselves best to render the pure and fresh colours of the plants.

Before starting to spread the dominating colours with a large and supple marten brush, I like to soak a French hand-made paper thoroughly. Some green is put where later on the foliage has to be painted in detail, various shades of blue where the delphiniums will be, and for the roses, I need a few yellow and pink spots of colour. On the moist paper, the colours run well into each other, and blend most beautifully. As soon as the paper is almost dry, I work at the details and complete the painting with some very fine brushes. This stage of working is usually accompanied by vibrating restlessness. I try, haunted by nervous haste, and yet with intense concentration and alertness, to capture the vision of the picture with soft and light brush strokes.

As soon as the paper is completely dry, the brush strokes become more hard and stiff, and the somehow painful delight of painting on moist paper is gone. It is impossible to make good if I am not able to finish my drawing during this short time, lightly, yet very exactly. That is why this technique is so difficult, but exciting and thrilling as well.

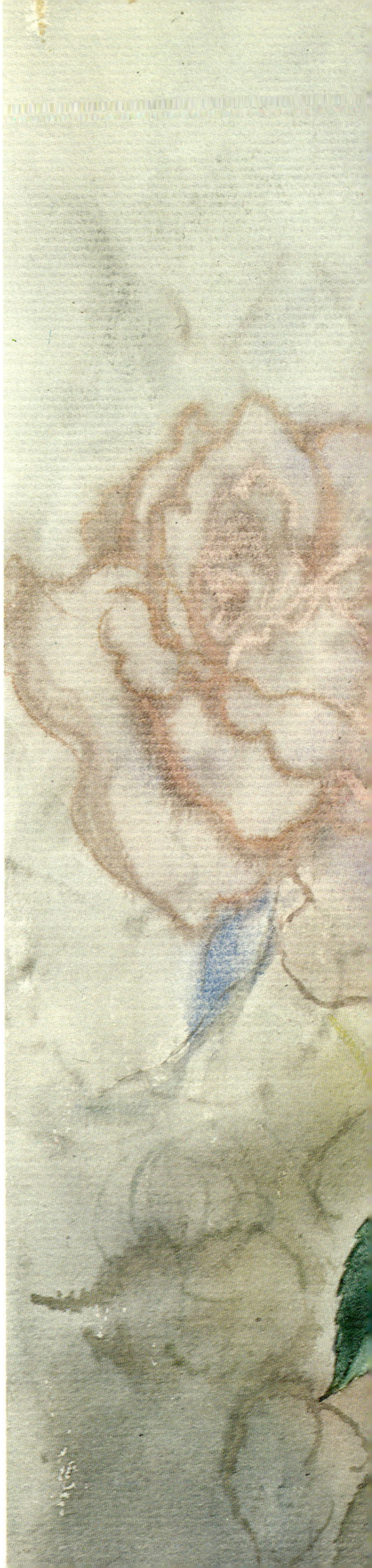

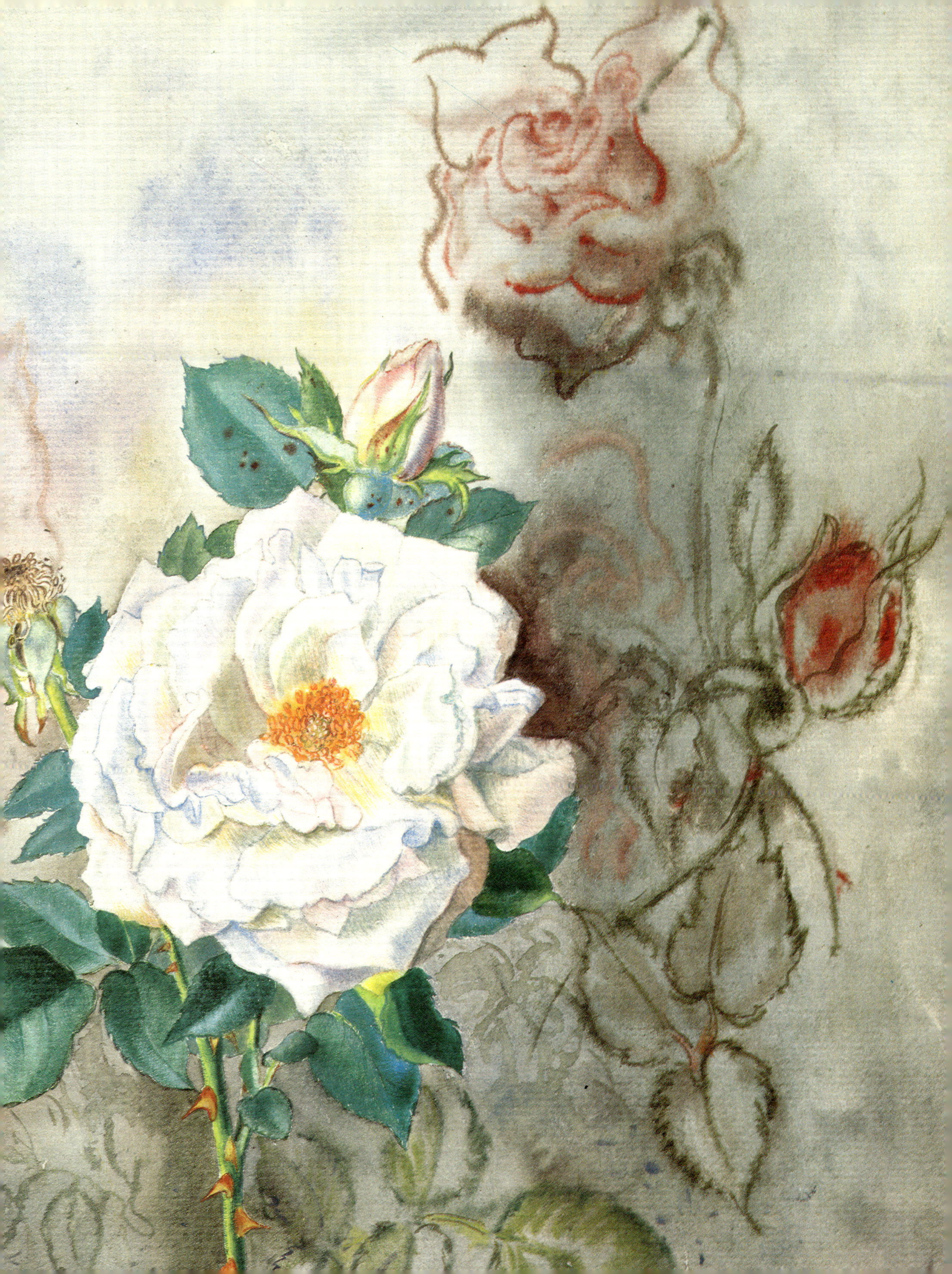

Once saturated with intense bright colours, the supple brush yields to my hand. As part of myself, it draws the last minute details of the plants so that they stand out against the mysterious background.

As I can express myself much better with colours and brush than with words, I would like to end my story with a "flower-letter" that my twenty year old daughter Lotti gave me with a bunch of flowers for my fiftieth birthday. She has the rare gift to let the flowers live freely and charmingly in the clear water of a wide glass bowl. And she arranges them according to colour and form that I feel as if her flower compositions had grown out of my heart. Like Lotti, I prefer to see flowers blooming in the garden, instead of putting them in a vase. She seems to feel the inner life of the plants and to know it, so she does not hurt them, and preserves their wilful charm, so that a bouquet from her means serene happiness for my eyes.

Her following words express my feelings about gardens, plants and flowers.

"I come from the garden. It is a warm, beautiful summer evening. The day was clear, but with the evening, a slight haze has come up, and some clouds are passing. It may rain tonight. I believe there are days and moods when flowers exhale more life and beauty, but maybe this is only because there are moments when I feel stronger and am more susceptible. This evening the flowers are very lovely. They give a breathless stillness to the garden. And when dusk is slowing falling, and a cooling light breeze is wandering through the garden, the flowers and leaves are subtly changing. The white rose glowing whiter than usual, and the red rose, now appearing almost black, is bending over its dark foliage The light wind draws a whisper from the lilies and the aquilegias, that are swaying like strange beings. Whilst lingering here in the dusk, I'm absorbed, watching the flowers, and the surroundings grow closer and denser. I'm trapped by a strange, peaceful magic. It's no longer the wind. The flowers whisper and dance by themselves, roused to their individual life. Spellbound I stand still and listen to this mysterious gentle and secret life. I am afraid to get close to the flowers, and leave the garden which is now perfectly still and dark.

In the early morning, the flowers are alive and beautiful. Only towards noon, especially on a bright, hot day, they close up and brood, quite absorbed with themselves, patiently longing for the evening and the night. Then their colours glow best; the yellow of the sunflowers, the red of the snap-dragons, and the blue of the clematis.

Flowers are beautiful when they stand in the garden, each one full of charm and grace. They make a free, but beautiful and clean impression in colour, shape, and size. They are lovelier when blooming in the garden, than in a vase. Yet, they challenge me, to combine their colours, form, and wilfulness after my impression and image. I experience a delicate pleasure when I pluck a rose, when it's vigorous stem lies in my hand, and I feel the heavy fullness of the open or opening bloom swaying. I hold the stem only lightly in my hand, because otherwise the thorns will hurt me. The rose becomes even more precious and fragile to me because its thorns force me to hold it gently. I look at the charm of the loose, light petals, made of an incomparably beautiful material, so clean and shimmeringly alive, that nothing in the world can compare with such beauty. I continue my stroll among the roses. The colour, the shape and the distinct aimless individuality of each flower excites me. I am full of joy, the morning seems to be clearer than before, I breathe deeply, and the faint fragrance of the roses makes me thirsty. I am getting wide awake and eager with excitement. There are moments when a single sound, a chord, is stirring within me. Such is now my experience with the colour shades, the expression and the movement of the plant. My thoughts are far away as I place rose after rose in my hand to an abundant, full bouquet. My eyes are searching further, perhaps I discover a dark violet clematis, a blooming shrub is attracting me, or I pluck some sprigs of asters under the dark tree over there, that are covered with a web of fine, tiny white blossoms.

Everything has to fit in my bunch of flowers, but not reluctantly and defiantly, as charm and fragrance would be lost. Here a dark twig is towering above the open, smiling roses; and there the sprig of delicate, tiny white asters is overshadowing the other blooms".

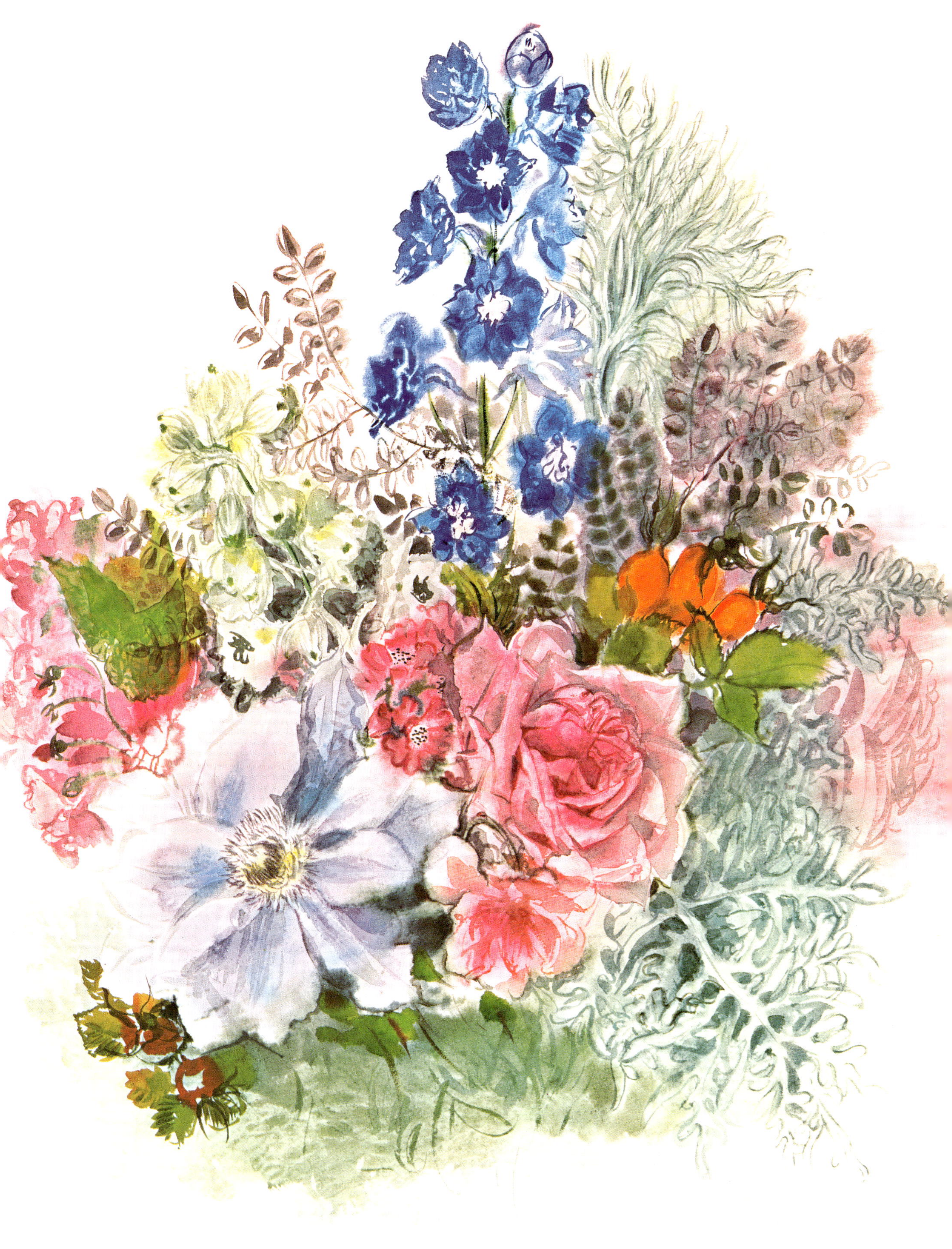

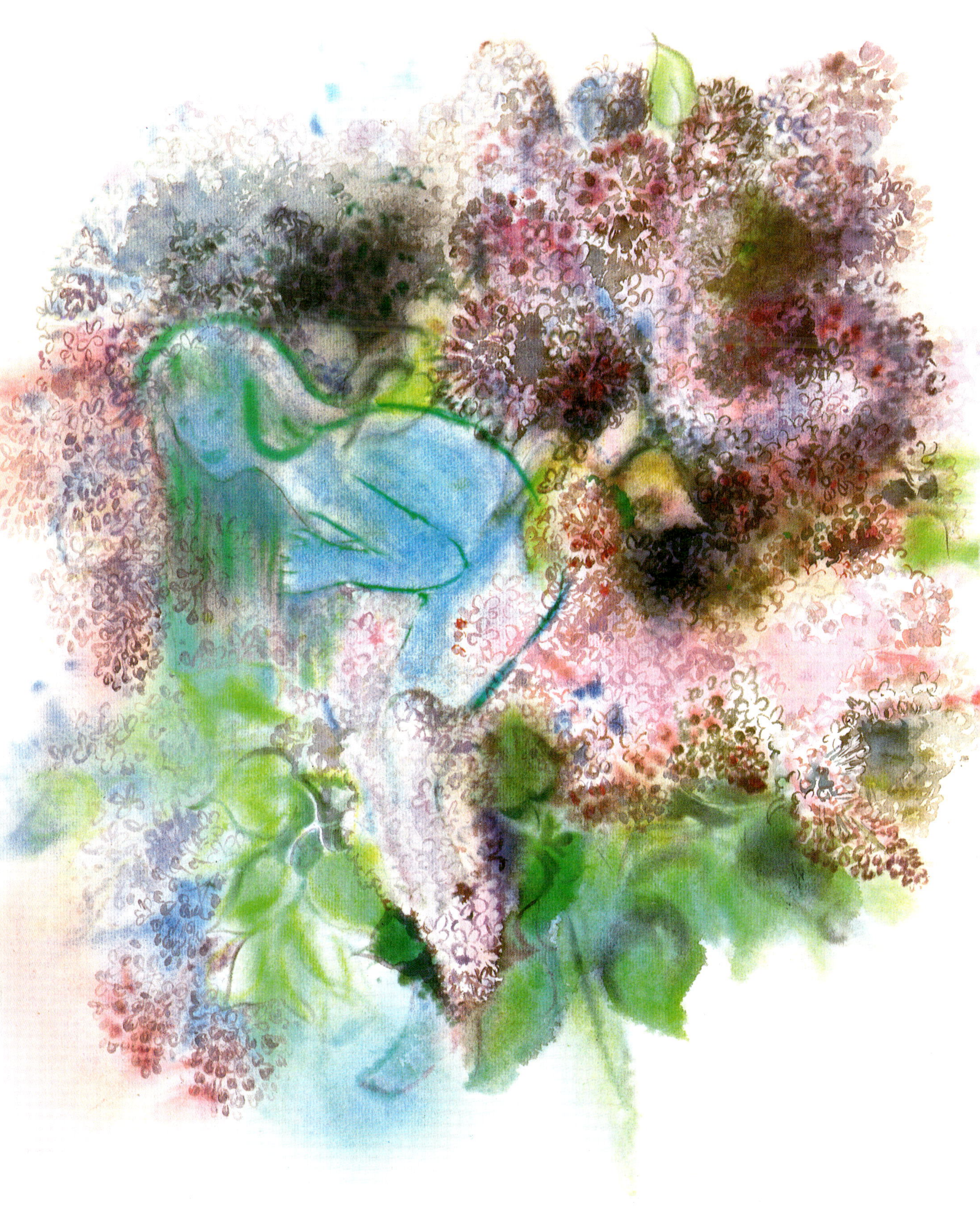

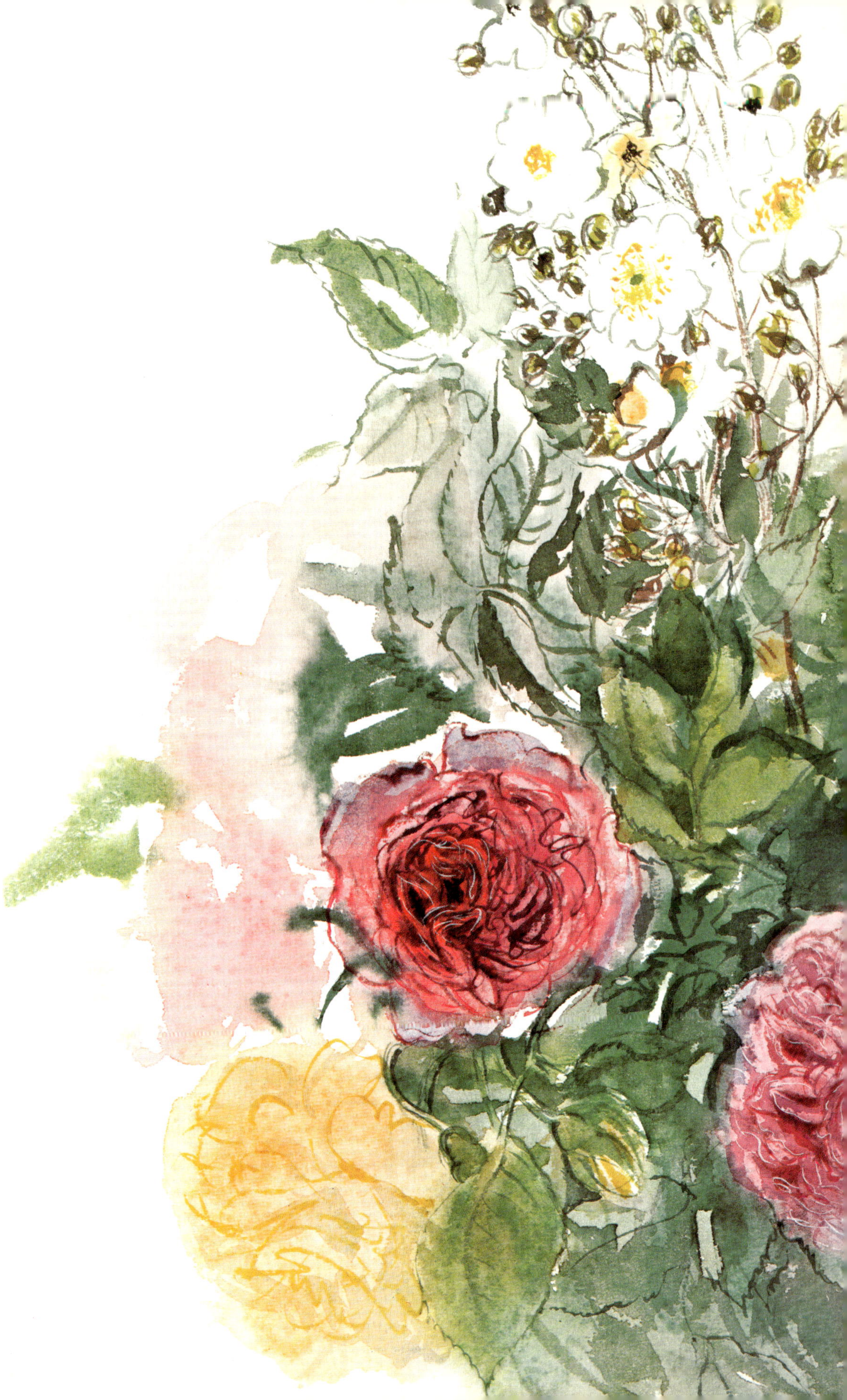

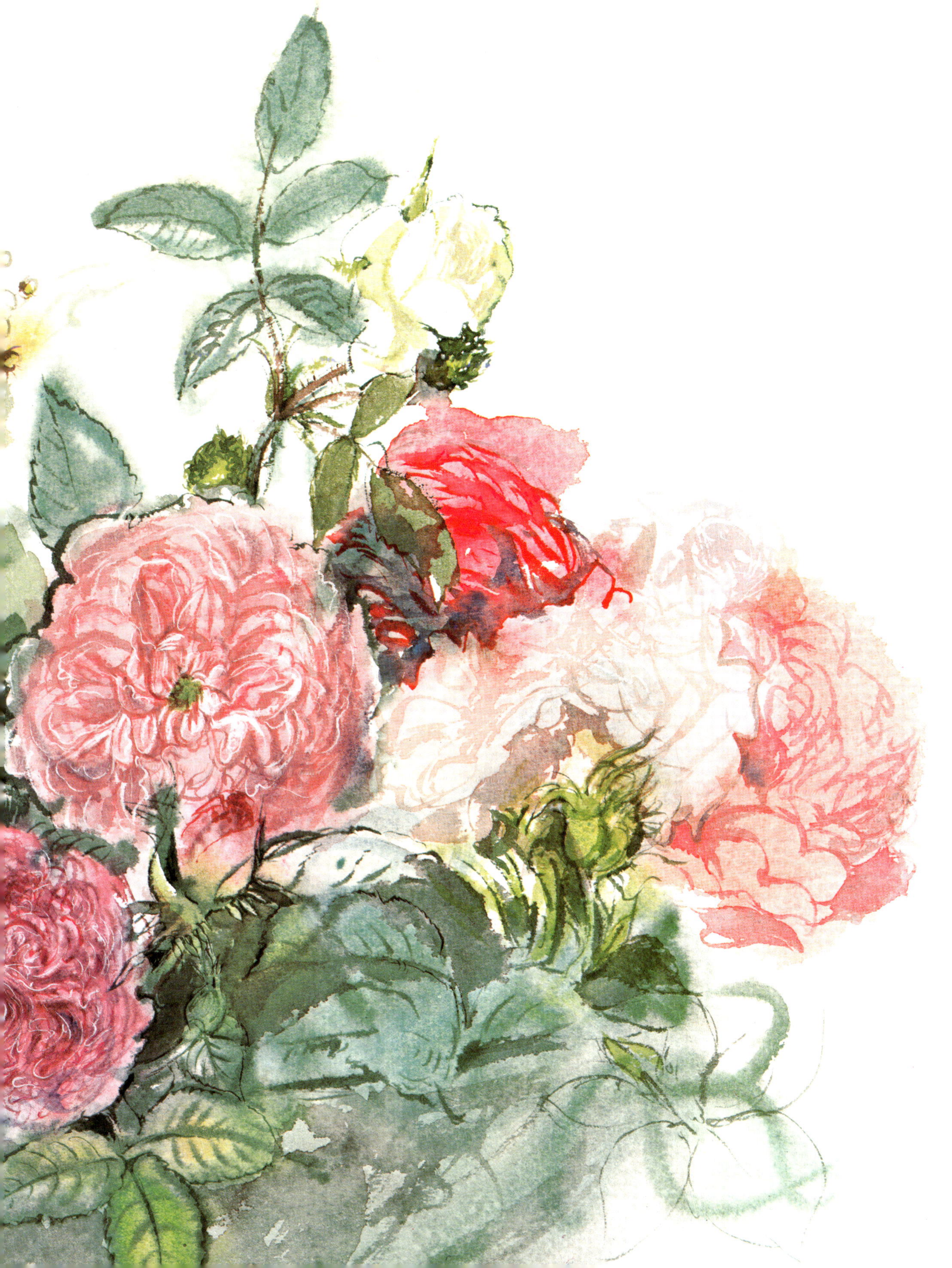

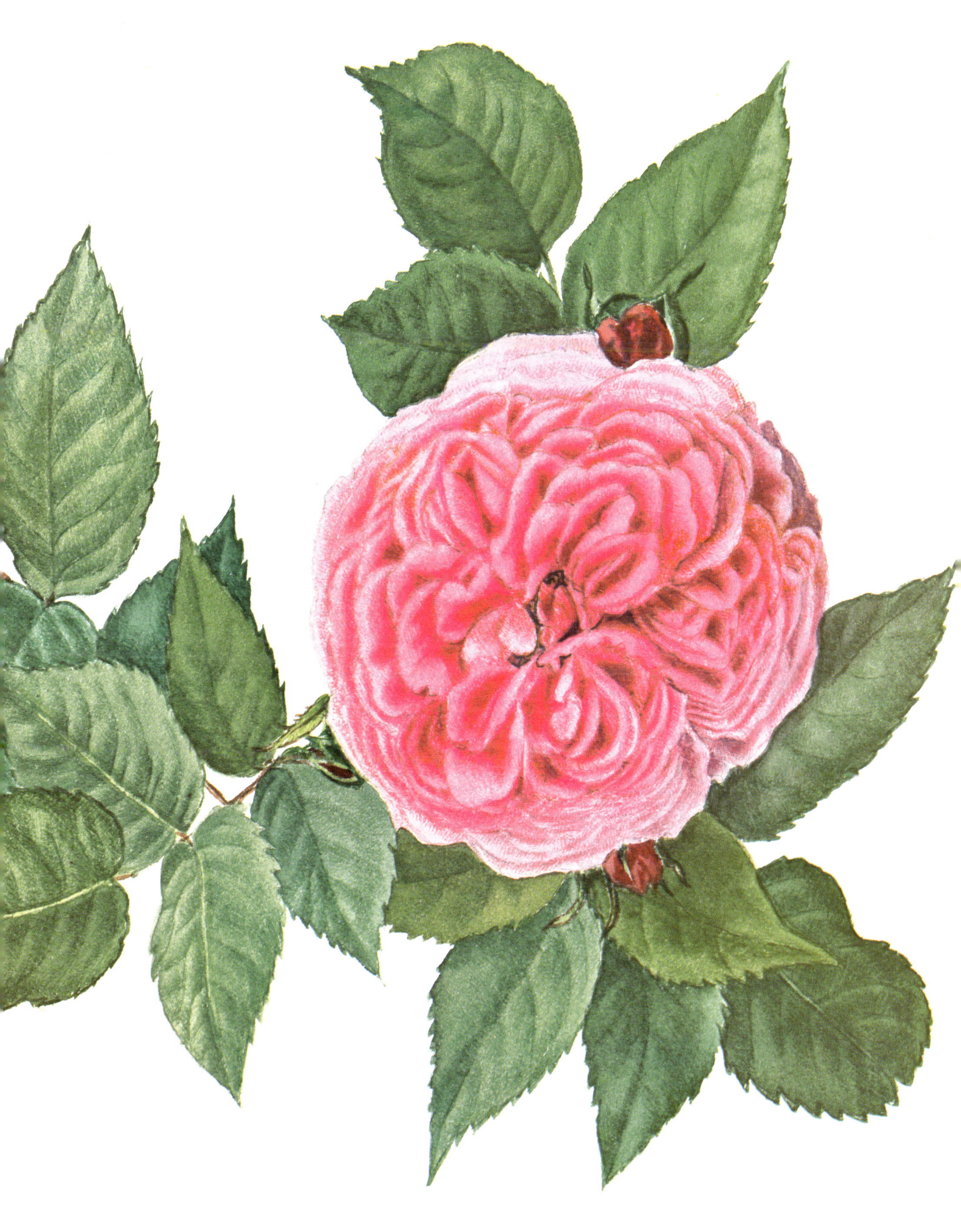

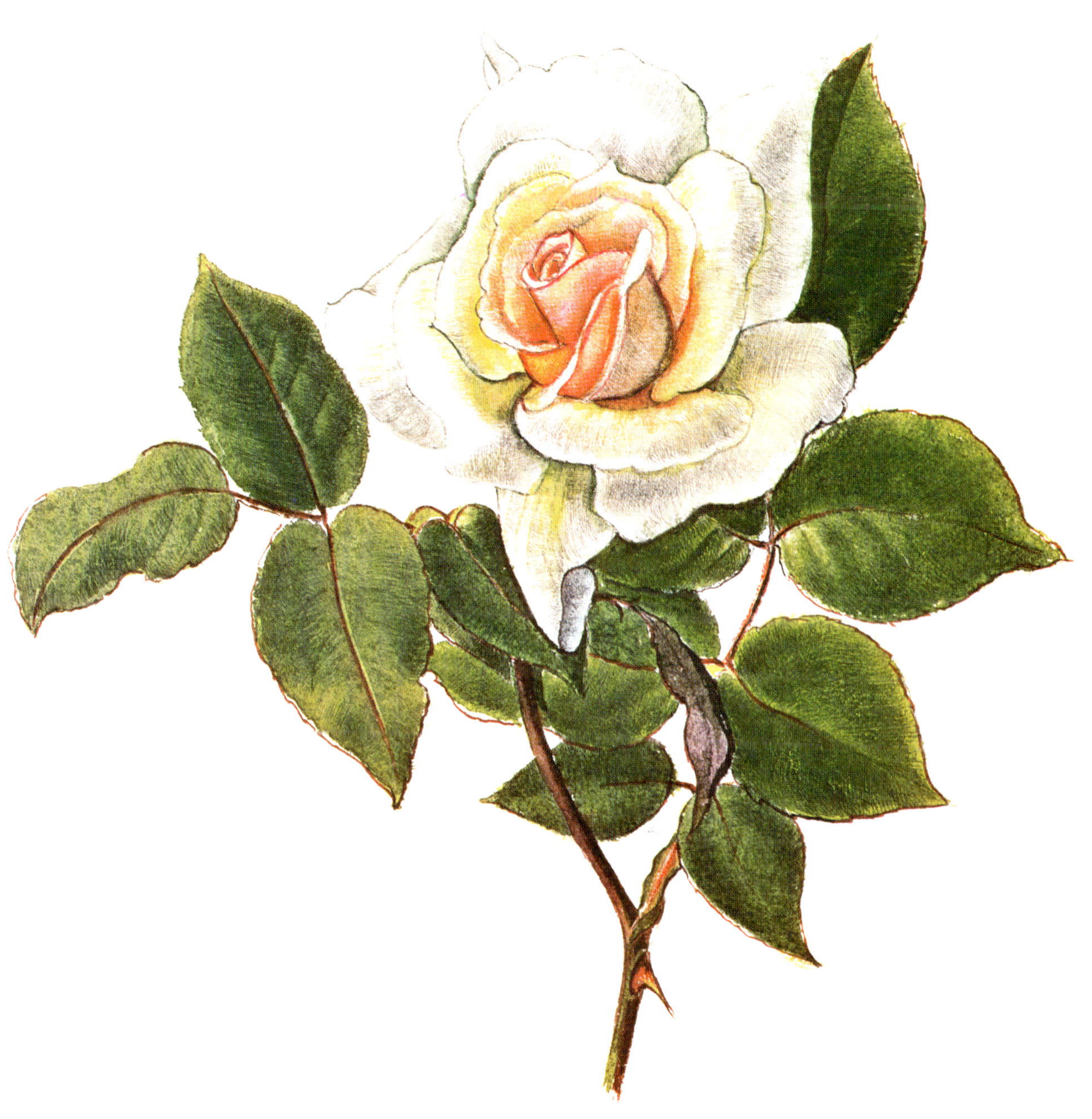

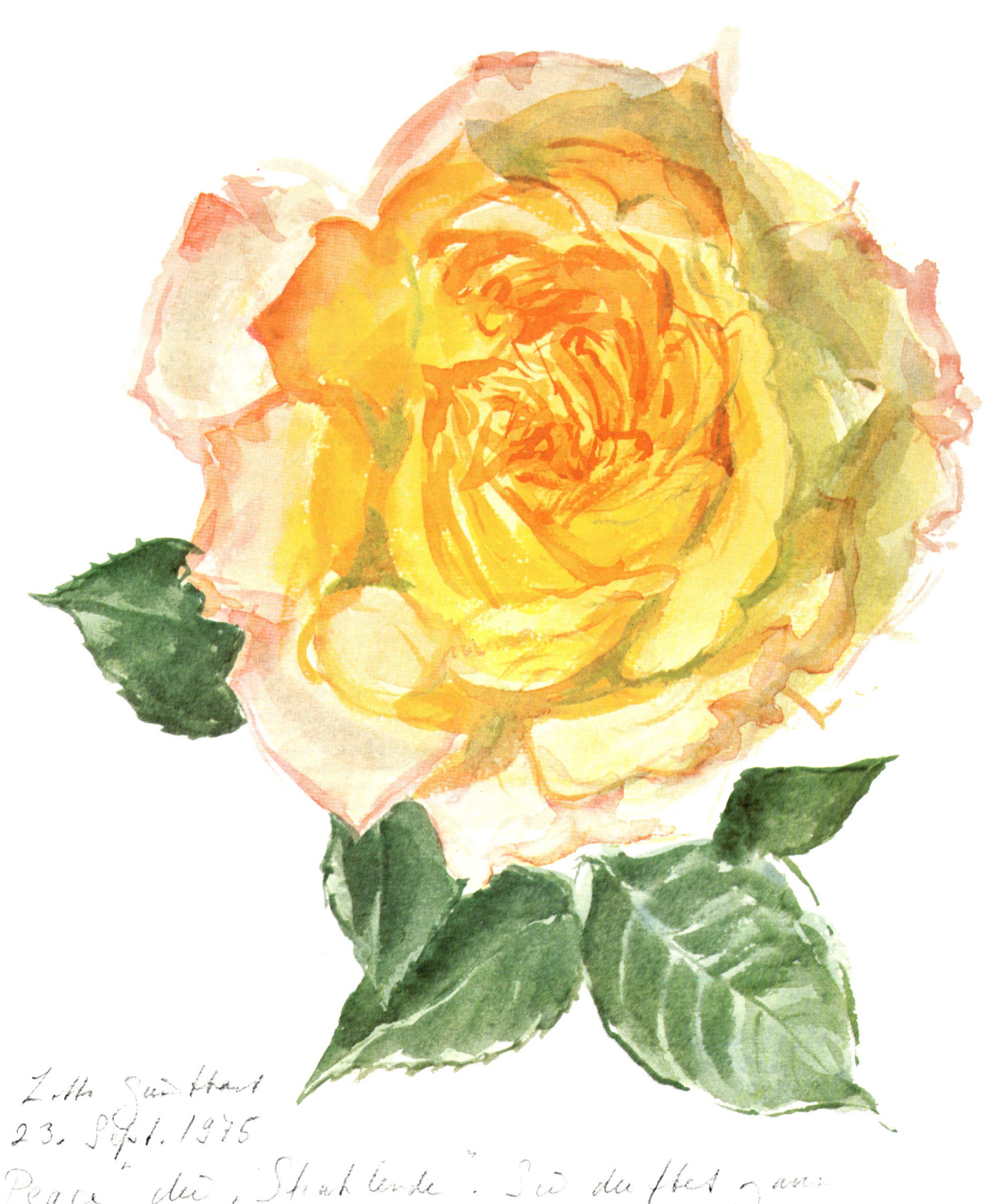

Lotte Guichhart
23. Sept. 1975
„Peace", die „Strahlende". Sie duftet ganz
rein und stark, ein „glockenheller Rosen-Apfel-Duft"

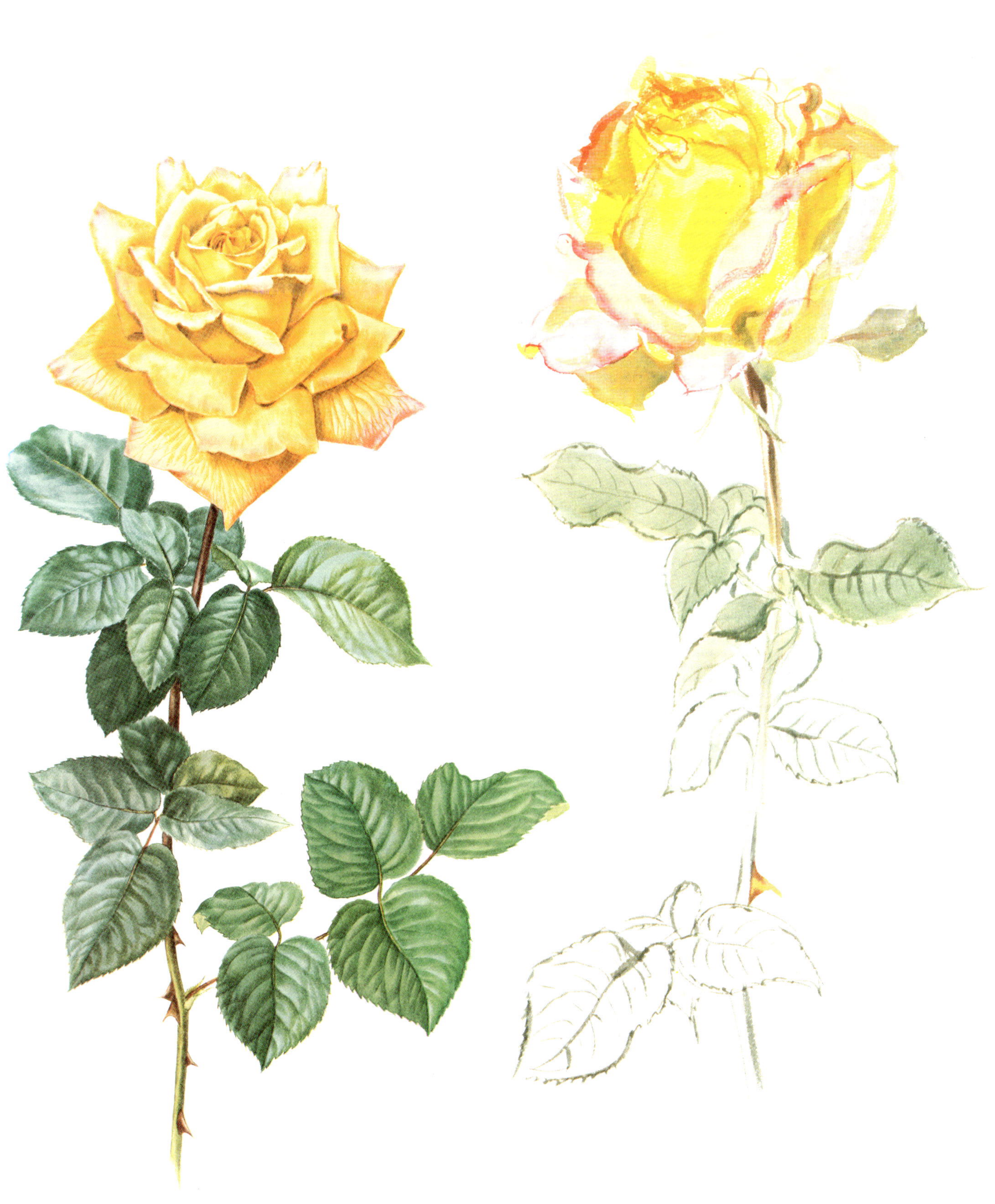

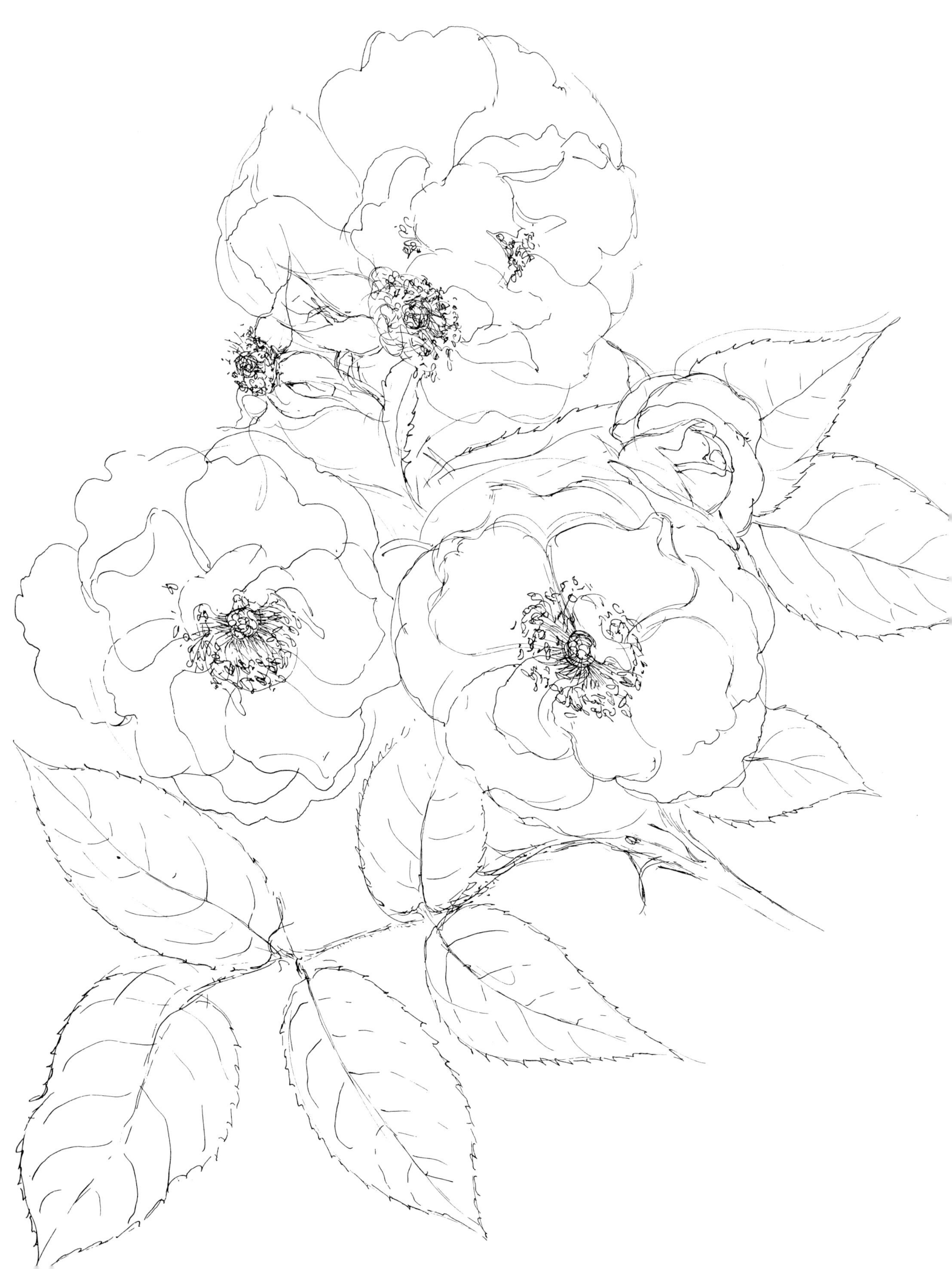

A fresh look at the yellow

Professor Conrad H. Eugster

The history of the yellow garden roses

The colour range of modern garden roses includes all variations, with the exception of the true blue tones. This is the result of continual breeding, and – unknown to many rose enthusiasts – it is relatively new. European and American roses prior to approximately 1830, were either red or pink, in many shades [1].
Of course, in addition there were white roses. A particularly fascinating aspect of rose breeding was to discover the colour YELLOW.
Even though yellow species have long been known, such as *Rosa foetida* ("Austrian Briar" from the Middle East, introduced in Europe before 1550), *R. foetida bicolor* (introduced before 1590), *R. hemisphaerica* (introduced before 1620), *R. foetida persiana* (1837), the China *R. banksiae* (introduced in England 1796), as well as *R. banksiae lutea* (1824), they had no influence whatsoever, for quite a long period of time, on breeding yellow garden roses by specific hybridization. This was also applicable for the European and Asian occuring types of *R. spinosissima,* from which yellow sub-species are long familiar, such as *R. spinosissima lutea.*
The first significant change in the colour spectrum was brought about by crossing "Park's Yellow Tea-scented China" *(R. X odorata ochroleuca,* introduced 1824) with other Chinese cultured species. Not only were the new colour tones in the region of soft primrose yellow and salmon orange, as we know from many illustrations of contemporary tea roses, but also the remontant characteristic (repeat flowering) was reliably transferred to many hybrids. Both the enlargement of the colour range, as well as the remontant factor, encouraged the rose breeders so much, that in a short time many new rose types appeared on the market. The fact that quite often imperfect varieties (weak growth, sensitivity to frost, disease prone) were introduced, worried the enthusiasts little.

[1] History of the garden rose, cf: [1–7].

The earliest yellowish and yellow roses which were grown in Europe in this way, included "Jaune Desprez" (red, buff, flesh and sulphur; 1830), "Lamarque" (white, centre deep straw colour; 1830), "Smith's Yellow" (pale straw colour; 1833), "Safrano" (pale buff; 1839), "Chromatella" (creamy white, centre yellow; 1843), "Gloire de Dijon" (yellow, buff, orange and salmon; 1853), "Maréchal Niel (deep yellow; 1864), "Rêve d'Or" (deep yellow, coppery yellow; 1869).[2]

Taking into consideration the contemporary colour descriptions, and the knowledge of the individual inherent scope of colour perception, then it is apparent that a true, intensive yellow, as we know today, did not exist.

Neither the brilliance nor the colour intensity and stability comparable to the standard of today was achieved. From many confirmations, we know that a seemingly deep yellow bud of a certain variety became paler upon opening, or that a fully opened yellow rose blossom faded in the sunlight or because of a temperature change. This problem is still being evaluated by present day breeders [cf: 9 and 10]. This is not intended to be a judgement on the aesthetical and exclusive delicacy of the yellow colour tones previously available, in particular the common mixture filled with pink, but only to emphasize their comparison with the true, intensive yellow colour of *R. foetida.*

The closest comparison to the yellow tone of *R. foetida* was obtained by the once flowering shrub rose "Harison's Yellow" (*R. X harisonii* – fine golden yellow) originating in New York about 1830.

The break-through to the variety in the colour range of our modern garden roses was achieved in 1900 by Jean Pernet-Ducher (1858–1928, Venissieux, Lyon, France) with "Soleil d'Or", an F_2- or F_3-hybrid from "Antoine Ducher" X *R. foetida persiana.* Today, it is obvious that "Soleil d'Or" is in the family tree of nearly all the newer yellow, salmon, peach, copper and orange coloured garden roses.[3]

[2] All colour descriptions according to [8].

[3] Compare [1–7] and [9–11]. This statement is applicable, as only recently known, also for several red roses, whereby the connection to "Soleil d'Or" is not immediately apparent.

It should also be noted that already prior to Pernet-Ducher, successful crosses had been made with *R. foetida* and with *R. foetida persiana,* namely "Gottfried Keller" (F. Müller, 1894), *R. X. penzanceana* ("Lady Penzance", Penzance, 1894), "Lord Penzance" (1894), and "Agnes" (Saunders, 1900). However, these roses hardly had a role in the following main lines of the breeding work.

Since "Soleil d'Or", also *R. foetida, R. foetida persiana* and the yellow species *R. ecae* (Afghanistan, introduced 1880), *R. hugonis* (China, introduced 1899) and *R. xanthina* (China, Korea, introduced 1906) have been utilized for further hybridizations.

What does the colour tone YELLOW mean in chemistry?

Until recently, it was believed that roses are coloured yellow because of their flavonole content [12]. This is, however, not true: Since about 1970, we know that the real cause for the yellow colour lies in the carotenoid content.[4]
Although flavonoles are abundantly present in rose flowers, above all in white roses, where they cause the often observed light yellow hue in dried petals, they hardly contribute to the colour in fresh petals.
Carotenoids are unsaturated terpenes, which are built up biosynthetically to a symmetric basic structure from eight isoprene units. With an increasing degree of unsaturation (number of "conjugated" carbon-carbon double bonds), light absorption shifts from the near UV (ultraviolet) range (about 300 nanometers [nm]) towards 600 nm, which leads to the conclusion that carotenoids in daylight may appear either colourless, pale yellow, deep yellow or orange. More rarely, carotenoids can also contribute to light red, dark red or even purple tones. This colour intensification is correlated to the number of conjugated double bonds (separated only by one single bond each); cf: Table I Carotenoids are insoluble in water and are synthesized and stored in substructures of plant cells (chromo-plasts). In contrast to carotenoids, the true red rose-pigments (anthocyanines) have different structures and, moreover, they are dissolved in the cell sap or bound to membranes.

[4] Proof [13] [14], older assumptions [15–18].

Table I shows the structure formulae of some carotenoids found in rose petals. The part of the molecule responsible for the light absorption, ie: for the resulting colour appearance (conjugated double bonds), is pointed out in formulae 1 to 5. It is evident that the absorption consecutively moves from UV to longer wave-lengths with an increasing number of conjugated double bonds, and that, parallel, the colour changes from yellow to red. Carotenoids have an intensive colour. Already traces in a rose flower have an effect which is readily recognizable.

It is useful to differentiate between the following types:
1. non-cyclic carotene hydrocarbons (1–5),
2. cyclic carotene hydrocarbons (6, 7),
3. polar carotene alcohols (8, 9),
4. epoxycarotenoids (10–12).

This sequence also reflects the biogenesis of the carotenoids in the plant: First 1 is built up and then, step-by-step, the others; eg: 12 is biogenetically a very late product.

Analyses of the carotenoids from yellow roses

A complete analyses of the carotenoids in rose flowers requires, besides experience, suitable technical equipment in order to obtain reliable and reproducible results. A modern procedure is the High Performance Liquid Chromatography (HPLC) combined with continuous, very fast spectroscopy.

Table II shows the separation of carotenoids from *R. foetida*. Every numbered peak represents an individual carotenoid, whose structure was determined. It follows that our visual impression of the colour of a yellow flower of *R. foetida* is the result of a complex mixture of carotenoids, in which, however, the intensively yellow epoxy carotenoids, eg: 10 dominates.

Table III schematically shows the results of the analyses of carotenoids in roses, summarizing for simplicity's sake, the types 1–4 mentioned above.[5]

In the "Maréchal Niel" (Tea Noisette; Pradel 1864), practically only non-cyclic carotenoids (type 1) were found, the majority being colourless compounds 1–3. The colour of the blossom is mainly caused by some neurosporene (4) and a trace of lycopene (5). About 20% of the carotenoids could not be identified. Similar results were found in "Albéric Barbier" (*Wichuraiana*-Rambler; Barbier 1900).

An altogether different picture is presented by *R. foetida, R. X harisonii* and "Gottfried Keller"! Here carotenoids of the type 1 are almost completely lacking. In their place, we find cyclic carotenoids (type 2), polar alcohols of type 3 and, above all, epoxides (type 4). In other words, the biogenesis is much more advanced than in "Maréchal Niel" and comprises the complete dehydration, cyclization, hydroxylation and epoxidation.

This result is also found in all modern deep yellow garden roses, which could be analysed up to date [6], eg: in "Allgold" (Floribunda; LeGrice 1958), "Bellona" (Floribunda; Kordes 1976), "Aalsmer Gold".
The discovery of carotenoids in the pure white "Virgo" (Hybrid Tea; Mallerin 1947), the orange-red "Sarabande" (Floribunda; Meilland 1957) as well as in "Super Star" (Hybrid Tea; Tantau 1960), "Alexander" (Hybrid Tea; Harkness 1972) and other roses, which show the striking vermilion tone, came as a surprise. The carotenoids of "Virgo" belong to type 1, however, the number of conjugated double bonds being insufficient to achieve visibility. The results in "Super Star" and "Alexander" show that carotenoids contribute substantially to produce these modern colour tones.

[5] New results from the author's laboratory; for details cf.: latest publications in Helvetica Chimica Acta.
[6] The high epoxy content of modern tea hybrids was first observed by Valadon and Mummery [13]. Our more recent results, however, do not agree as regards the correct identification of the individual carotenoids and the determination of their quantity.

Conclusions

The modern analyses of carotenoids from rose petals is in an early stage. However, the results have been so surprising that some conclusions may be made. The soft lemon-primrose hue of "Maréchal Niel" is due to the carotene hydrocarbons type 1. These belong to the less stable carotenoids and are readily degraded in the presence of light to colourless products. Possibly similar results may be found in other yellow tea and noisette roses.[7] In comparison, *R. foetida* is very different: due to the high degree of epoxidation, the colour tone is shifted to pure yellow and, at the same time, the stability of the carotenoids increases.[8]

One is led to the following conclusions: By crossing *R. foetida* with a remontant rose, it was possible to transfer the yellow colour tone to the offspring, also dominantly transmitting the abilities of cyclization (type 2), hydroxylation (type 3) and epoxidation (type 4)!

Since epoxidation of carotenoids also occurs in green leaves, there however, being reversible (oxygen transport in the so-called violaxanthin cycle), yellow roses have a deficient violaxanthin cycle, whereby the de-epoxidation does not take place, either completely or partially.

From our analyses of the carotenoids of "Gottfried Keller", the same facts were found. The conclusion is obvious that one of the parents was actually *R. foetida persiana*. "Gottfried Keller" unjustly played a minor role in subsequent rose breeding. Well known is only its offspring "Poulsen's Yellow" ("Mrs W. H. Cutbush" X "Gottfried Keller"; Poulsen 1938). This is considered to be the first true yellow floribunda rose [11].

[7] An investigation is urgent, but not easy because old yellow tea roses are not readily available. Whether the fading of carotenoids in petals happens for the same reasons as in *in vitro* trials, remains an open question.

[8] The colour tone of *R. foetida* is very similar to *R. foetida persiana*, however, a chemical analysis of the latter has yet to be done.

For morphological reasons, one has assumed, that for *R. X harisonii,* often identified as the popular "Yellow Rose of Texas", one parent could be *R. foetida.*[9]
The other parent might be a form of *R. pimpinellifolia* [1–3, 6, 7]. Our analyses confirms this assumption, for the carotenoids found correspond in structure and composition to those of *R. foetida,* with one restriction: *R. pimpinellifolia* belongs botanically to the same group as *R. foetida* (Pimpinellifoliae) and is probably capable of synthesizing carotenoids; which types occur in their yellow forms, eg: *R. pimpinellifolia lutea,* has not yet been studied.

The new analyses of carotenoids in numerous modern yellow garden roses (hybrid teas, polyantha hybrids, floribundas) have regularly brought to light the basic pattern observed in *R. foetida,* thereby reflecting again and again the extraordinary influence of this rose on its offspring "Soleil d'Or". The influence is also clearly recognizable in the most famous newer tea hybrid "Peace" (Meilland 1945). However, here an additional observation has been made: In "Peace", the catabolism of the carotenoids, ie: the degradatin to smaller fragments, the so-called apocarotenoids, is noticeable more strongly than in other roses.

Among connoisseurs of roses, the opinion is wide-spread that the modern colour tones "orange-scarlet", "coral-orange", "vermilion", etc., which appear so strikingly first in "Gloria Mundi" (Polyantha Hybrid; de Ruiter 1929), and later in "Princess von Orange" (de Ruiter 1935), "Independence" (Floribunda; Kordes 1950), "Super Star", "Alexander" and many other varieties, originated by mutation. Supposedly, the brick-red anthocyanidin pelargonin was herewith produced for the first time in a rose. The positive evidence for pelargonin "Gloria Mundi", etc., is certainly correct [19], however, our analyses have shown that it occurs already in the old "Dorothy Perkins" (*Wichuraiana* rambler; Jackson & Perkins 1901) though in small quantities. Therefore it cannot be a mutation. It is now also certain that the real reason for the brilliant colour tone of "Super Star", "Alexander" and others is a mixture of anthocyanines with carotenoids. For "Gloria Mundi", the results of the analysis are not yet available. In many red roses, the carotenoid content can be recognized visually from the yellowish base of the petal.

[9] *R. foetida persiana* is excluded, since it was only introduced in Europe in 1837.

However, it is a miracle that it was possible to mix two such fundamentally different pigments, such as the water soluble anthocyanines and the water insoluble carotenoids, so that our eyes cannot distinguish between them.

A further noteworthy result of our analyses is the proof that carotenoids occur also in white roses. Hence, the biosynthesis of the fundamental compound, eg: 1 and 2, is intact. However, the formation of a sufficient number of conjugated double bonds to bring the light absorption from UV to visibility is blocked in white roses. Either the enzymes for the desaturation are lacking or they are inactive.

Undoubtedly, the analyses of the various pigments of roses will shed more light on the complexity of rose breeding.

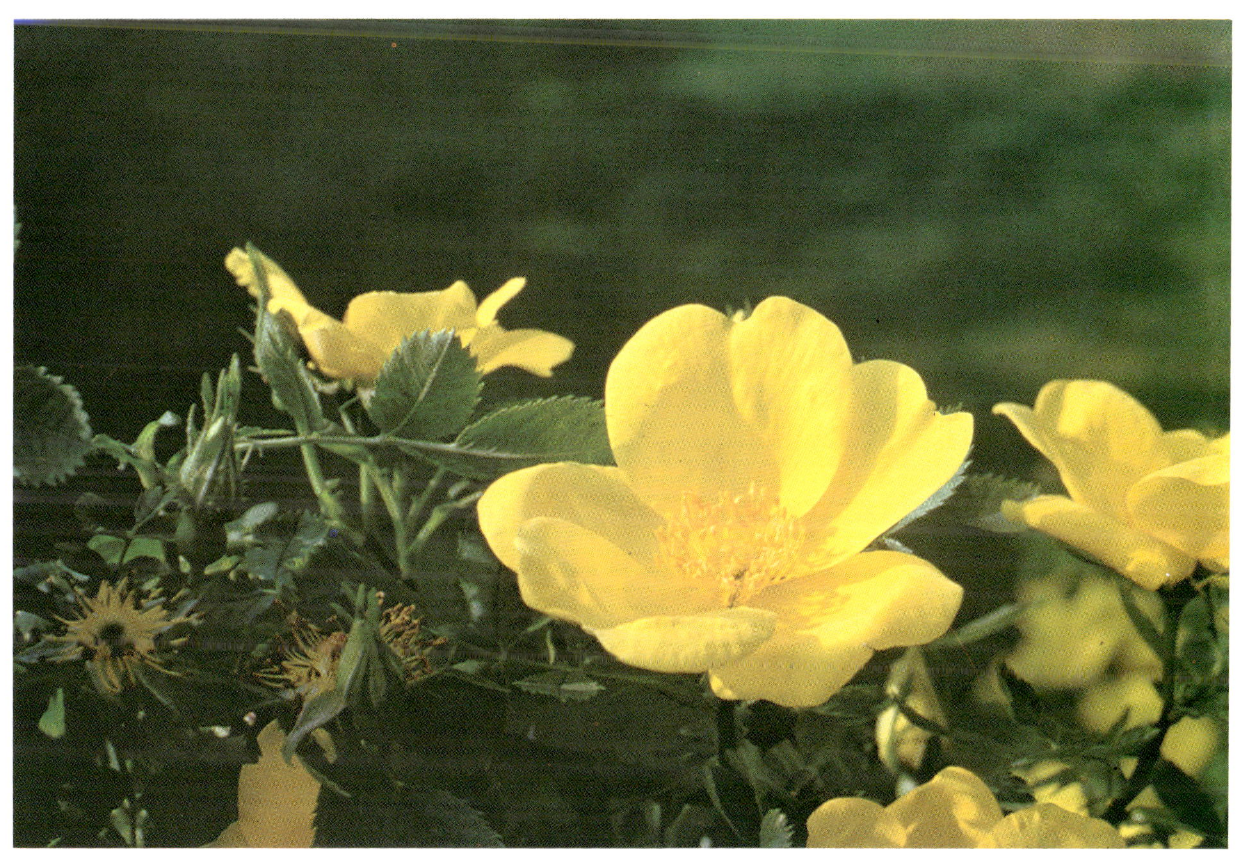

Rosa foetida HERRMANN

Table I Structures of Carotenoids from Rose Petals
(Conjugated Double Bonds in Bold Type)

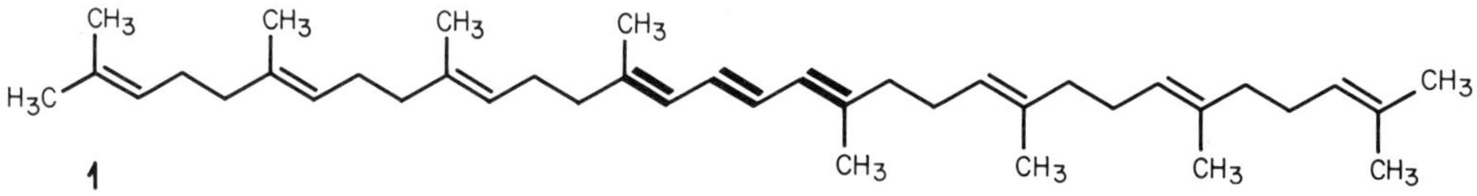

1

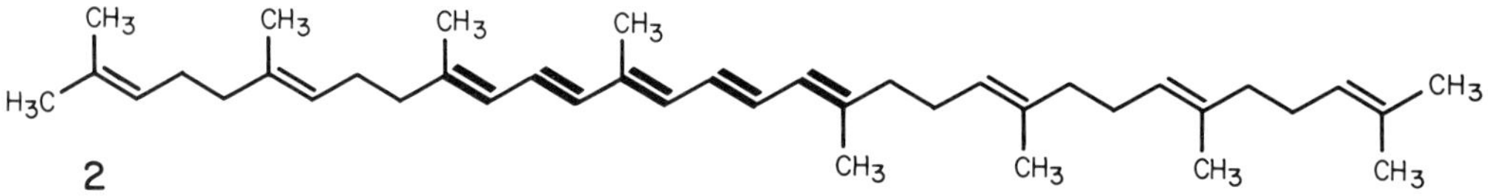

2

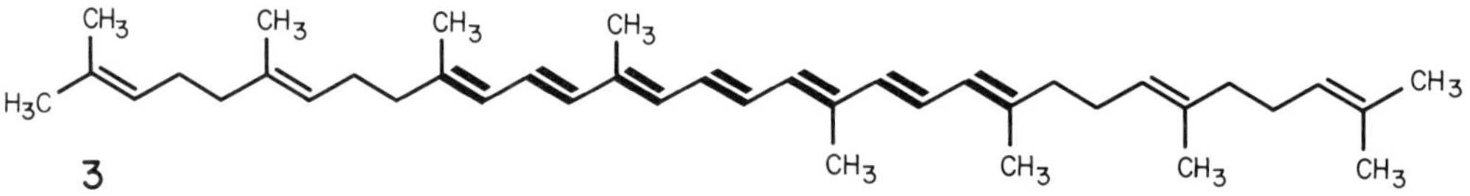

3

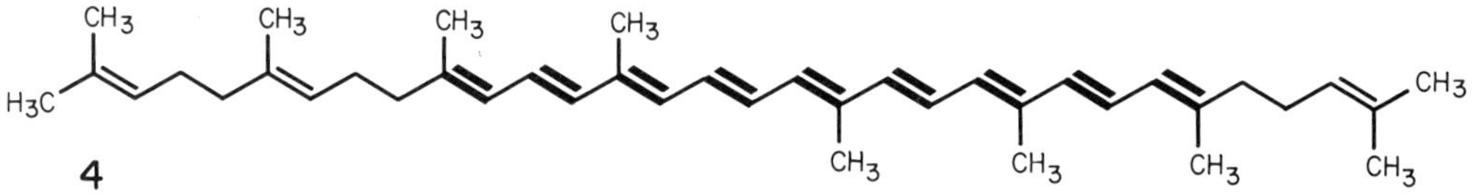

4

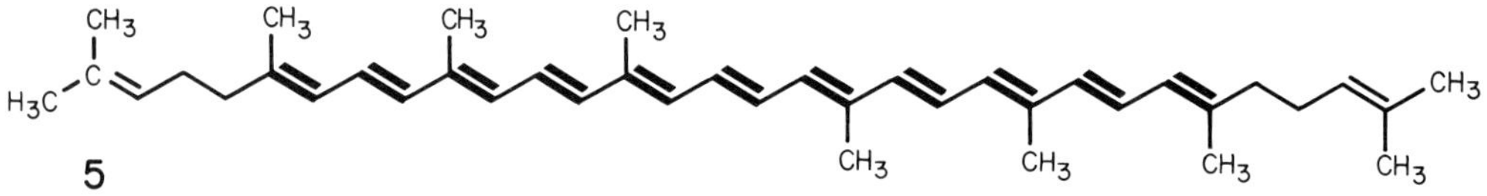

5

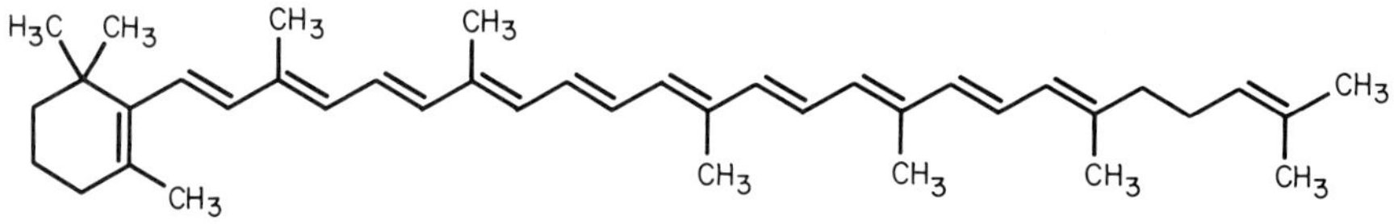

6

name	hue of a dilute solution	λ max.
Phytoene	colourless	300 nm
Phytofluene	colourless	367 nm
Zetacarotene	faint yellow	425 nm
Neurosporene	orange	467 nm
Lycopine	red	505 nm
Gammacarotene	red	492 nm

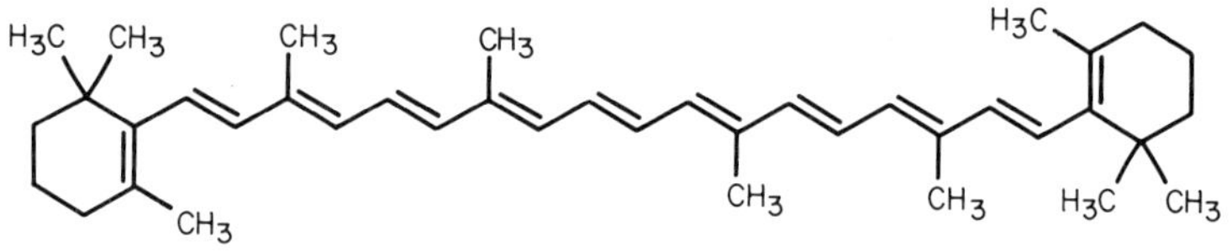

7

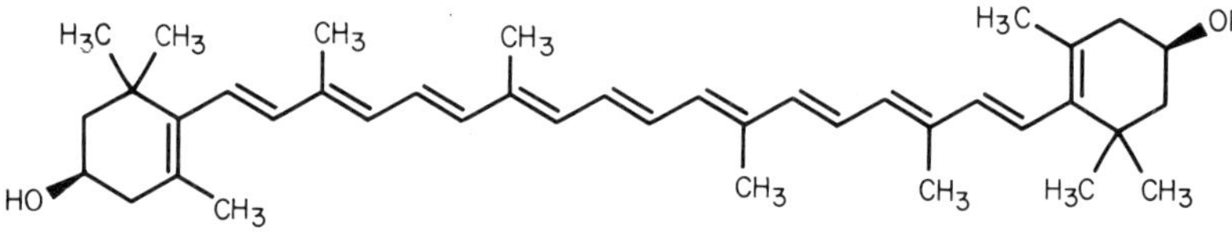

8

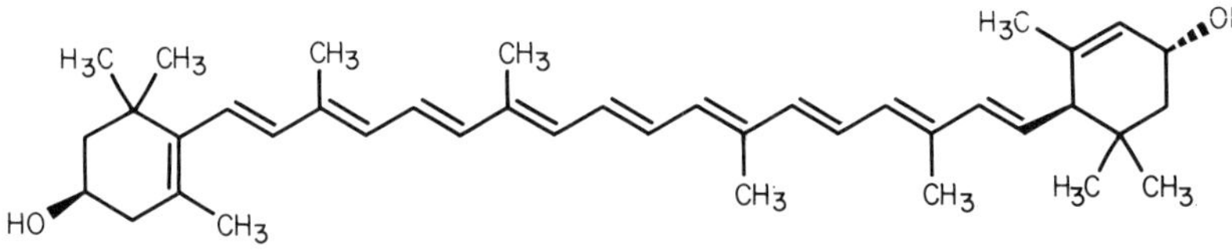

9

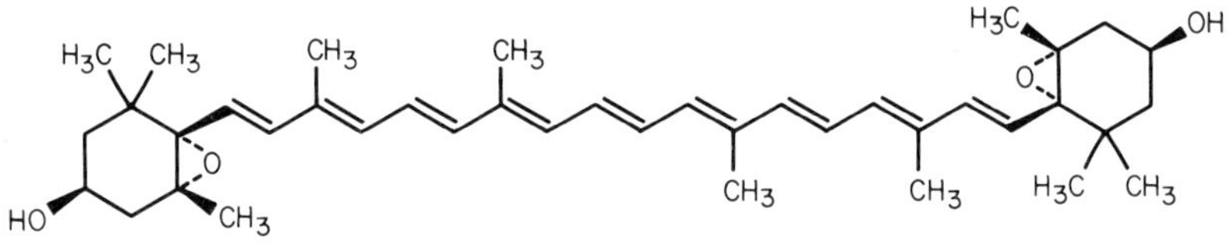

10

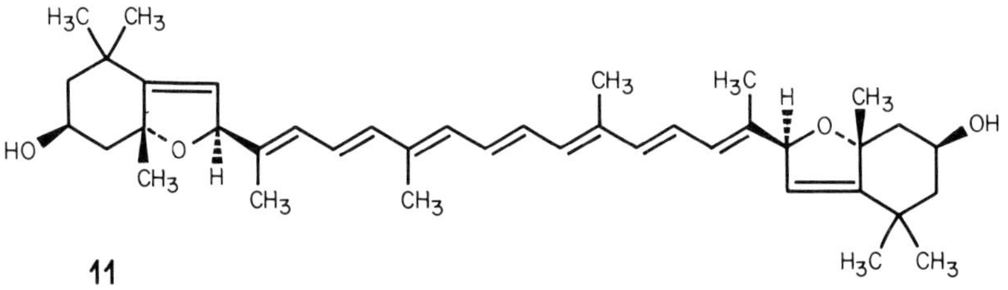

11

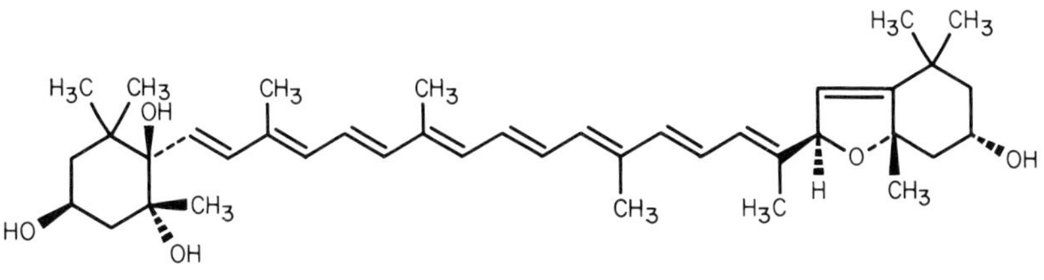

12

Betacarotene	orange	477 nm
Zeaxanthin	orange	476 nm
Lutein	orange	474 nm
Violaxanthin	orange	466 nm
Auroxanthin	bright yellow	425 nm
a new carotenoid from yellow roses	yellow	448 nm

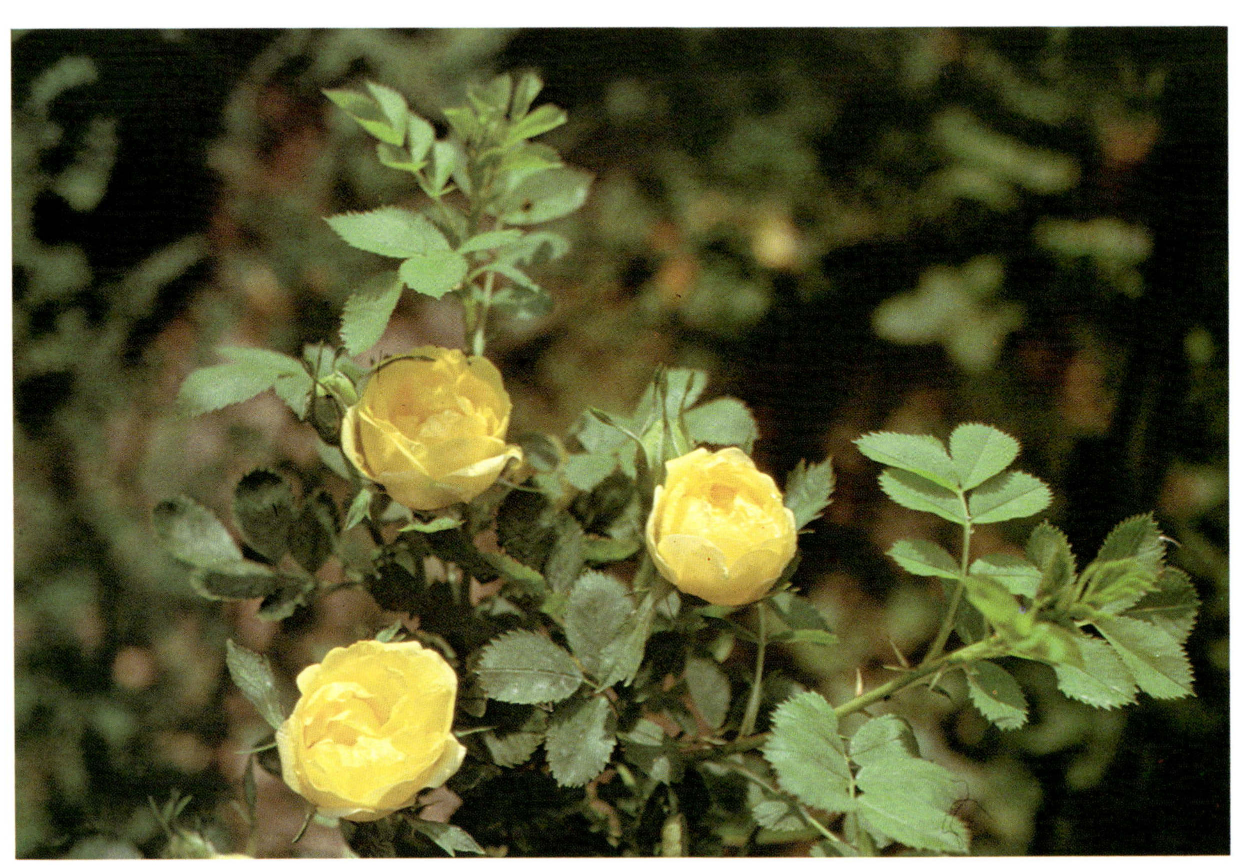

Rosa foetida persiana (LEMAIRE) REHDER

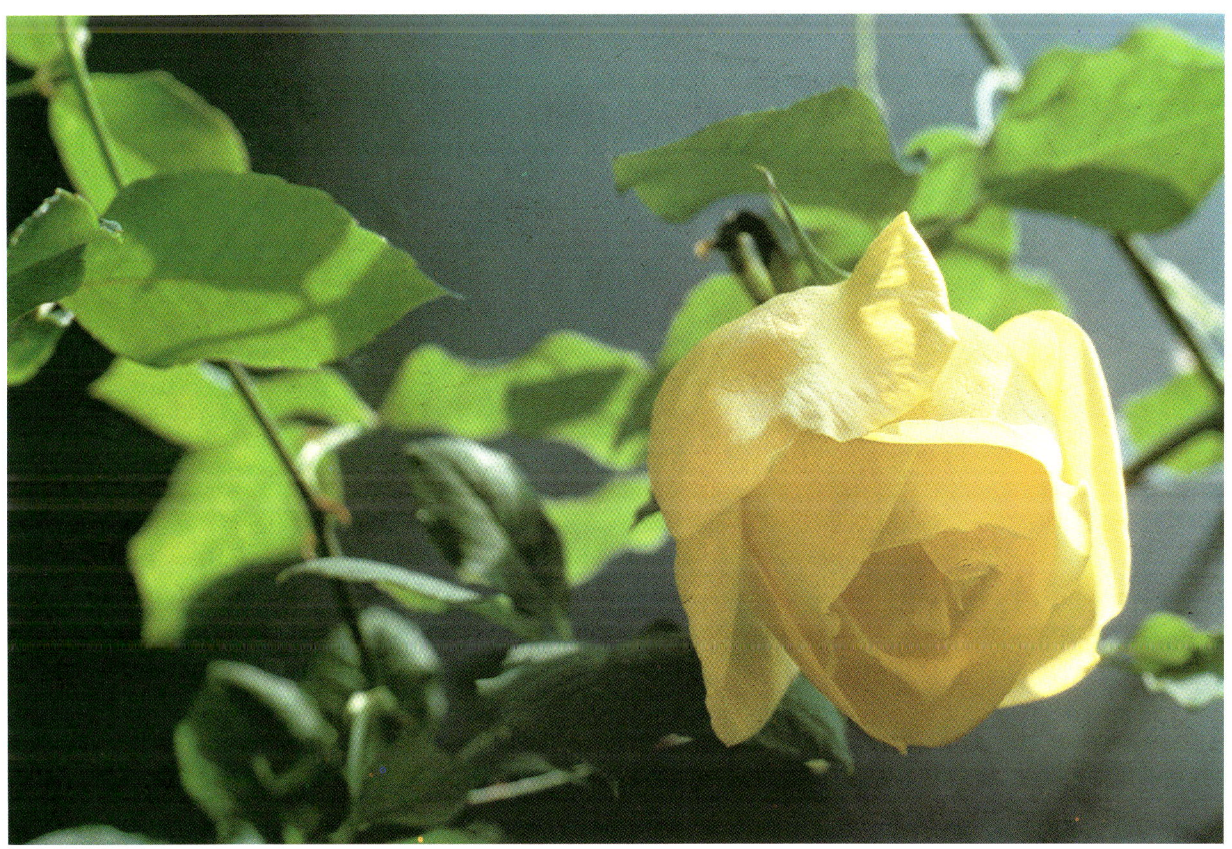

"Maréchal Niel"

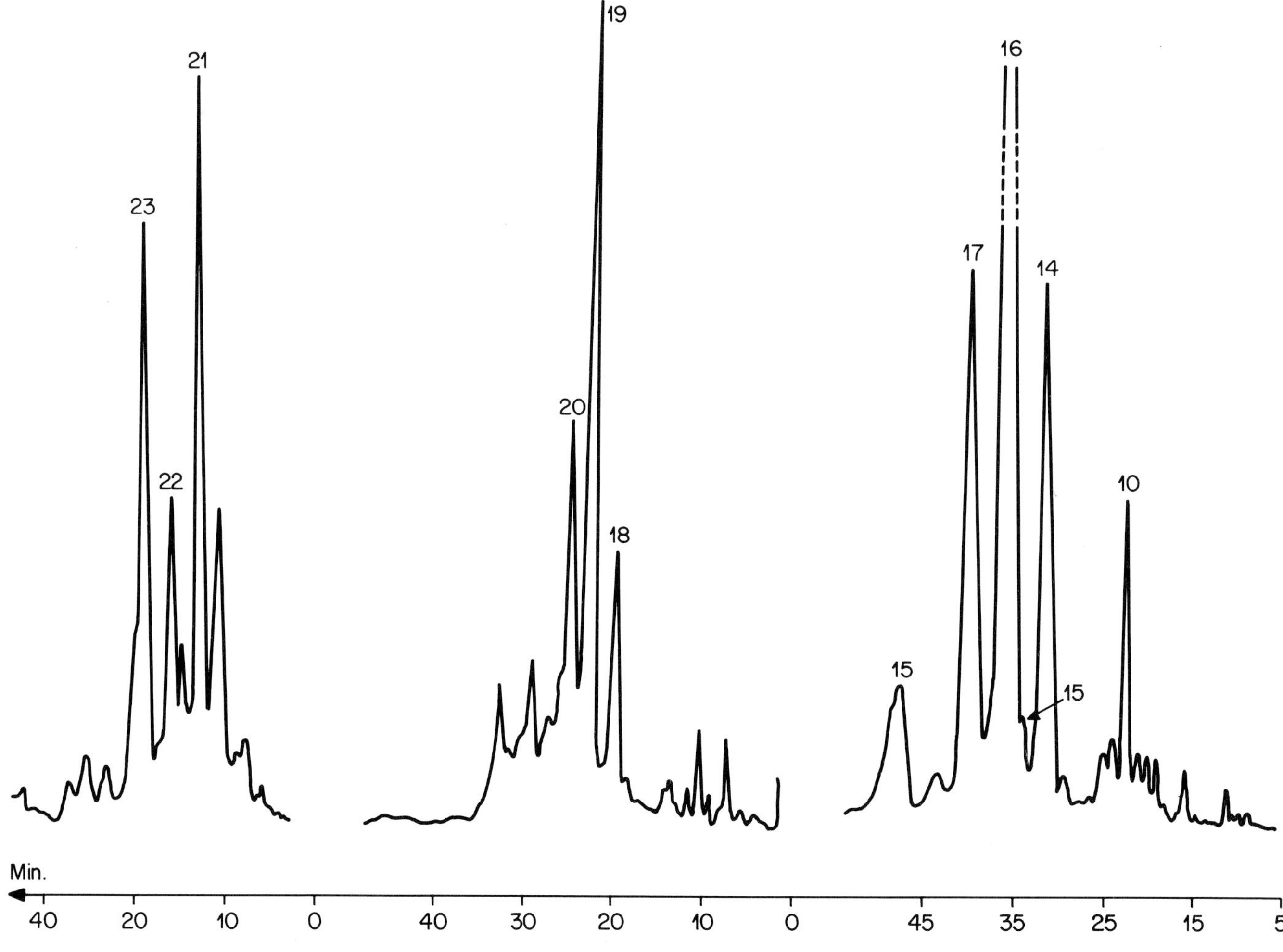

23
21
22
19
20
18
16
17
14
15
10
15
Min.
40 20 10 0   40 30 20 10 0   45 35 25 15 5

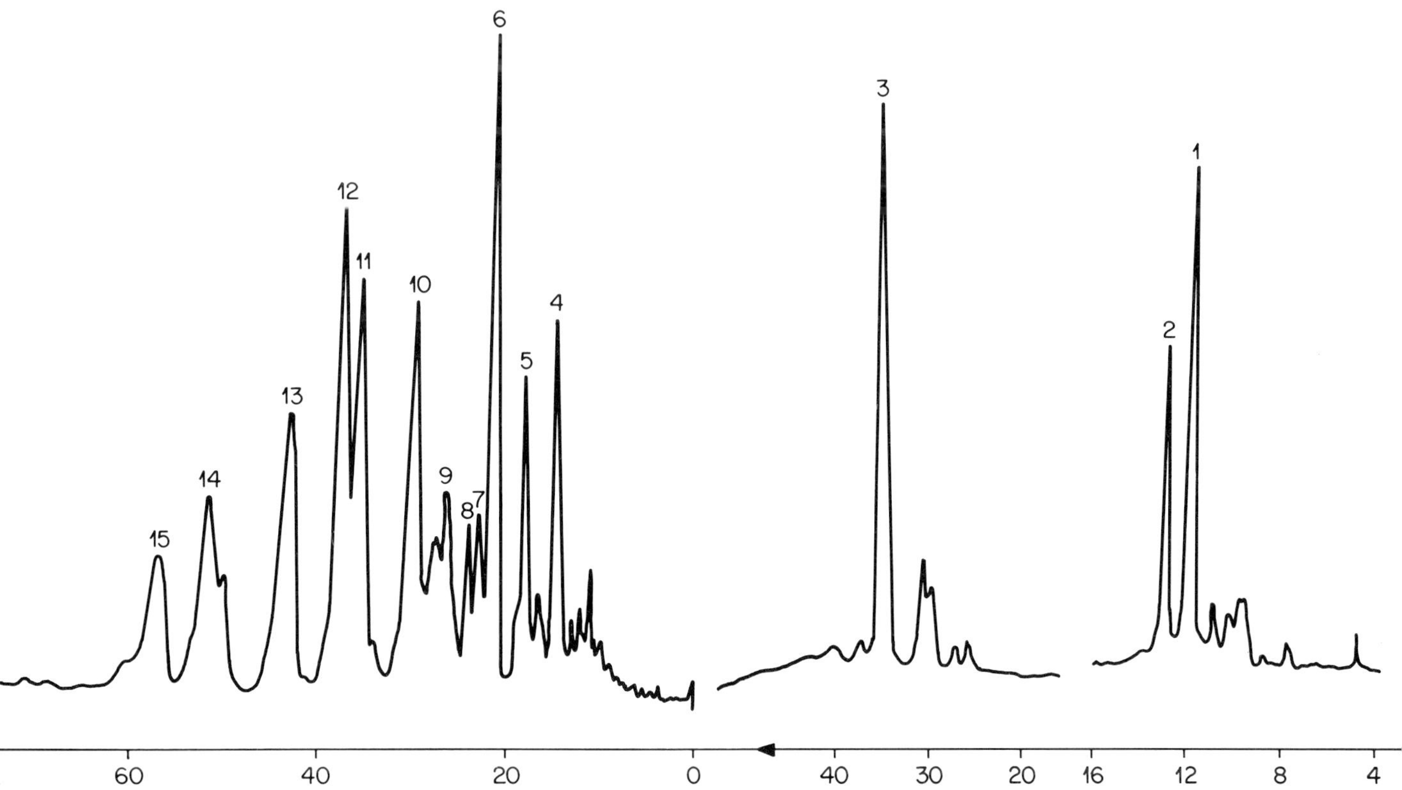

Text for Table II.

HPLC separation of the carotenoids from *R. foetida.* Pre-separation on Mg0 columns in six main zones, then six individual HPLC separations. Carotenoids of the types 1 and 2 are almost completely lacking. Nr. 3 belongs to type 3. All the other identified peaks are epoxides (type 5).

Identity:
1) 2) epimeric mutatochromes,
3)   β-cryptoxanthin,
4)   mixture,
5)   antheraxanthin,
6)   mutatoxanthins,
7) 8) unknown,
9)   (Z)-auroxanthin,
10)   mixture,
11)   (8*R*)-luteoxanthin,
12)   (8*S*)-luteoxanthin,
13)   (8*R*, 8'*S*)-auroxanthin,
14)   (8*S*, 8'*S*)-auroxanthin (shoulder) and (9'*Z*, 8*R*)-luteoxanthin,
15)   (8*R*, 8'*R*)-auroxanthin, 10) violaxanthin,
16)   (9*Z*)-violaxanthin,
17)   (9'*Z*, 8*S*)-luteoxanthin,
18)   (9*Z*, 8*R*, 8'*R*)-auroxanthin,
19)   neoxanthin,
20)   neochrome,
21)   (3*S*, 5*R*, 6*R*, 3'*S*, 5'*R*, 6'*S*)-5', 6'-epoxy-5, 6; 5' 6'-tetrahydro-β, β-carotene-3, 5, 6, 3'-tetraol,
22)   (3*S*, 5*R*, 6*R*, 3'*S*, 5'*R*, 8'*R*)-5', 8'-epoxy-5, 6; 5', 8'-tetrahydro-β, β-carotene-3, 5, 6, 3'-β, β-tetraol,
23)   (3*S*, 5*R*, 6*R*, 3'*S*, 5'*R*, 6'*S*, 9'*Z*)-5', 6'-epoxy-5, 6; 5' 6'- tetrahydro-β, β-carotene-3, 5, 6, 3'-tetraol).

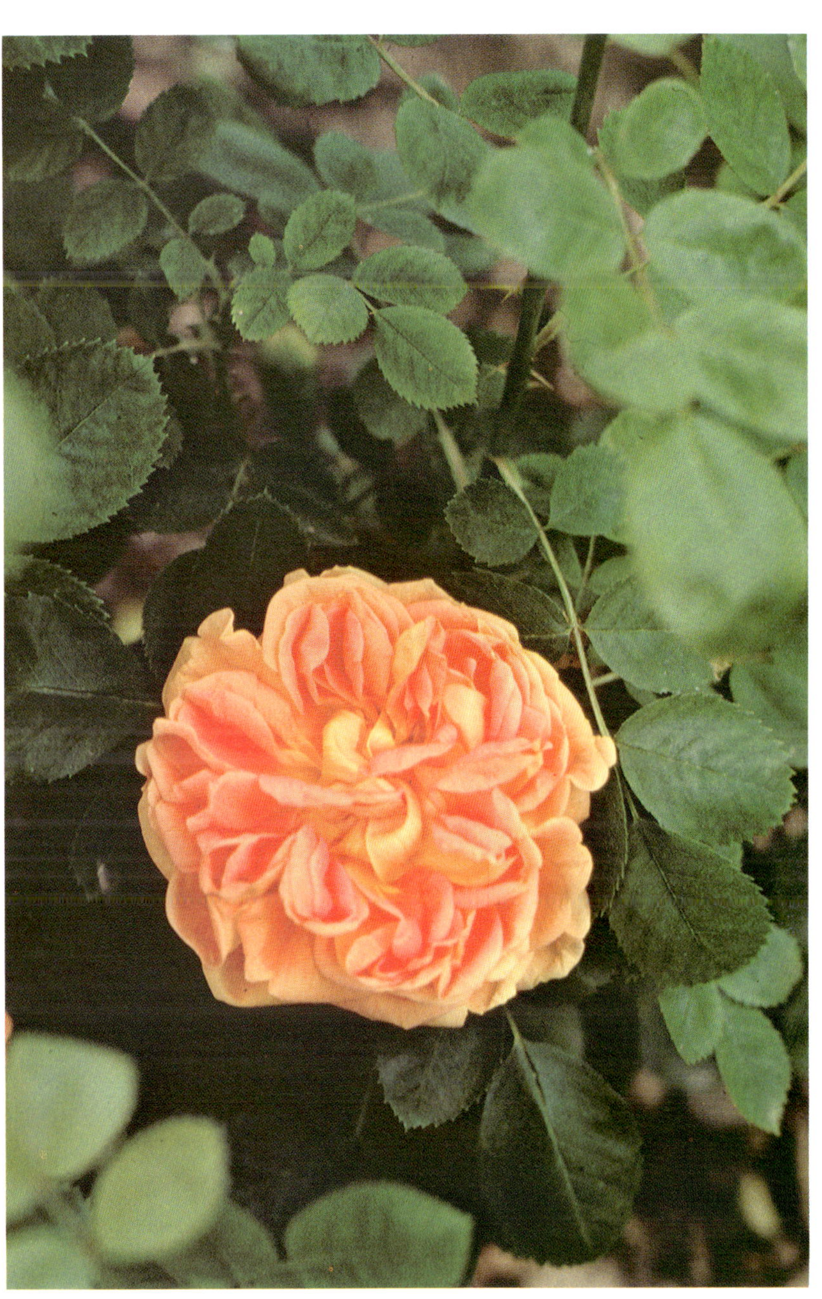

"Soleil d'Or"

Table III

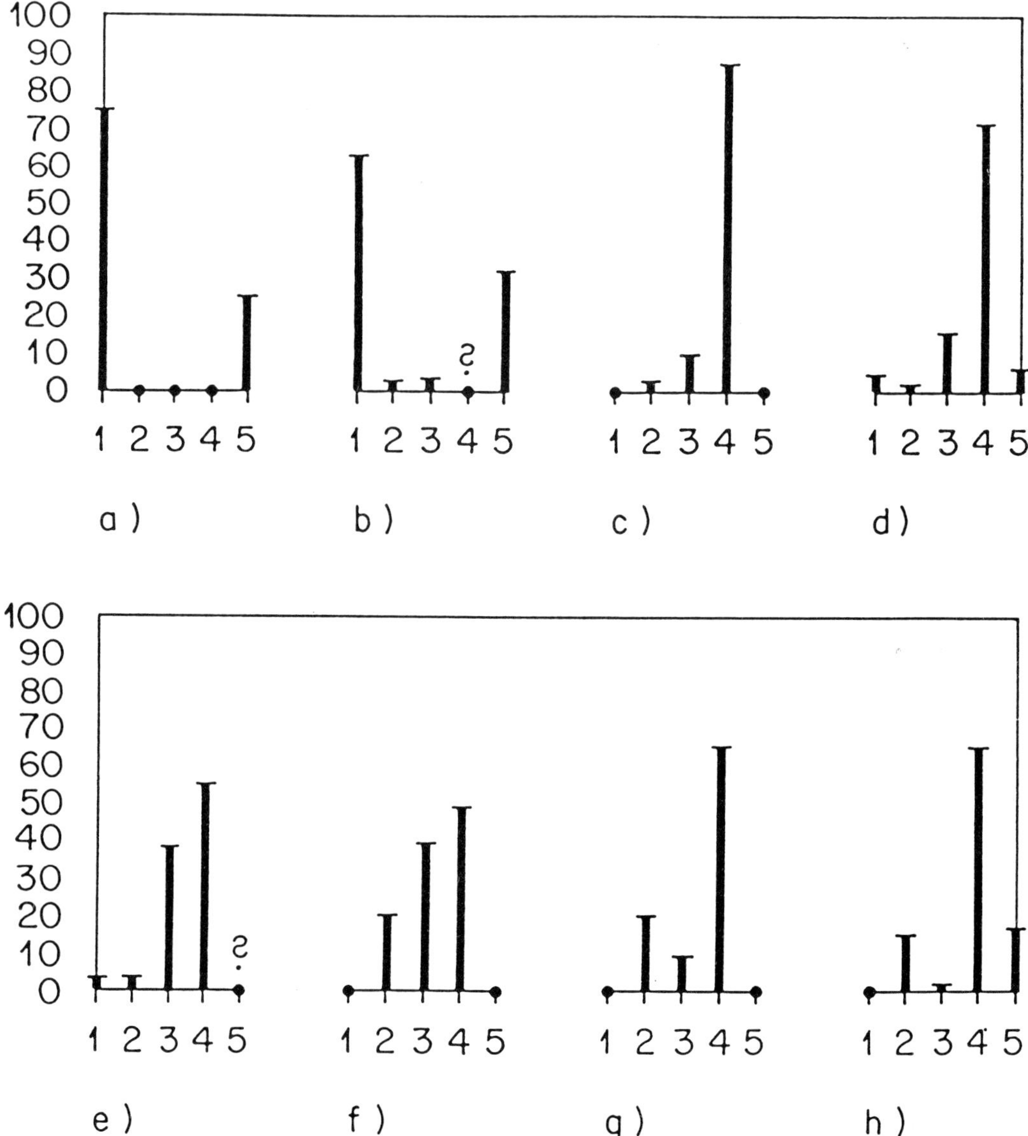

Text for Table III

Carotenoids in roses, divided into types 1 (non-cyclic hydrocarbons, 2 (cyclic hydrocar-bons), 3 (alcohols), 4 (epoxides), 5 (unknown)

a: "Maréchal Niel",
b: "Virgo",
c: *R. foetida*,
d: *R.* x *harisonii,*
e: "Gottfried Keller",
f: "Peace" ("Mme Meilland"),
g: "Allgold",
h: "Alexander"

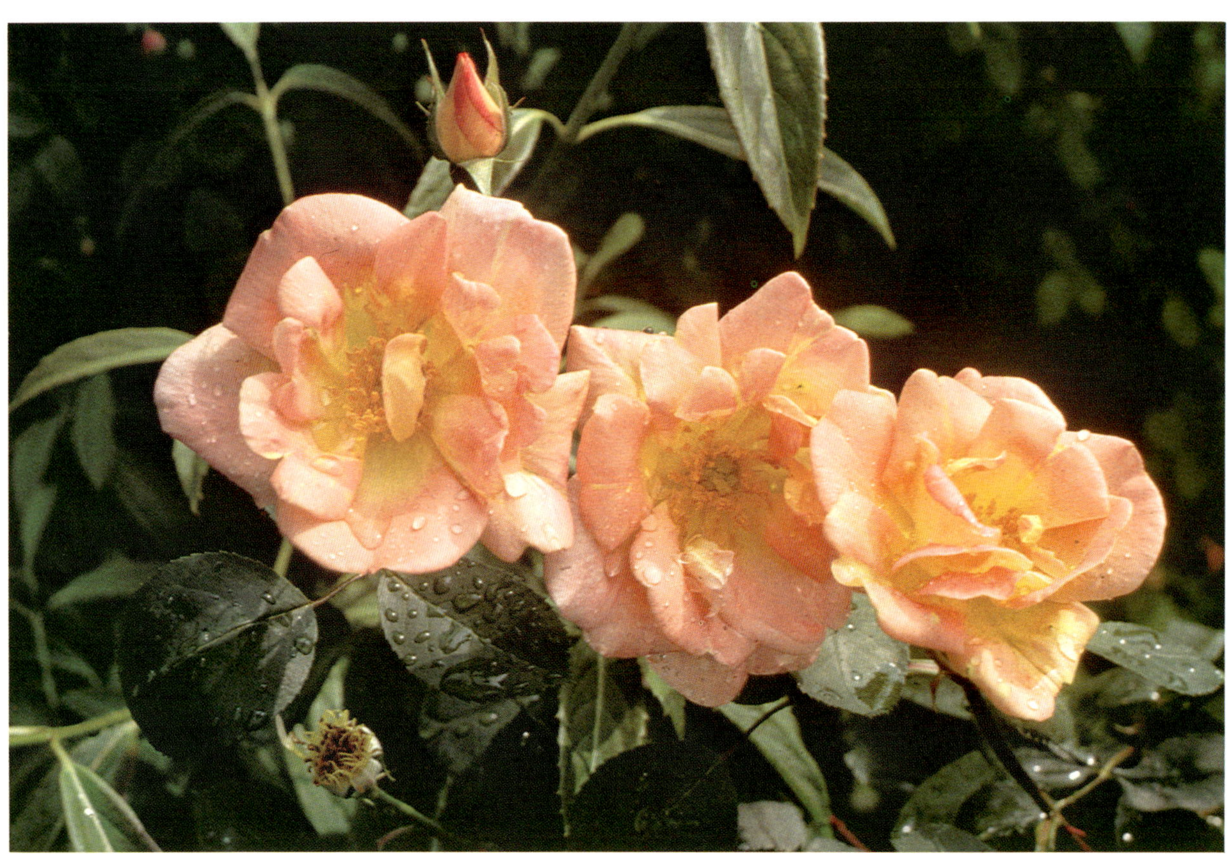

"Gottfried Keller"

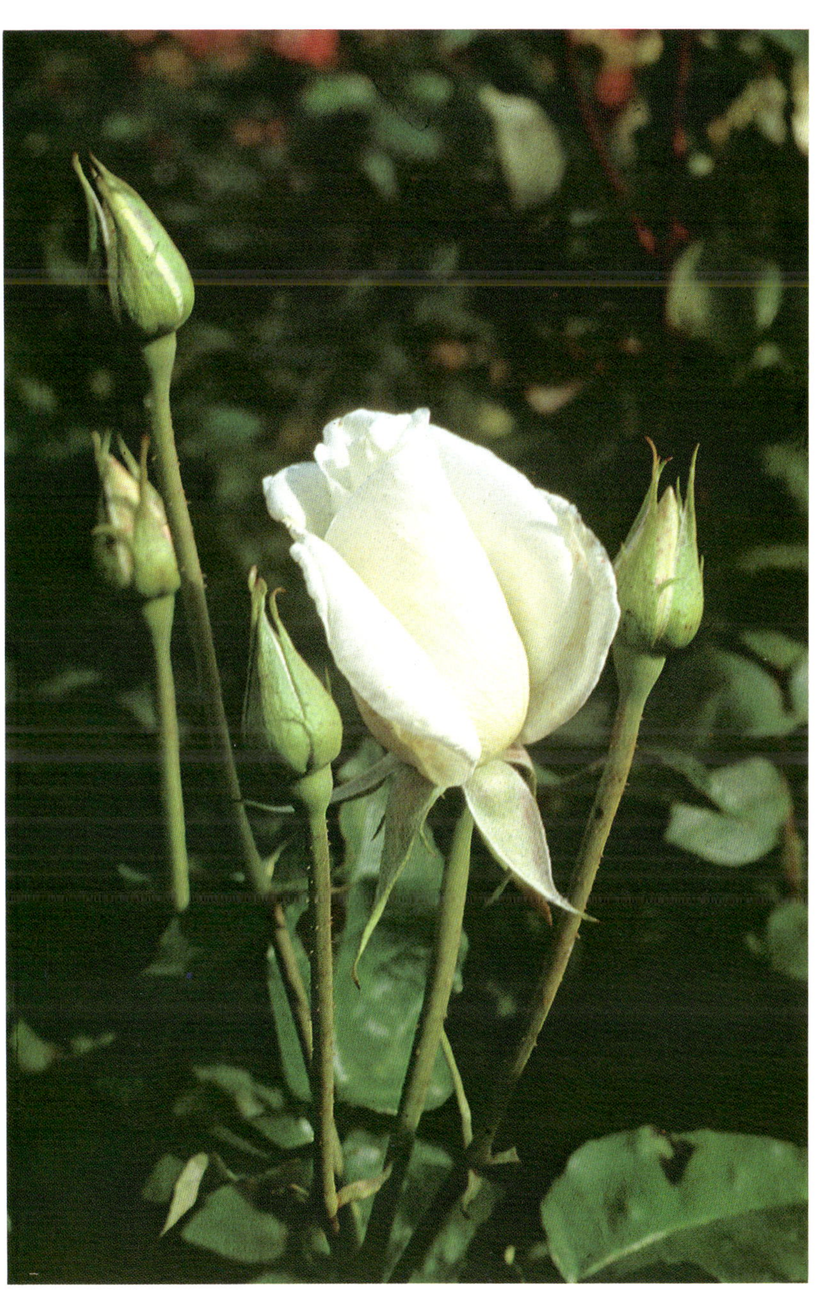

"Virgo"

REFERENCES

[1] E.E. Keays, "Old Roses", McMillan, N.Y. 1935.

[2] E.A. Bunyard, "Old Garden Roses", Country Life Ltd., London 1936.

[3] R.E. Shepherd, "History of the Rose", McMillan, N.Y. 1954.

[4] Ann P. Wylie, "Zur Geschichte der Gartenrosen", Endeavour (London) Vol. *14*, p. 181 (1955); *eadem*, "The History of Garden Roses", J. Royal hortic. Soc. Vol. *79*, p. 555 (1954), Vol. *80*, p. 8, p. 77 (1955).

[5] G.S. Thomas, "The Old Shrub Roses", J.M. Dent, London 1971; *idem,* "Shrub Roses of Today", Phoenix House, London 1962.

[6] G. Krüssmann, "Rosen, Rosen, Rosen", Paul Parey, Berlin 1974.

[7] J. Harkness, "Roses", J.M. Dent, London 1978.

[8] W. Paul, "The Rose Garden", 3rd. Edition, Kent, London 1872.

[9] B. Park, "The Yellow Roses", Rose Annual, p. 76–80 (1961).

[10] N. Young, "The complete Rosarian", Hodder & Stoughton, London 1971.

[11] E.B. Le Grice, "The Development of Modern Yellow Roses", Rose Annual, p. 106–113 (1972); *idem*, "Colour Development in Floribunda Roses", *ibid.* p. 66–69 (1975).

[12] J.B. Harborne & G. Rowley, Rose Annual, p. 47 (1959); *iidem,* Gardeners Chronicle, p. 427 (1958).

[13] L.R.G. Valadon & R.S. Mummery, Phyton (Buenos Aires) Vol. *25*, p. 151 (1968).

[14] R. Buchecker & C.H. Eugster, Helv. Chim. Acta Vol. *60*, p. 1754 (1977).

[15] K. Arisumi, Sci. Bull. Fac. agron. Kyushu Univ. Vol. *20*, p. 131 (1963), Vol. *21*, p. 169 (1964).

[16] M.C. Jain, T.R. Seshadri & R.K. Trikha, J. Sci. Indust. Res. (India) Vol. *30*, p. 77 (1971).

[17] M. Yokoi & N. Saitô, Phytochemistry Vol. *12*, p. 1783 (1973).

[18] D.P. de Vries, H.A. van Keulen & J.W. de Bruyn, Euphytica Vol. *23*, p. 447 (1974).

[19] R. Robinson, Endeavour Vol. *1*, p. 92 (1942).

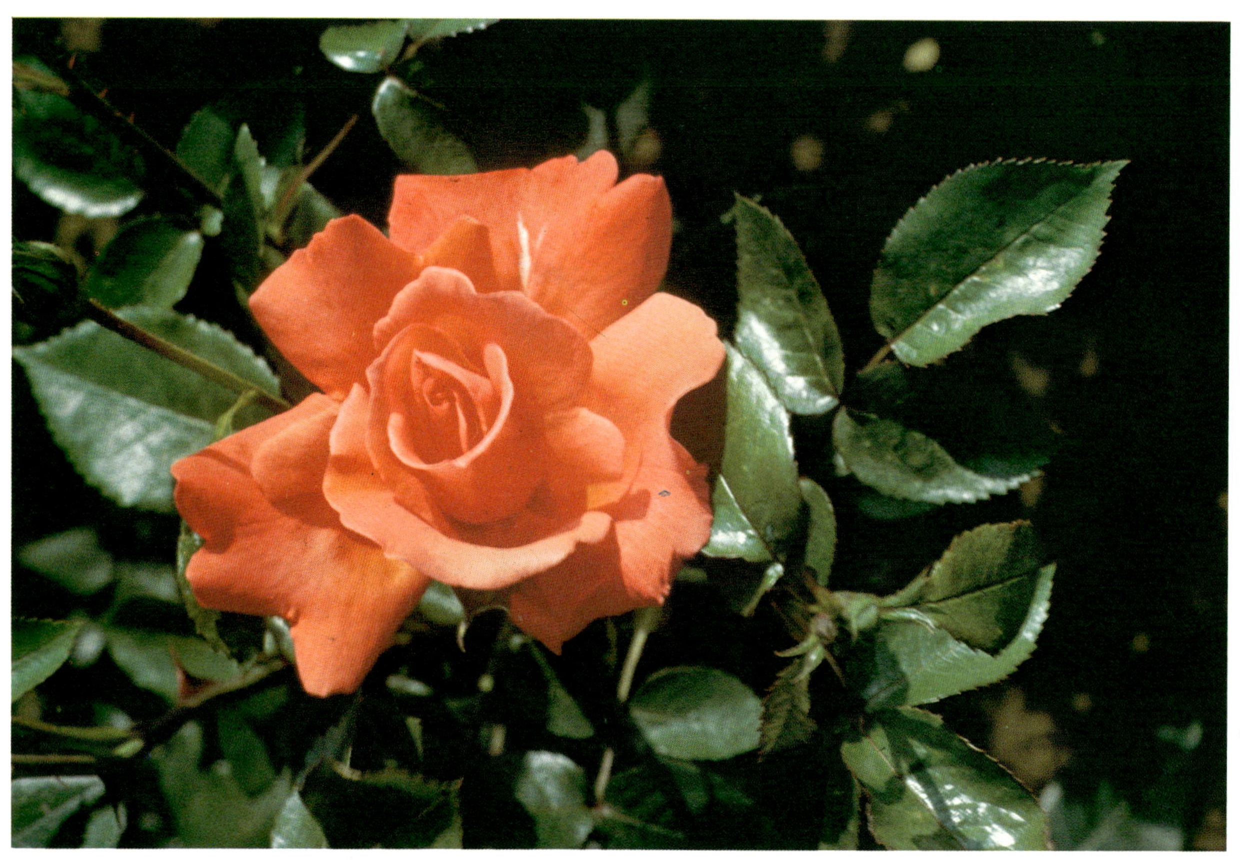

"Alexander"

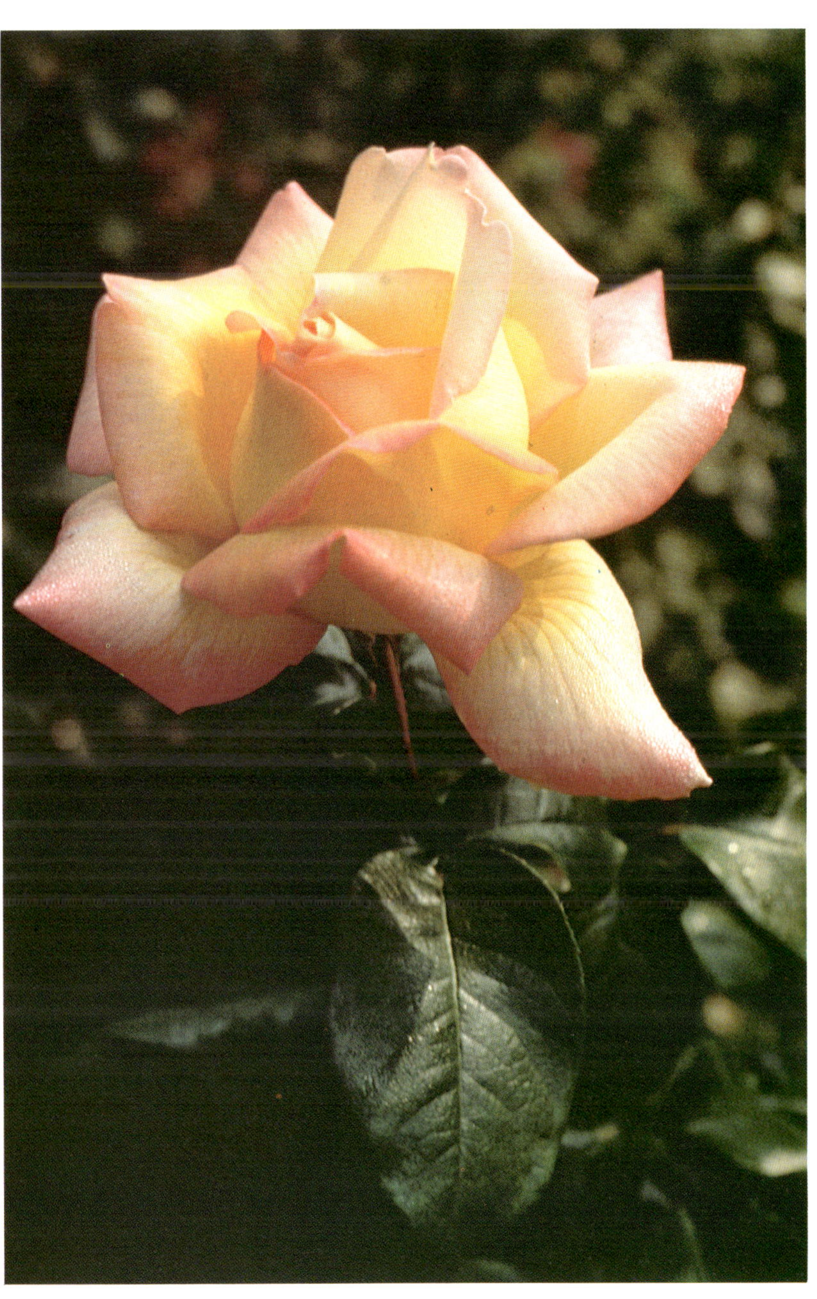

"Peace" ("Mme Meilland")

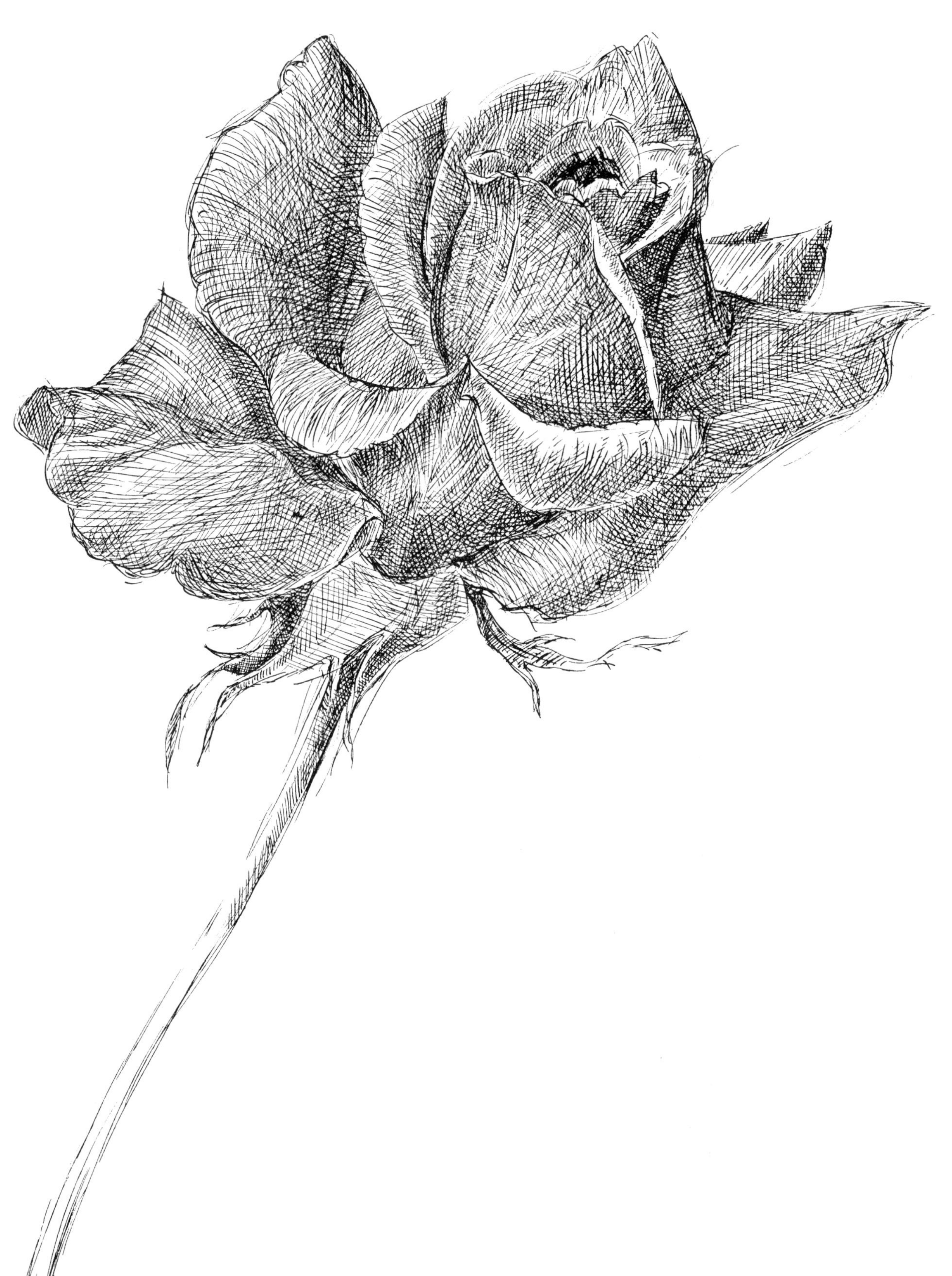

Granolitho®

The new printing technique.

Till a few years ago, collotype was considered to be the best half-tone printing process to produce reproductions of the highest quality. Nevertheless, the high cost and the limited number of copies possible, have nearly brought about the disappearence of this method; in the meantime, most firms specializing in collotype have closed down.
Only LICHTDRUCK LTD still continues with the collotype process. However, supplementary to collotype, they have developed an exclusive new half-tone printing technique qualitatively adopting the modern collotype process, but of more importance, also with outstanding additional advantages.
This new screenless printing technique, named GRANOLITHO®, is excellently suited, due to its trueness to colour and structure, to produce reproductions of the highest quality. The following comparison clearly shows the qualitative differences between the conventional multi-coloured printing process and the screenless GRANOLITHO®.

TRUE TO STRUCTURE
Conventional printing technique

Letter press, heliogravure, offset printing etc. are all characterized by a screen structure. Four dots next to each other form a screen circle whereby each dot is black, blue, red or yellow. This, together with the white background paper, results in a coloured impression. If two additional dots are added to the screen circle, a moiré effect is achieved.
The screen defines the position of each dot towards each other independently of the structure of the original.
The reproduction loses the character of the original to be copied.

GRANOLITHO®

The GRANOLITHO® print has a grained structure which follows each colour separation. Because the grains are not symmetrical, the number of colours which can be printed is almost unlimited, without resulting in an irritating moiré pattern. The GRANOLITHO® print also gives a much finer decomposition of the picture, which thereby results in a more true reproduction.

In addition, the colour impression is not the result of the screen dots on the white background paper, but through the combined activity of each separate colour, exactly the same as the original.
The original characteristics of the picture are retained.

TRUE TO COLOUR
Conventional printing process

The reproduction of colour values is limited to the 4–6 colours predefined in the screen circle. Certain corrections to emphasize a colour in separate areas of the picture are possible, but cannot achieve all colour shades.
This is particularly the case with hot and cold colours when next to each other.

GRANOLITHO®
As a result of the dense tonal value (fine grain) and the independence from a defined screen circle, an almost true to colour copy of the original is possible.
Each original to be copied is divided according to an individual colour chart into colour separations. During this procedure, the hot and the cold colour shades contained in the original are considered separately.
Since there is no danger of producing a moiré effect, eight or more different colours may be used without further thought.
Therefore, even the slightest variation in a colour shade is obtainable. And, only then, does a facsimile or an art print reach its true value.
This process has been successful not only with facsimile copies of the historical "Gutenberg's Bible", "The chronicle of the crusaders of Jerusalem", the German "Haggadah Shel Pessah" of 1462, but for prints of famous contemporary art works by Beuys, Chagall, Christo, Dalì, Picasso, etc.

US Patent Number 4374913

Comparison: Screen and Granolitho® (sections from supplement, both enlarged fivefold).

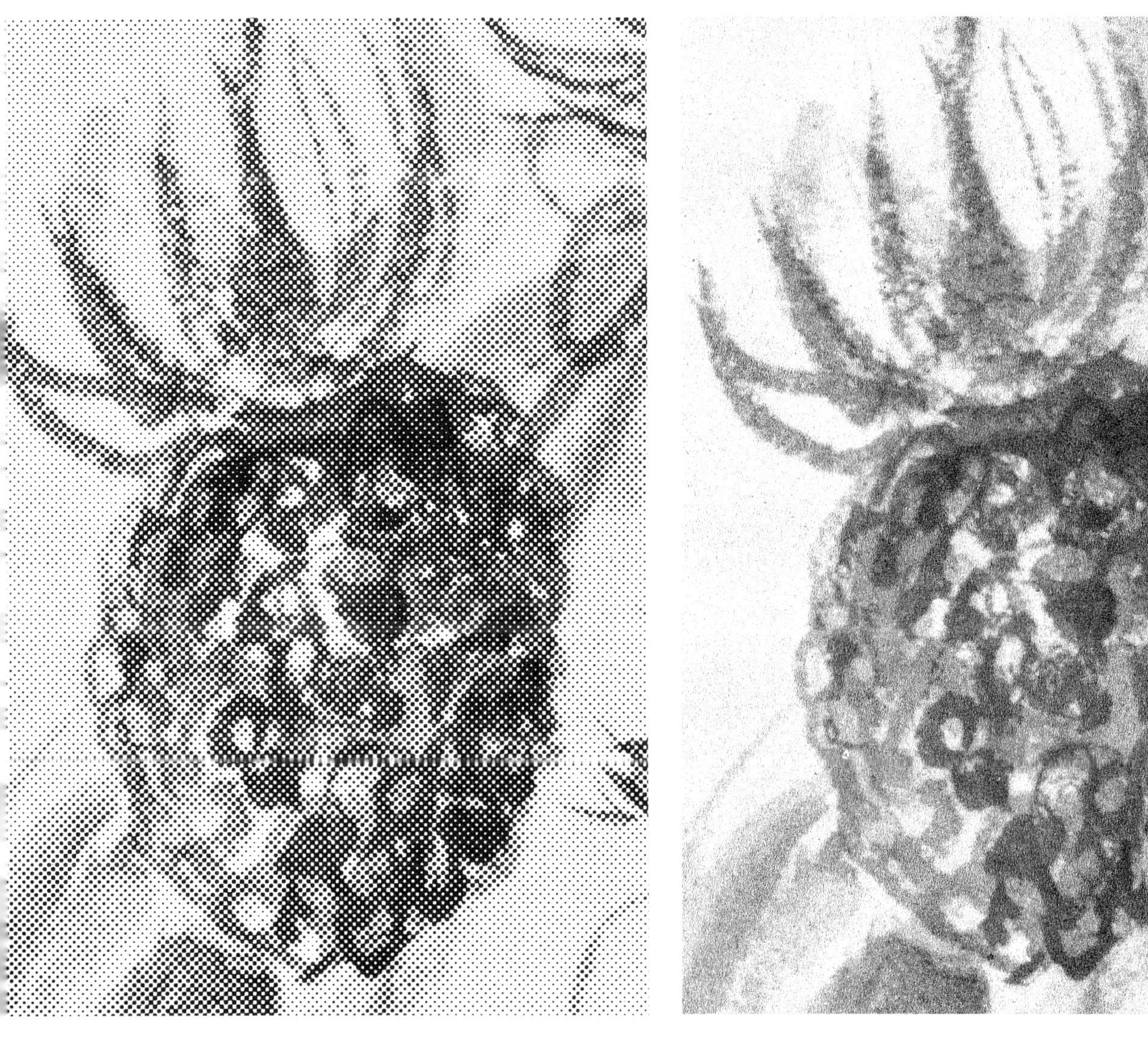

Screen   Granolitho®

Supplement:
Granolitho® on handmade paper in back sleeve.

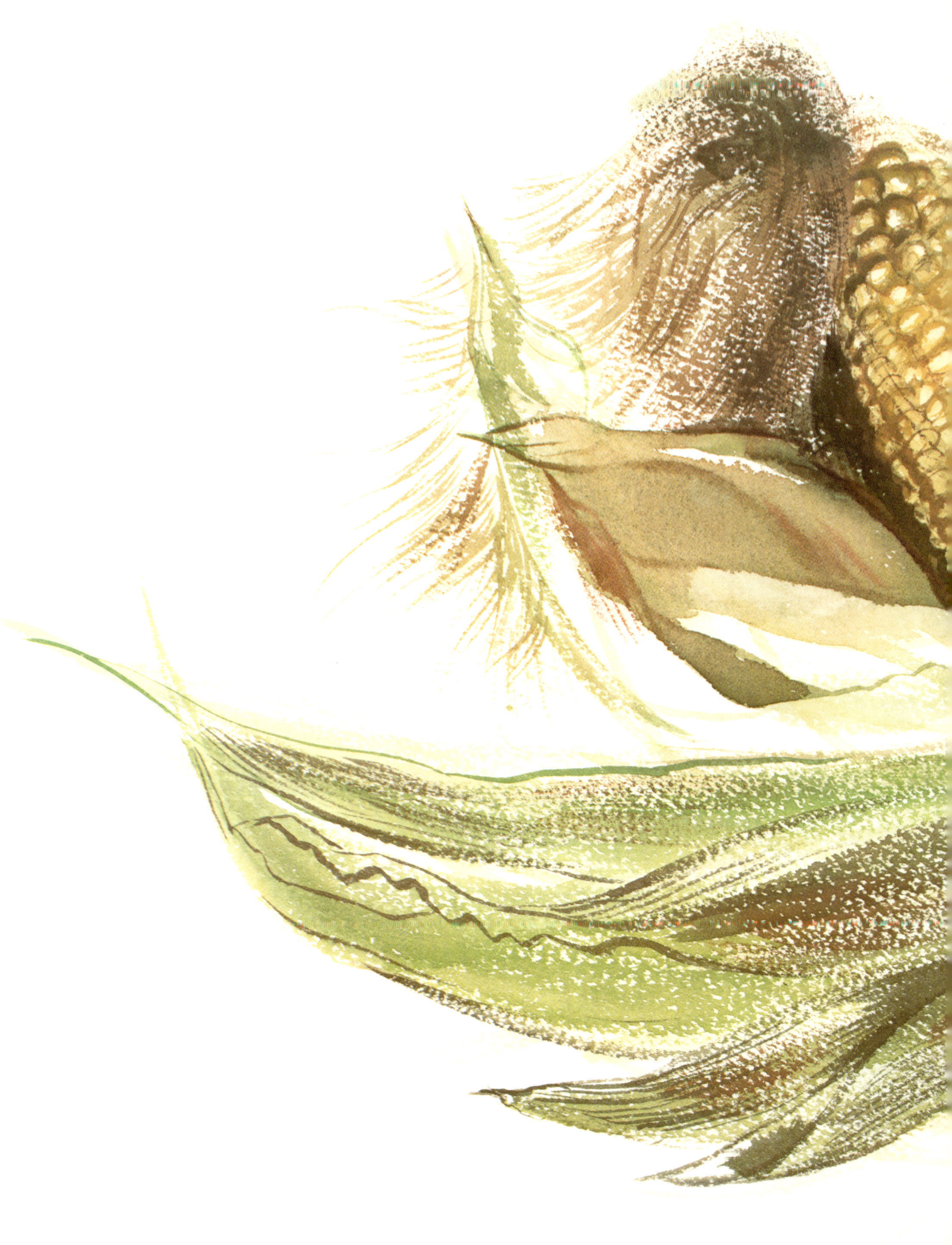

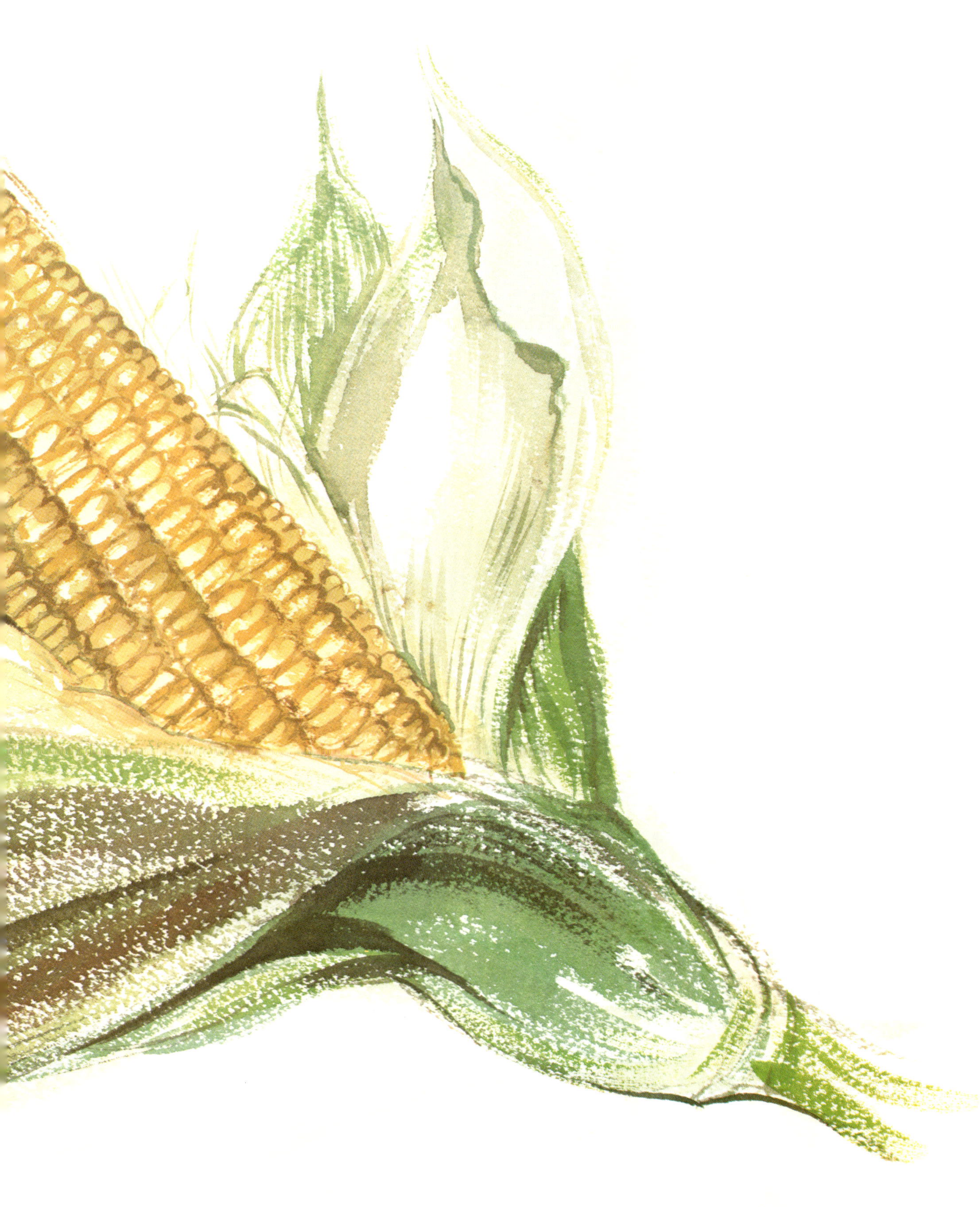

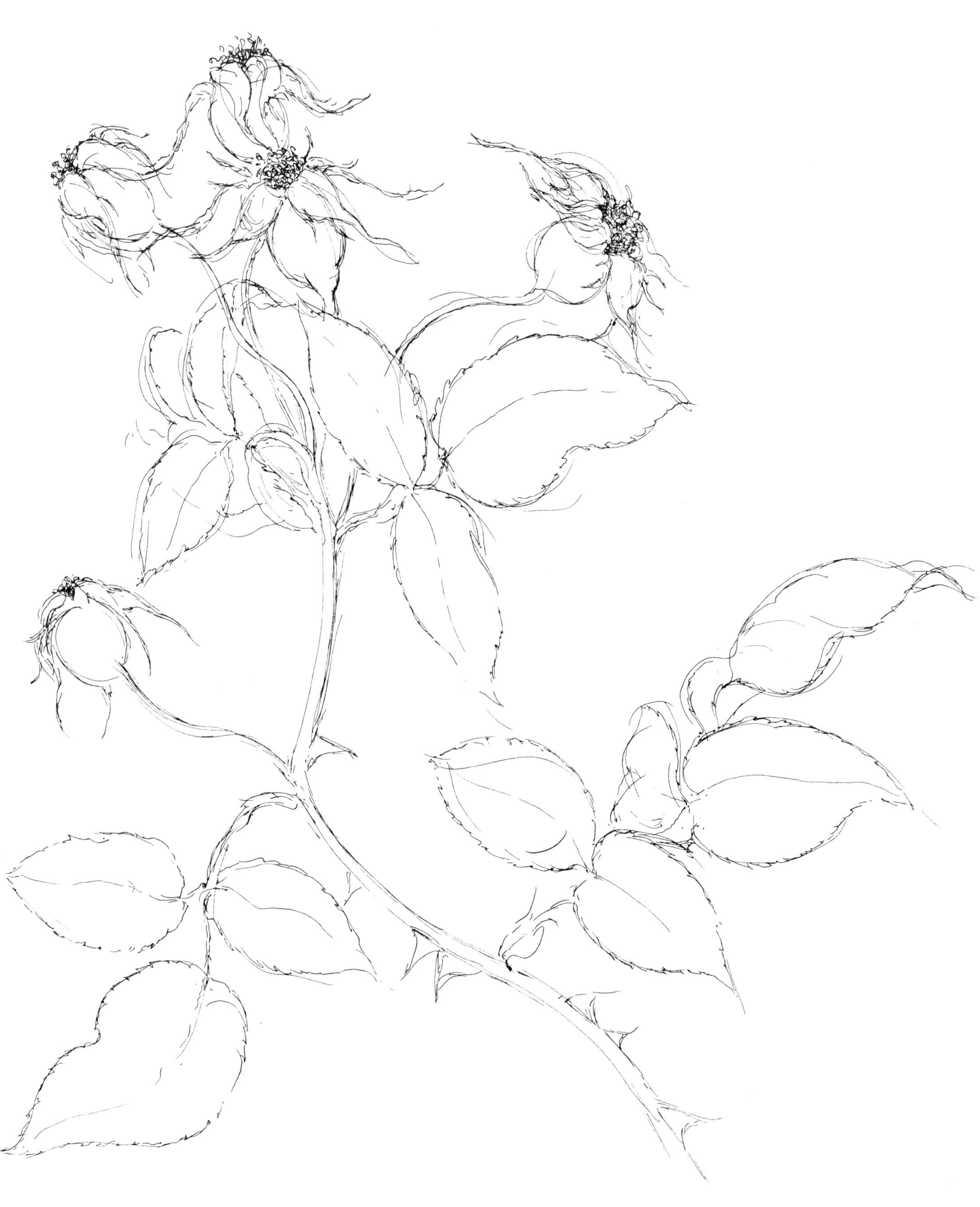

Bibliography

Year

1942   "100 Years of Zürich's Agricultural Kanton Society".
       Illustrations by Lotte Günthart. Brugg, Schweizerisches Bauernsekretariat.
1947   "50 Years Swiss Farmers Society"
       Illustrations by Lotte Günthart. Brugg, Schweizerisches Bauernsekretariat.
1954   Small pocket diary with 12 pictures of roses with fairies. Zürich, Gebr. Fretz Ltd.
1955   Large calendar with 12 roses, Heidelberg, Popp.
1959   Full-time collaboration as illustrator with The Swiss Rose Society, of whom she is
       Vice-President.
1959–
1977   Rose calendar of DR. R. MAAG LTD Dielsdorf
1961   "A McCall's Portfolio of Great American Roses".
       10 water colours by Lotte Günthart. New York, McCall's Magazine (May edition)
1962   "Rose oh reiner Widerspruch." Illustrations by Lotte Günthart.
       Text by Prof. Gottfried Boesch. The rose in prose by Rainer Maria Rilke.
       The Swiss Rose Society.
1962   "Vom Ruhm der Rose". Forty large size rose pictures by Lotte Günthart.
       Text by Prof. Gottfried Boesch. Introduction by Richard Katz.
       Zürich, Albert Müller
1964   "La Nobilità della Rosa". Illustrations by Lotte Günthart.
       Text by Prof. Gottfried Boesch. Introduction by Conte Carlo Gola, President
       of the Società Orticoladi Lombardi. Gozzano/Milan, Bemberg, s. p. a., and Milan,
       Editore Goerlich.
1965   "The Glory of the Rose". Illustrations by Lotte Günthart.
       Text by Prof. Gottfried Boesch. Introduction by James Laver.
       London, George G. Harrap & Co.
1965   "Die Rose des Strassburger Münsters". Illustrations by Lotte Günthart.
       Text by Prof. Gottfried Boesch. The Swiss Rose Society.
1966   "Romance of the Rose". Illustrations by Lotte Günthart.
       Text by Richard Harrity. New York, This Week Magazine.

1966   "Noblesse de la Rose". Monographies des roses par Armand Souzy, président de la
        société française des roses. Préface par Louise de Vilmorin.
        Généalogie des roses par Robert Kohli. Paris, Flamarion

1966–   "Rosenbogen", Various illustrations by Lotte Günthart.
1976   (The magazine of The German Rose Society.)
        Edited by K. H. Hanisch ("Mein schöner Garten"). Germany, Burda

1967   Gold and silver medals issued by the Rose Town of Rapperswil under the direction
        of Town Councillor Mr Hans Rathgeb.
        Designed by Lotte Günthart. Sold by Swiss banks.

1967   "La Femme, le poète et la rose". Illustrations by Lotte Günthart.
        Poems chosen by Hubert Gravereaux. (Limited facsimile edition of 200 copies.)
        Lausanne and Paris, Payot

1968   "Roze". Illustrations by Lotte Günthart.
        Tekst i podpisy pod rysunkami Prof. G. Boesch. Introduction "Roza w Polske"
        by Izabella Kilianska. Translated by Mgr Barbara Zolkowska.
        Warsaw, Panstwowe Wydawnictwo Rolnicze i Lesne

1968   "A l'heure de l'amour et des roses". Illustrations by Lotte Günthart.
        Poems chosen by Hubert Gravereaux. Lausanne and Paris, Payot.

1968   "Alte Rosen und Gedichte". Illustrations by Lotte Günthart. The Swiss Rose Society.

1969   "Tulpenglück" – a fairy tale. Illustrations by Lotte Günthart. Text by Dino Larese.
        Amriswil, Amriswiler Bücherei (1970).

1970   "Water colours and drawings".
        Catalogue for an exhibition at the Cargnegie-Mellon University.
        Pittsburgh, The Hunt Institute for Botanical Documentation.

1971   "Gedanken über dies und jenes".
        78 pen and ink drawings by Lotte Günthart. Text by Anita. Basle, Birkhäuser.

1971   Quellenbüchlein "Springs of Hope". Illustrations by Lotte Günthart.
        New York, Herder.

1975   "Bel appetit". Water colours by Lotte Günthart. Text by Anita. Regensberg, Rosula.

1975   "Was Bärbel auf der Chilbi erlebte".
        Hand coloured drawings by Lotte Günthart. Text by Onkel Karl.
        Regensberg, Rosula.

1976 "Springs of Hope". Illustrations by Lotte Günthart.
(An exquisite and valuable bibliophile, bound in silk.) St. Gallen, Leobuchhandlung.

1976 "Vergiss mich nicht". Illustrations by Lotte Günthart.
(Everlasting calendar and book of memories.) St. Gallen, Leobuchhandlung.

1977 Rose calendar of SWISSAIR, Zürich.

1977 "US Virgin Islands National Park, St. John, 1976". Sketches by Lotte Günthart.
Fascimile edition. Zürich, Foundation Lotte and Willi Günthart-Maag.

1979 "Rose d'amour". Description of a garden in New Zealand.
Text and illustrations by Lotte Günthart. Regensberg, Rosula.

1981 "Meine Tiere". Text and illustrations by Lotte Günthart.
(28 stories experienced personally by the authoress about animals)
Regensberg, Rosula.

1981 "The History of the Rose in the Holy Land Throughout the Ages". Illustrations
by Lotte Günthart. Text by Asaph Goor. Jerusalem, Massada and Am Hassefer.

1982 "The Paradise Island". Text and illustrations by Lotte Günthart.
Zürich, Foundation Lotte and Willi Günthart-Maag.

One Person Exhibitions

Year

1941	Zürich, Neupert Gallery
1943	Zürich, Orell Füssli Gallery
1962	Basle, Musarion Gallery
1962	Zürich, Congress House
1963	Lucerne, Court Gallery
1963	Zweibrücken, Oskar Scheerer, President of The German Rose Society
1964	Los Angeles, Fernando Valley Gallery
1964	Milan, Palazzo Serbelloni
1965	London, Foyle's Art Gallery
1966	Paris, Bernheim-Jeune Gallery
1967	Schaffhausen
1967	Lucerne, Castle Heidegg
1967	Lucerne, Annual Meeting of The Swiss Rose Society
1967	Rapperswil, Castle and Hotel Swan
1967	Karlsruhe, German State Garden Show
1968	Kreuzlingen, Swiss Eastern Division of The Rose Society
1968	Amriswil, Bahnhofstrasse 19 Gallery
1969	Saverne, Valentin Ruch, (France)
1969	Paris, av. de Villar 4, Hubert Gravereaux
1970	Pittsburgh, "Lebenswerk" (Retrospective), The Hunt Institute for Botanical Documentation, Carnegie-Mellon University
1971	Hamilton, New Zealand, 1st World Congress of The Rose Societies
1972	Baden-Baden, Casino
1979	Isle of Mainau, Castle Mainau
1979	Bonn, German State Garden Show "Haus am Rhein"
1979	Kilchberg and Lugano
1981	Lucerne, Castle Heidegg

Group Exhibitions

Year

1941	Lucerne, Museum of Art
1942	Zürich, Museum of Art
1943	Basle, Museum of Art
1967	Geneva, Museum of Art and History
1968	Gent, La Baronne de Gerlache de Gomery, President of The Belgian Rose Society
1971	Zürich, Swiss Federal Institute of Technology (dry-points)
1972	Castle Lüdingshausen, Germany
1974	Kyoto, Japan, Annual Meeting of The Japanese Rose Society Mr Kameoko (President)
1976	Pittsburgh, Carnegie Music Hall, New York, Hotel Waldorf Astoria, Detroit, General Motors Company, (Presentation of large coloured etching), Bicentennial of America
1976	Oxford, 3rd World Congress of The Rose Societies
1980	Basel, "Grun 80"
1981	Jerusalem, 5th World Congress of The Rose Societies
1983	Baden-Baden, Germany, "Rose Romantic", 6th World Congress of the Rose Societies
1983	Zürich, Stadthaus

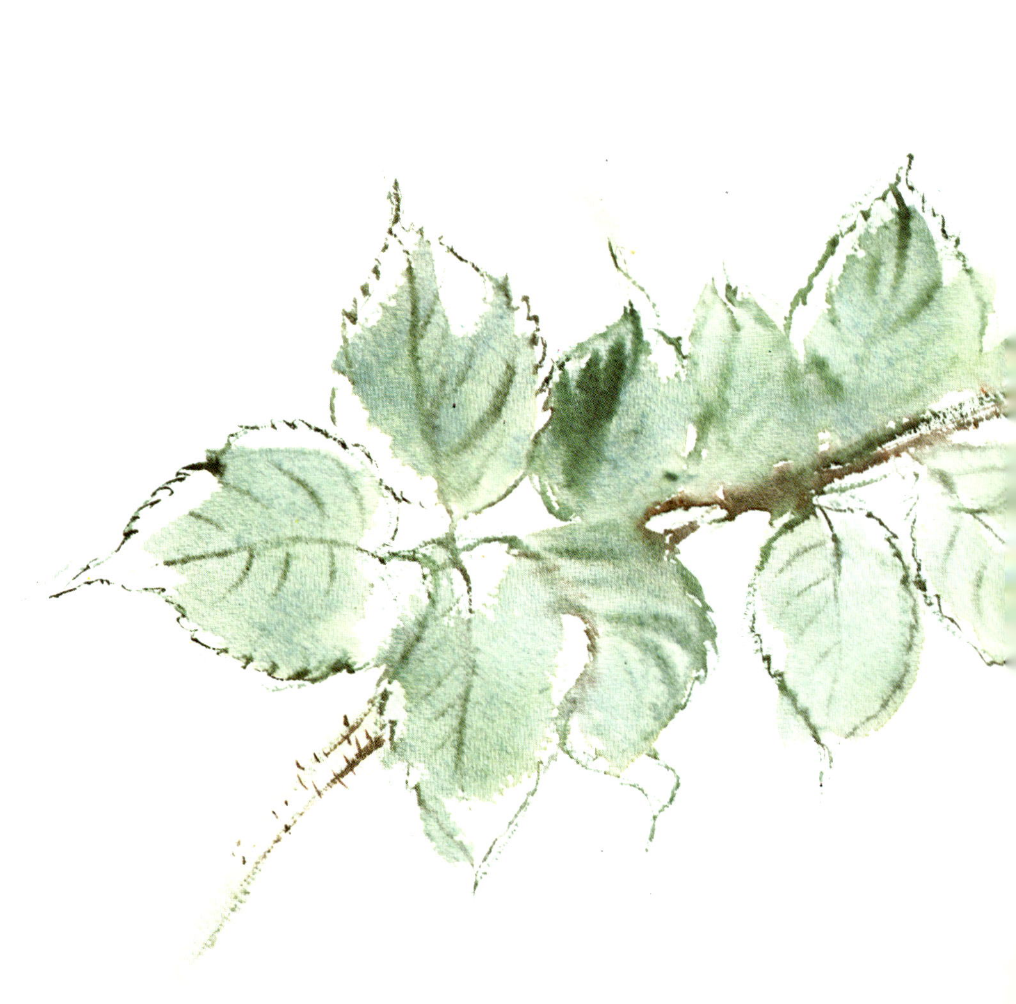

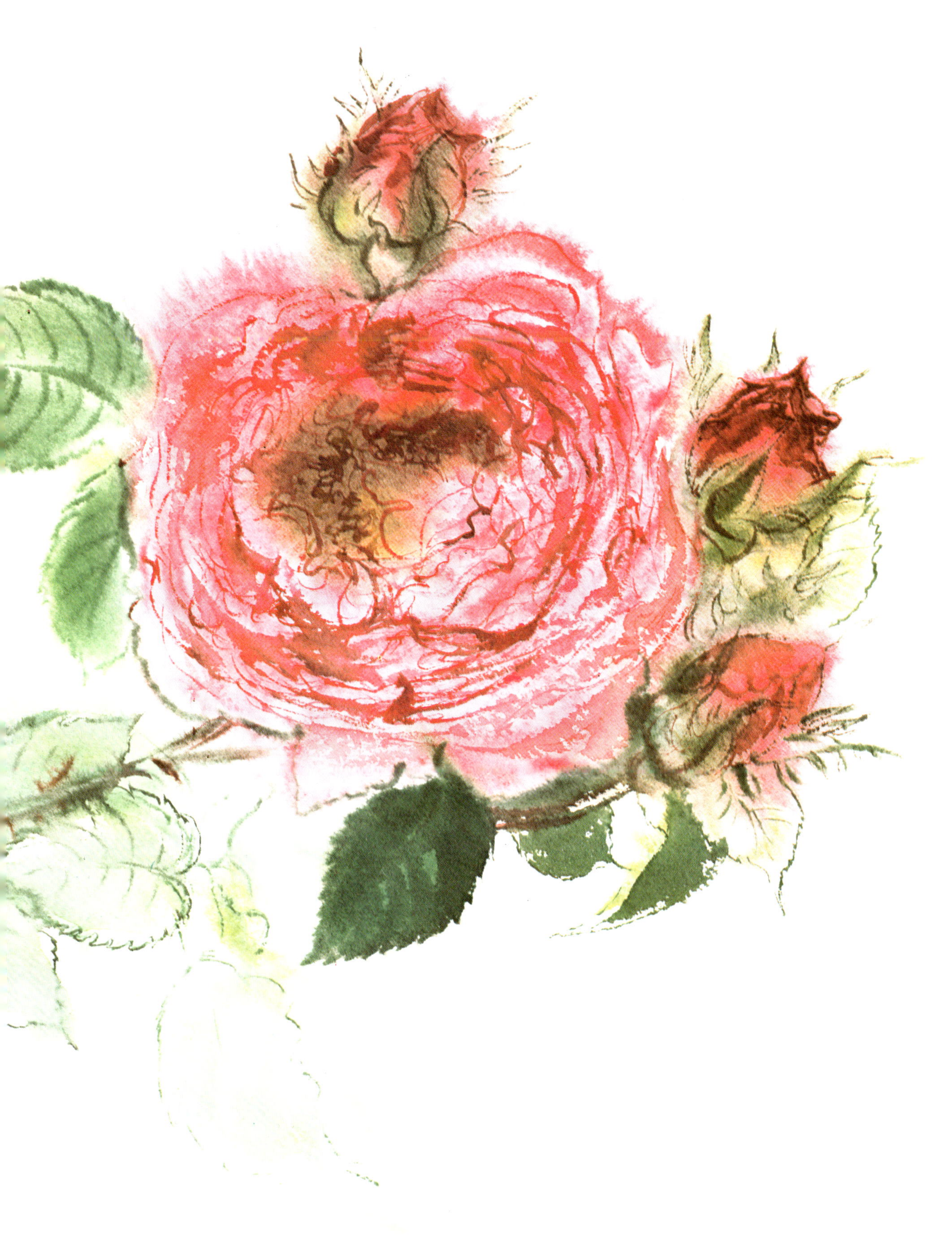

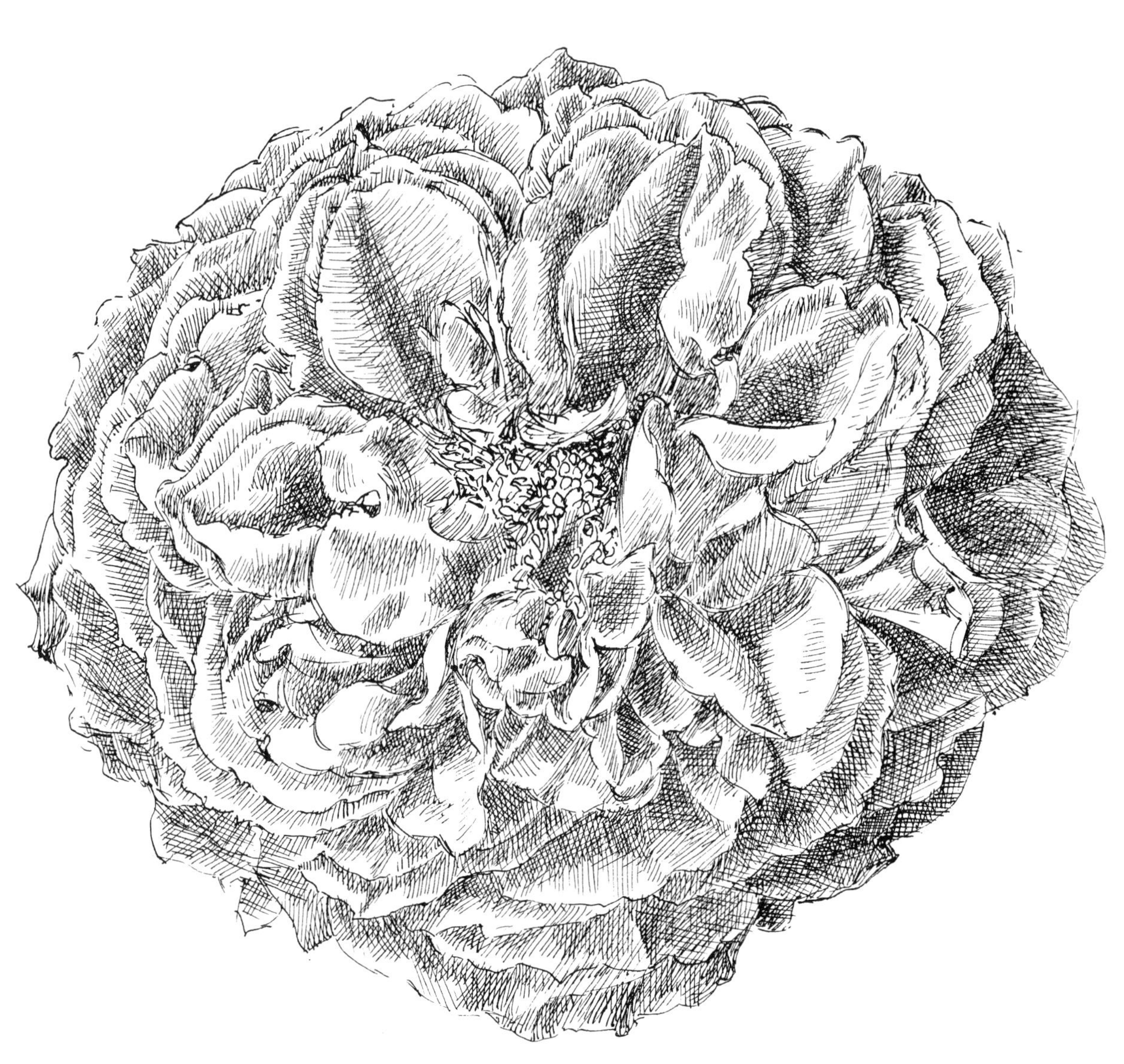

Awards

1940   onwards: active member of the Gesellschaft Schweiz. Malerinnen, Bildhauerinnen
       und Kunstgewerblerinnen
1967   Golden Rose of The German Rose Society
1968   Golden Rose of The Swiss Rose Society
1980   Gold medal from The World Federation of Rose Societies
1984   Honorary member of The German Rose Society and The Swiss Rose Society

Media

Water colour, dry-point, tempera, pastel, pen and ink, pencil, oil, brush and ink

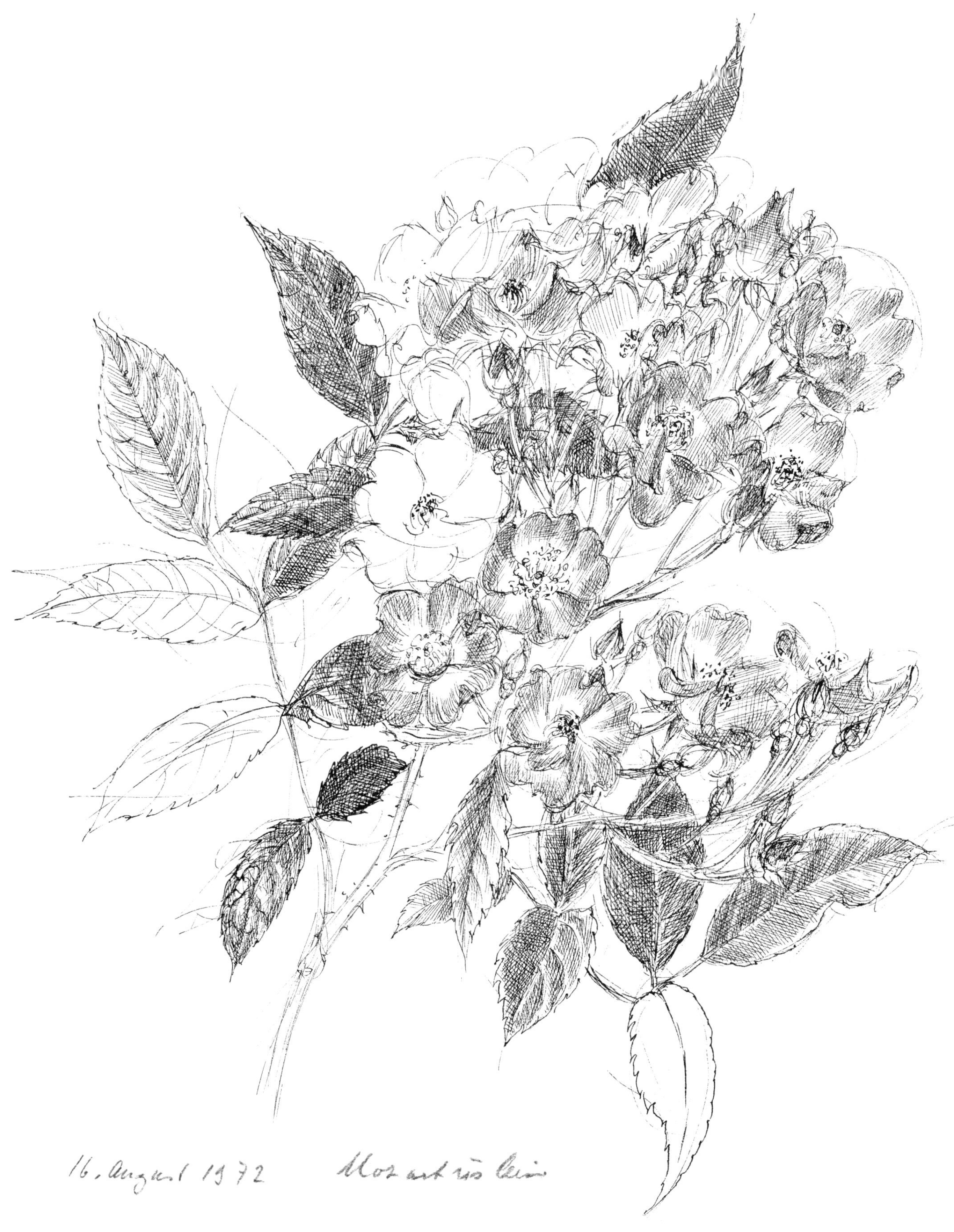

16. August 1972   Mozartröslein

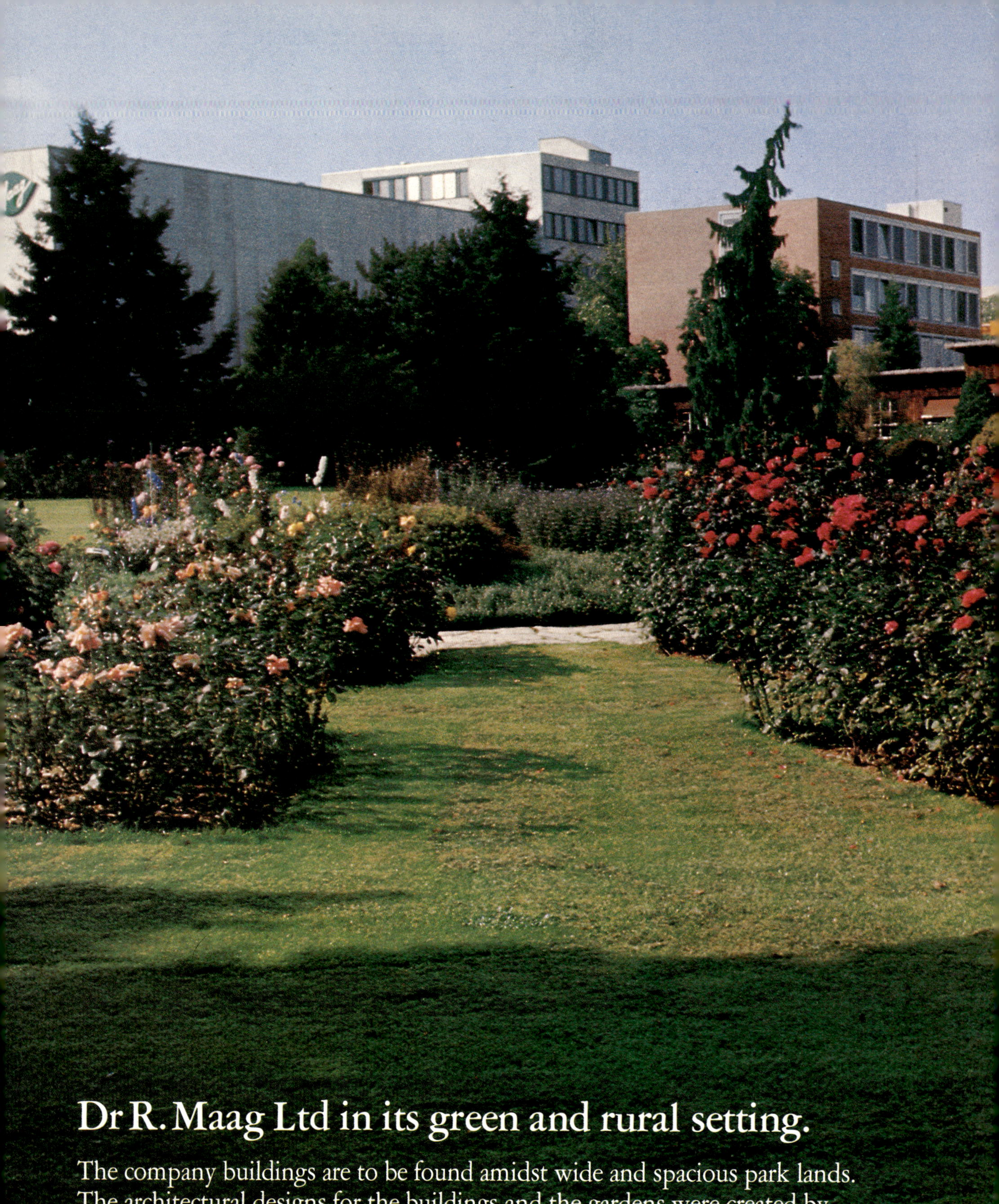

Dr R. Maag Ltd in its green and rural setting.

The company buildings are to be found amidst wide and spacious park lands.
The architectural designs for the buildings and the gardens were created by

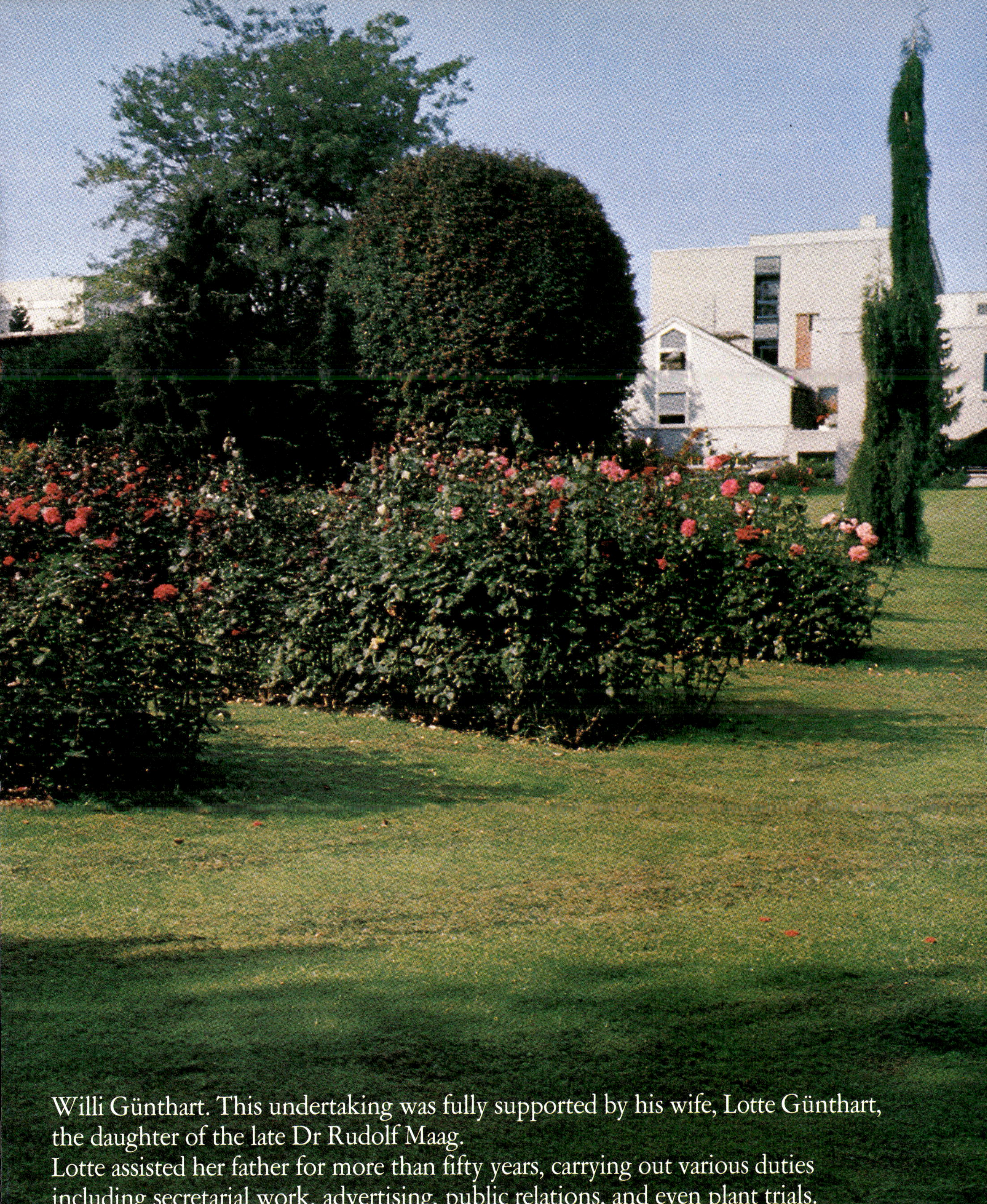

Willi Günthart. This undertaking was fully supported by his wife, Lotte Günthart, the daughter of the late Dr Rudolf Maag.
Lotte assisted her father for more than fifty years, carrying out various duties including secretarial work, advertising, public relations, and even plant trials.

First published in the United States of America in 1984 by
Carnegie-Mellon University,
The Hunt Institute for Botanical Documentation,
Pittsburgh, Pennsylvania

Text	Lotte Günthart-Maag
Translation	Julia Stierli-Large
Artwork	Willi Günthart
Printed by	Lichtdruck/Matthieu AG, Dielsdorf-Zurich
Typesetting	Englersatz AG, Zurich
Colour separations	Giezendanner, Regensdorf-Zurich Lichtdruck/Matthieu AG, Dielsdorf-Zurich
Cover	Hch. Weber AG, Winterthur

Printed in Switzerland